LONG DISTANCE
INFORMATION

LONG DISTANCE INFORMATION

JULIE WELCH

MACMILLAN

First published 1999 by Macmillan

an imprint of Macmillan Publishers Ltd
25 Eccleston Place, London SW1W 9NF
and Basingstoke

Associated companies throughout the world

ISBN 0 333 73883 7

9 8 7 6 5 4 3 2 1

A CIP catalogue record for this book is available from
the British Library.

Typeset by SetSystems Ltd, Saffron Walden, Essex
Printed and bound in Great Britain by
Mackays of Chatham plc, Chatham, Kent

To the East End Road Runners

'When I am an old woman I shall wear purple, and a red hat that doesn't go.'

Jenny Joseph

'I get knocked down, but I get up again.'

Chumbawumba

PART ONE

PEDAL TO PARIS

Runner's World Training Log.
Day: Thursday. **Distance:** 6 m. **Time:** 61 min.
Weather: Dusty. **Course/notes:** Le Touquet seafront
to Cucq. Big shady trees, pavements stippled with dog
shit and blocked by cars, shops smelling of pain au
chocolat and fish. Counted four other runners. We criss-
crossed at the roundabout by the Hôtel Westminster.
Life quality: Golden.

If ever you have to cycle 320 miles in 4 days with 263
complete strangers, here is a tip. Take a tube of Germolene and you will never be short of friends. The blistered,
the grazed, the sun-fried and the saddlesore will beat a
path to your door.

Let me explain. In September 1996 in a moment of
vainglory I had decided what a brilliant idea it would be
to cycle from London to the Arc de Triomphe. Pedal to
Paris was being organized by the Royal British Legion to
raise funds in its seventy-fifth anniversary year, and the
start date was my birthday. I couldn't think of a better
way to clock up another year on the tripmeter of life.
They were going to set off at eight o'clock from the Royal
Naval College in Greenwich, half a mile from where I
lived. All I had to do was wake up and ride through the
park.

In those days I was working for the *Sunday Telegraph* on

a section called 'Active: The Essential Guide To Taking Part'. 'Active' featured a new kind of sportswriting. Instead of being bums on seats, pontificating about the state of British tennis or the moral fibre of the England cricket team, 'Active' reporters had to get in shape and go out there and walk the walk themselves. (The old kind of sportswriters were of course known as Passive or sometimes Falling Off Their Bar Stool And Being Carried Out By Their Friends.) I had been on 'Active' for five months and I was very happy.

However, as the day of my departure to Paris approached, certain problems manifested themselves. These were nutshelled by my husband as 1) We had been married for twelve years and in all that time he had never once seen me riding a bike and 2) I didn't have a bike to ride.

It was the opportunity I had been waiting for. 'You seem to have forgotten,' I said, 'that you are married to the great-niece of Charles Kingston Welch.'

This is going to take a bit of explaining, but here goes. The reason I started supporting Tottenham Hotspur (as opposed to West Ham or Leyton Orient which were geographically nearer to where I lived as a child, or Manchester United which had a tragic glamour derived from the recent Munich air crash) was down to three North London Jewish girls with whom I became friends at the school I attended between eleven and thirteen. Historically Tottenham had a bedrock of North London Jewish support and in the '60–'61 season it also had the team of Brown, Baker, Henry, Blanchflower, Norman, Mackay, Jones, White, Smith, Allen, Dyson and Medwin who played sometimes. This was the team which performed the never-before-accomplished feat of the Double, and my three friends and I spent a happy old time shutting ourselves in the end toilet in the basement cloakrooms to listen to the Cup draw, and carving DANNY on the inside of our desk lids and all the other stuff which we thought was really iconoclastic fun as twelve-year-old girls at the start of the sixties.

Anyway, that was how I came to support Spurs and, much later, support myself and my son after I was divorced from my first husband and I could use my knowledge to become a football reporter. What I didn't know then was that my family originated from Tottenham. My grandfather was the youngest of the ten children of Charles Welch, plumbing engineer, which was no doubt just the Victorian version of the man in overalls who charges £172.10 plus VAT to unblock your sink. Long before I was born, of course, the family had become part of London's diaspora of the upwardly mobile to Essex, and I grew up unenlightened about our roots.

No, the Spurs thing was just coincidence. Or maybe not. I like to think that in some part of the brain reserved for stuff you know that nobody's ever told you about was the information that my genes had passed down the line from people who had brought the fruits of the inspiration of Sir Thomas Crapper to Stoke Newington, Seven Sisters and White Hart Lane.

But I knew about Uncle King from early on from my mum, who was curator of family myths and legends. Uncle King was my grandfather Fred's oldest brother and, as Mum said, a true Welch. By this she meant he was blue-eyed and chubby and had trouble reaching the top shelf of the wardrobe. In their time Welches have displayed many varied and remarkable abilities – Grandpa Fred rode a unicycle and also invented a type of hand grenade, though with typical familial mistiming it was on the day after the First World War ended – but common to us all is an economy in the inches department. No true Welch will ever attract the eye of the basketball selectors.

Uncle King's is not a story I get to air very often because basically most people couldn't care two figs whether the beaded rim of the pneumatic tyre was invented by Marie Curie or an orang-utan. They just get on a bike and pedal away. What they don't realize is that if my great-uncle hadn't spent months fiddling around his garden shed in 1893 we'd all still be bouncing around on wooden wheels.

Furthermore – I'm not boring you, am I? – this is only the first interesting fact about Uncle King. The second is that at the age of fourteen he fell in love with a girl named Anne who was even more bijou than him. As a testament to his affection he invented the tandem so they could ride round Tottenham side by side. One day – this is true – they were spotted by a songwriter called Harry Dacre who was so inspired by the dinky pair that he dashed home and rattled off the song which goes:

> Daisy, Daisy, give me your answer do.
> I'm just crazy, all for the love of you.
> It won't be a stylish marriage.
> I can't afford a carriage.
> But you'll look sweet
> Upon the seat
> Of a bicycle made for two.

Isn't that nice?

What would have been even nicer, give or take a century later, would have been to have had Uncle King right there beside me. He wouldn't have been casting doubt on my ability to cycle 320 miles in 4 days, and saying, 'Not only do you not ride bikes, you haven't even got a bike to ride.' He would have gone into his garden shed and turned a surplus trug, a broken shrimping net and a handful of old washing machine parts into an 18-gear tourer with titanium frame. But all we had was the family heirloom, a thirty-year-old shopper which in its time had been the *dernier cri*, one of those low-to-the-ground jobs which whisked you around on wheels the size of bagels. Three decades on, when I tried it out it was like trying to travel on the Stone of Scone.

Then, a week before I was due to set off, I remembered a guy called Mick Morrison, encountered briefly in 1991 when he was team manager of Raleigh and I was interviewing one of his cyclists for *Cosmopolitan*. I'd liked him a lot; I'd only spoken to him by phone but I like to think I am a good reader of character, one who can instinctively spot the sterling worth of a chap who says, 'If you or your kids ever want a bike, give us a call.'

Let's cut a long story short. Mick Morrison was still on the same mobile, if not with the same outfit. He was now looking after Team Ambrosia – I suppose he was now the man to call if I ever needed some tinned rice. But he pointed me towards Raleigh marketing from whom the promise that I would mention Raleigh in every second sentence of my copy brought forth the loan of a factory-fresh Jaguar 12 with grip-shift gears, skinwalled tyres and mercifully gel-filled seat. It was the purplish colour of a vamp's lipstick and like nothing I had ever ridden before.

I took it for a spin round the block. 'The saddle's too high,' I said, then stood around looking daffy and helpless. Because here's an odd thing. I can change a car wheel, put up a tent, mend a fuse, but show me a bike that needs fixing and I turn into Raquel from *Coronation Street*. Ron, youthful pedaller round the countryside of Nottingham and son of George the one-time Raleigh nightwatchman, rubbed his hands and got out the spanners and gadgets and did all those serene, tinkering activities men do with bikes. He put away the spanners and gadgets and dusted his hands, and I rode round the block again.

'The saddle's too low,' I said. Ron got out all the spanners and gadgets and tinkered again but we couldn't get that bloody saddle to stay up where we wanted it, and it was now twenty minutes off midnight. But it didn't feel too bad and anyway it was too late to do anything about it because the next day was when I set off.

Our journey was to take us on Kentish B-roads, via villages with names like Sellindge and Peene to the ferry at Dover. We would pedal off into Calais and beyond, through the battlegrounds of the Somme, past fields of poppies and cows the colour of crème brûlée. It sounded idyllic when I thought about it but as usual a fault line was about to open up between expectation and experience.

The first morning was excruciating. I toiled up one-in-two hills while everyone else's backsides disappeared over the horizon. Nobody had ever told me Kent was in the Andes. I rued the holiday I had just spent in Le Touquet where instead of rigorously cycling at least three times a week for one and a half hours as advised by the British Cycling Federation, I had lolled around in the Bar des Sports on a training diet of Tête de Veau avec Sauce Gribiche and that well-known isotonic drink Beaujolais.

I doubted I would even make the ferry, and imagined myself returning home that night, defeated. I told myself it was no big deal; it wouldn't be the first time I'd had to pack something in. I'd probably feel a bit embarrassed for a while but everyone would understand. They always did. Then I thought, possibly for the first time in my life, 'Bugger that,' and focused on a furiously pedalling man in head-to-foot Lycra. He turned out to be taking a short

LONG DISTANCE INFORMATION

cut. It was the M20. But ten minutes of jostling with juggernauts later I was racing along the sea front in Dover.

On board, exultant but stiff, sore and hungry, I phoned my sons. I conversed with two of them but my money ran out before I could speak to the third and youngest. Waddling away to tend my throbbing parts, it shot through me that I must find another pound coin, rejoin the queue and call again so he could be brought to the phone. One of the worst wounds you can inflict on a child is to make them think they do not merit listening to; I speak from personal experience.

I rejoined the queue and was presently hearing the reproachful sobs of someone who had indeed thought I had not deemed him worthy of an audience. I would have turned back there and then but I have not yet mastered the art of cycling on water. I had to go on. Besides, I had an unbreakable date in Calais that night. I had arranged to share a bottle of Gamay with myself in the Hôtel Meurice. It was my birthday and it would have been bad manners to call it off.

We had already begun to sort ourselves out into groups: the Supersonics, the Merely Fast and Other Ranks. The Supersonics were Lycra-clad zealots who had real racing bikes and conducted their own mini Tour de France. I only got to speak to the Supersonics when they needed my Germolene. It was not that they were unfriendly, simply that they did not notice you as they flashed by. You were just a blur, like a tree seen from a passing TGV train.

The Merely Fasts were older and heartier: enthusiasts who belonged to the Cyclists' Touring Club and were full of bike lore and bossy advice. Among them were men whom in normal life I would have crossed the M25 in rush hour to avoid, men who wore pink and white polka dot shirts with shorts of the same ilk. But there were also men with whom, at the time, I would gratefully have been joined in a form of marriage: shining knights of the road like Brian from Lincoln, who shepherded me through the first horrible hours, and John from Epsom who nobly dropped back from the *peloton* to encourage me through hill hell.

But I knew my place. Other Ranks comprised two sub-groups: the Quick Quick Slows, whose numbers were often swollen by temporarily winded Fasts and Supersonics with broken wings, and the Trundlers, those whose main goal was to make it to the towns where we were billeted at night before everyone else had left them in the morning. I was a Trundler.

So, through no fault of her own, was Min, who had already established her intrepidity quotient by doing the Three Peaks Challenge and an all-day Aerobathon and was already planning her next time out from the children, a walk through the desert. A Christian phlebotomist from Cambridge, Min was riding a borrowed bike with not enough gears. It went downhill at the rate of celery growing. She was my room-mate. It was a blind date organized by the British Legion, but how quickly you can forge a bond over Germolene and bath salts.

I thought you'd ask. A phlebotomist is somebody who takes blood samples from people's veins. But you could have guessed that anyway from the way Min fixed my number on the back of my T-shirt every morning, gently tapping my shoulder blade and saying, 'I'm going to put the pin in just here.'

By the second day, life wasn't so bad. I made friends – not just Min, but Joan the practice nurse from Godalming, Paula who was something in the environment, Derek the Spurs supporter. The only problem was my left knee. It was twice as big as the one I had started out with and the colour of a traffic light on red. From being Our Lady of the Germolene, I became a stalwart of The Knee Club. We would muster on the grass at control stops and rub our tubi-gripped cartilages. We would shake our heads over each other's patellas. Our conversation rippled with the brand names of magic unguents: Voltarol, Voltaren, Voltarene, rather like the chorus of 'The Happy Wanderer'.

On the third day, which began with a brass band and wreath-laying ceremony in the town square in Abbeville, my knee rose again from the dead. Again, I had Brian from Lincoln to thank. 'Your saddle's too low,' he said, on seeing my hideously deformed gait.

The tour mechanic was Nigel from the Sidcup Cycle Centre. He had bad news to break. The bolt which held saddle to frame was sheared. It meant you could turn it round and round for the rest of your life and still the seat wouldn't stay in place. There was nothing for it but crude surgery. As the strains of the Marseillaise died away he got to work with a hacksaw. My beautiful Jaguar 12 was scarred for life but now it had a saddle bolt which worked. A miracle took place. I could pedal on full power without begging for an anaesthetic. I didn't need a block and tackle to winch me on and off my bike. I was a real cyclist.

Thirty-six hours later we were racing through the Paris traffic, whipped into a pedalling frenzy by motorcycle outriders. Legs going round like circular saws, I didn't know how much longer I could carry on. A sign came into view: Place Charles de Gaulle. We started cheering and punched the air. All round the Arc de Triomphe, crowds were lined up to see us. We slid off our bikes and stood silently as old slow men wearing medals laid wreaths at the tomb of the Unknown Soldier, but it wasn't till I glimpsed Mike King, the *Sunday Telegraph* snapper, watchful and quiet with his cameras slung on his broad shoulders, that I knew this was real. All through the trip I'd been fretting in the back of my mind that there would be no photographer at the Arc, that the editor of 'Active', realizing I was unhinged, had decided the best thing was to humour me by sending me out to France with a load of other loonies on wheels. With any luck I'd forget why I was there and would be found ten years later by the side of the road, offering a Germolened fingertip to passing cyclists.

Mike is a big, gentle guy, a sort of cuddly bear who takes pictures. He is a man of simple tastes and a fondness for routine, which interface at a single point, the Little Chef restaurant. When you travel with him on a story, you know what you are going to get – pleasant conversation, superb photos and cod, chips and peas with two slices of bread and a pot of tea. I like him very much and hope it will not mar our friendship if I say that there are times when I've wished he'd remember to put film in his camera.

The plan was for the cyclists to peel away from the Arc and head off in convoy to a reception somewhere in Invalides. The directions were somewhat vague but that didn't matter because we would be led there by a police escort complete with outriders and blue flashing light. 'Don't worry, you've got plenty of time,' muttered Mike, snapping away while I posed with my bike in front of the Arc. Behind me the cyclists formed into a line and began a final triumphant circuit of the great monument. Mike's eyes began glinting behind his specs. I could see this was It for him – the definitive picture.

'Please, Mike, please, the police van's moving off and I don't know where the reception is.'

'Don't worry, I've nearly finished.'

'Mike, please, my passport is in the tour bus which is waiting for us at the reception and if I don't get there and pick it up I won't be able to leave the country.'

'Don't worry ... Ah. Hang on a minute. Wasn't any film in that camera.'

He was right. I shouldn't have worried. I lost sight of the cyclists but pedalled frantically after them, shouting, '*Vites! Où est* Les Invalides? *Où est*, no sorry, *où sont les bicyclettes?*' at people whose only crime had been to drink their coffee outside on a sunny afternoon on the Champs-Elysées. I got there in the end, in time for the ceremony at which we were given medals of our own. It was the only medal I have ever won apart from a bronze at Greek dancing. I knew I would keep it for ever.

I also had a holdall full of sweaty underwear and crumbling Hobnobs. The whiff of socks still lingers but so do the memories: riding into Montreuil up what seemed like a cobbled Alp, sharing baguettes the size of bollards at Poix de Picardie, slurping kir in the fire station at Beauvais in late afternoon, the camaraderie and freedom. On Sunday night Min and I travelled home on Eurostar, medals round our necks, doped with happiness, our backs to the engine so we could see the roads we had travelled so effortfully recede rapidly into the dusk.

It was on that journey back to England, on the cusp between forty-seven and forty-eight, that I started to make peace with my limitations. I knew now I would never be King of the Mountains, not at anything, but for the first time I could see maybe that wasn't so terrible. I felt drunk with achievement. At Waterloo, I thanked Min for being such a brilliant co-Trundler and kissed her goodbye. That night I didn't fall asleep till after one. Twelve hours later I was having to go on all fours up the stairs and people were buying tickets to watch me sit down. And the week after that it was back to real life and the old kind of sportswriting: motorways, football grounds, trying to arrange interviews with managers who didn't want to be interviewed by me.

Mike King and I were driving back from Manchester late one afternoon when we got to talking about what it was I did. 'I'd say you were an adventuress,' he volunteered.

I let out a 'Whaaat?!!!' the way you'd shout, 'Yessss!'

Mike began to duck below the verbal parapet because he thought he'd offended me. 'I mean, the way you take yourself off to press boxes up and down the country,' he stuttered.

I told Mike it was the most brilliant thing anyone had ever said to me. I may even have simpered. What amazed me, though, was that I hadn't scowled or fobbed him off. I've never been very graceful about compliments. Perhaps it's because I thought someone was trying to manipulate me into doing something I didn't want to do, or because I sensed I was being patronized. Maybe I just felt more comfortable with hurled insults, so I could hurl them back. You can spend an awful lot of time in the middle of the night wondering why you're the way you are. But I'd noticed that in the last few weeks I didn't seem to do it so much.

I had set out to ride a bike to Paris and I had done it. Most of the people I did it with were faster and better than me, but what I had achieved was all mine. Nobody could claim any rights to it. No one had gone and rewritten the second draft of it over my head, or put in a good word for me with the right person. I won't claim that one cycling trip to France rid me of all self-hatred, sorrow, boredom, rage and fear for ever, but the moment when I slid off a bike and wheeled it to a war monument in a foreign city was when forty-eight years of failed exams, abandoned novels, missed deadlines and rejected scripts began to slip off my back. A sore bottom and a red peeling nose seemed a very reasonable price to pay.

LOSING IT

Runner's World Training Log.
Day: Wednesday. **Distance:** 4 m. **Time:** 45 min.
Weather: Dry and cold. **Course/notes:** Hare &
Billet–Clarendon Hotel–Liskeard Gardens. Wore my
new thermals and was mocked by men in a van. I
arranged for them to crash in a ball of flame on the
Sidcup bypass.

If you'd asked my mum about the years when I was
growing up, she would have said we were happy. Whenever I did something antisocial or became overwhelmed
with grief and despair, which happened quite often during
my adolescence, she would say, 'I don't know why you're
being like this. We've got such a happy home.' She
couldn't bear anyone to be angry or miserable, because at
heart she was one of the most sympathetic people I ever
knew. This made it even worse, somehow, that I managed
throughout a great deal of my childhood to make her
thoroughly pissed off.

Her own childhood had been a mixture of freedom
and neglect; one of seven siblings, she was hardly more
than a baby when her mother died. Her father got
married again, to her mother's sister, so her aunt became
her stepmother. The auntie produced two more children
whom Mum perceived as being petted and given preference. Highly intelligent, her desire to go to university

ignored, my mum channelled her ambition, disappointment and sense of loss into me.

That wasn't anything remarkable; most of my friends had mothers like that. As Elaine Dundy sort of said in *The Dud Avocado*, it wasn't easy to be a Woman in those stirring times. But most mothers didn't have a daughter like me, who having excelled at eleven-plus and won a scholarship to a London public school went and blew it totally. Within the space of a year, I turned into a dolt.

Mum blamed it on the television which I watched obsessively when I wasn't shut in my room reading the *Daily Mirror*, which I had to smuggle into the house on account of it being what she called common. I bought the *Mirror* on my way to school because it had good coverage of horse racing, which along with Spurs was my consuming interest. And while we're on the subject of consuming, I also put on twenty pounds in weight. Bored out of my skull by lessons, I was soon recording bottom marks in most subjects and eventually it was suggested to my parents that they might remove me before the school had to take my scholarship away.

I was sent to a boarding school for country Sloane Rangers where for a while at least I recovered enough of my wits to top the class again. For years, though, that first failure took lodgings in my psyche. Even into my thirties, it wasn't unusual for me to dream about the school in London: empty labs, ugly teachers, ink blots, frightening children, rows of scuffed desks. Often they featured the giant stairwell from which, in my dream, I was always trying to escape by finding the narrow staircase on one side that even in real life had led to a skylight just out of reach.

The building has gone now, pulled down like the house where I grew up; there's a commercial block on the site in Carmelite Street. Meanwhile I'm nearly fifty years old and I can still enjoy moments of guilty moroseness when I feel I conned the headmistress at the interview. Even as a ten-year-old I could exude a sort of effervescent charm, just as at other times I could and can be the acme of charmlessness. At some level I suppose I decided that the clumsy, fat, not very intelligent person who lost her scholarship was the true me, but with a bit of luck there were occasions when I could act out the role of someone clever, vivacious and successful. My secret was that I was a counterfeit. I felt bad about pulling the wool over that headmistress's eyes; I also felt triumphant, as if I had got away with something, and a bit scornful that she had let herself be duped by a crafty ten-year-old girl.

Once when I was seventeen years old my mother and I were having one of our many rows. (I was in every way a very *difficult* teenager.) It was shortly before I was due to go up to Bristol University. Mum had badly hoped New Hall, Cambridge, would offer me a place but my interview did not go well, and wishing to have the last word in this row, Mum told me I had failed.

Anyway, I nurtured this riposte. One part of me rebelled against being so dismissed and set out determined to prove her wrong. Another part, of which I was unconscious, decided to use it as a curse. I would become my mother's victim. She so badly wanted success for me, so as revenge I would deprive her of it. I'm not proud of that, but it just seems to have been how it was, the story of my life: one part manoeuvring myself into a position where I could succeed, the other part somehow contriving to fuck it up.

Like I said, the bike ride to Paris was the first time in ages I'd stuck something out to a successful conclusion. It didn't rank very high in the scale of grand achievements, but it was a big thing for me and I liked it very much. So much, in fact, that I wanted more. If I could cycle to Paris I could do anything: write another book, have that TV series up and running, get together all those pieces of paper with phone numbers scribbled on them in my desk and bag and pockets and write them down in my contacts book. And then I would actually be able to ring people I wanted to speak to without having to make six calls first to track them down. And then I would be a normal, organized, functioning human being in the world of work. It was in this spirit of omnipotence that I set out to walk the Three Forests Way, a journey which was going to take me back to the scene of my childhood.

WALKING THE WALK

Runner's World Training Log.
Day: Friday. **Distance:** Running equivalent – 5 m.
Course/notes: Tried out a new class. I raised my step to the highest level. Obviously, in my ignorance, I'd committed a solecism; a thin woman with crested hairdo and big teeth, all smiles, asked did I know how difficult Cathy's class was. Noticed this before when you go anywhere new – there's always one devoted pupil, usually female, who owns it. Calls the instructor by her first name in a casually irrelevant tone, like a Christian with a bit of a crush on God who refers to 'the man upstairs'.

Three things not to be confused with long-distance walking:

1) Rambling
2) Competitive race-walking
3) Having a nice time

The name 'Three Forests Way Challenge Walk' says everything you need to know about it: a 64-mile non-stop round trip of the arboreous wilds of Epping, Hainault and Hatfield. The Long Distance Walkers Association put it on in November because many of those who do it have completed so many Ultrahikes that they crave the underfoot goo and pitch darkness of late autumn to make it challenging enough.

It starts and ends in the Storm Hut at Gilwell Park, the headquarters of the Scout movement, and beats a path along bridleways and farm tracks, past hedgerows studded with fat blue berries which scream, 'Eat me!' but are probably as nourishing as arsenic. You cross fields mined with cowpats and yomp a late-night half mile beside the River Stort on a towpath no wider than a ribbon. You have twenty-six hours to get out alive.

I know now I should have picked on something easier for my first long-distance walk but I was still full of myself from the Paris trip and, anyway, I wanted to go home. I grew up in a large house overlooking Epping Forest and spent a lot of my childhood roaming round it with a terrier and my friend Jo, a diminutive, very efficient girl who later became a diminutive, very efficient GP. My dad, who had died in May, had been what we thought of as a local Personage; for two years (unprecedented) he was Chairman of the Local Council and sat on committees a lot. In fact one way or another he seemed to have banged a gavel on every cabinet table in Essex. His death notice in the *Daily Telegraph* of 29 May 1996 was at least a centimetre longer than anyone else's, though I think if my mum had realized what it would cost she might have subbed out Epping Forest District President of the Rural Angling Society.

Route map in hand, kitted out head to foot from the Field and Trek catalogue, I set out from Gilwell at nine on a crisp Saturday morning along with 135 others. Gilwell was childhood territory too. In the late fifties, its Chief Scout was the father of one of my schoolfriends. He always wore shorts so looked like an enlarged boy. Mrs Chief Scout put lettuce in her Marmite sandwiches which was considered quite adventurous for her time. With them I attended the 1957 Gang Show, and a Guy Fawkes Night Pow-Wow and Sing-Song Round the Fire.

Within half an hour of leaving Gilwell we were pounding up the wide grass track which ended in the road where I had once lived. Our house had been at the other end. As I said, it's gone now, pulled down in 1984 and replaced by three modern ones. My parents moved near by, somewhere smaller and easier to warm. Mum, who I've always felt has far more guts than me, has been to see the new houses and says they are quite nice, but till the day of the Three Forests I had never gone back and even then I carefully looked the other way.

There wouldn't have been time to look, anyway. You either like the sport of long distance walking or you don't, and I loved it from the start, but it's always fast and additionally, in winter, it's wet, muddy and often brutal. It also involves a lot of deciphering of route maps. These are three or four pages of instructions carefully typed in a language similar to English. What are you to make of 'BR (80 degs) towards scrub between posts, BL (93 degs) through gap in trees (school on L). Continue on permissive FP 200 mtrs'? Try 'Cross field (30 degs) (no defined path) aiming for pole in hedge corner' and see where it gets you. And if you just stand there scratching your head it's all over. The walkers have gone. You're left alone in a frozen beet field at 83 degs from nowhere.

In the end I did what I always do in the press box when it's time to get the quotes; I followed the people who looked as though they knew where they were going. At football grounds it's the tabloid reporters; on the Three Forests Way it was a bunch of elderly blokes in anoraks.

And like the guys from the redtops, who as a broadsheet journalist you always look down on till you actually try and do their job and realize it requires skill and wits you don't begin to possess, these scrawny greybeards were so much better than me it was excruciating.

After half an hour of trying to keep up with them every single muscle from my hips down seemed to be turning to concrete. More wizened old guys sped past me like Michael Johnson. One of them slowed long enough to hand me four Anadin and tell me I'd be all right after a nice cup of tea at the next checkpoint.

I limped into the barn at Little Forest Hall, where everyone rallied round offering blister plasters even as I kept saying, 'I haven't got blisters.' (Blisters are an obvious hazard of long distance walking, though not as widespread as you'd think from the way everyone talks. What happens is, you twist your ankle or stagger around because you've let yourself become dehydrated, and you call it blisters. It doesn't necessarily mean, 'I am suffering from small bubble-like elevations of my feet produced as a reaction to mechanical irritation', it's just walker-talk for a range of conditions from being a bit off colour to needing urgent hospital admission. Thus, if you're a long distance walker and go into cardiac arrest, you say, 'I'm going to have to slow down a bit, my blisters are killing me.')

It was at Little Forest Hall, after nearly 22 miles, that the first of the walkers jacked it in, but not, I was proud to think, me. Boots carrying a handicap of several kilos of Essex and Hertfordshire clay, I blundered on in the fading light. Regrets set in, about the night before when instead of going to bed early with a cup of Horlicks I was dancing on the table at Ron's birthday party. I began to fantasize about being picked up in a Rolls-Royce and swept off to a hot soak. Another mile went past, by which time I was so desperate I would have settled for being rescued by a Lada.

My luck was in. I fell in with Bobby, a Norwich vet, and her boyfriend, who had both done the Three Forests before and knew the way. We caught up with Trish, Joan and Karen from the East End Road Runners. It was their first long distance walk too. Karen said they ran several marathons a year but nothing, *nothing*, had prepared them for this.

We emerged into a village high street. It was odd to see people leading normal lives, shopping, going into pubs, listening out for the football scores while we had spent eight hours crashing around in the bushes. In the White Roding Sports and Social Club it was warm and welcoming, and the Refreshments were of a very high order. (Refreshments are a very necessary part of long distance walking and quite frankly if you aren't offered tinned fruit and cold rice pudding on at least one checkpoint my advice is to vote with your feet.)

Outside the Sports and Social Club, night fell. We put on our head torches and streamed out like a line of miners, heading for Hatfield Forest. I had a new group of guardian angels – Janet and her companions from the Surrey group of the LDWA, who said that as I was slowing down a bit they might be able to keep pace with me. After half a mile at a punishing gallop, Janet very decently dropped back to keep me company, jollying me along with tales of walks past when she had to be fished out of a river and was pursued by drug-crazed youths in remote woodland at dead of night. She had just got to the bit when she hallucinated towards the end of a 100-miler when I slipped in a gully in the dark. My right ankle started telling me it was time we weren't here.

Janet became a bobbing torch-beam which I followed like the Star of Bethlehem into the depths of Hatfield Forest. At the checkpoint, motherly women dispensed chocolate cake and sympathy. A walker who had been sitting at the tea counter quietly nursing his Beverage suddenly went the colour of Polyfilla and crashed to the floor. Someone else threw in the towel, a martyr to cramp. I too announced my retirement.

'You can't give in now,' shrieked Bobby the vet. 'Half an hour from now you'll be in the loo crying your eyes out. You'll hate yourself. You'll never be able to hold your head up at your newspaper again.' Then she added the clincher. 'You get a hot meal in Sawbridgeworth.'

Fortified by two Mars bars and the last of the Anadin, I set off for Sawbridgeworth with the East End Road Runners. We spent ten minutes on a damp heath, peering at the route map which counselled us to 'cross driveway with white house on L and old trees on R'. This was complicated by the fact that every house on L was white and every single tree for miles was old. Around us, the good people of Hertfordshire were celebrating Guy Fawkes night, oblivious to our strivings. Fireworks exploded in the starry darkness. Rain started tipping down. We marched across a glistening beet field, turned R as instructed at Hopper Between Sheds and piled straight into a large black mound not mentioned in the OS map. This turned out to be a sleeping cow.

By then the only way I could walk was on the front of my feet. I reached Sawbridgeworth Scout Group HQ at a rather fetching mince and collapsed in a chair. It was tattered, it was grubby, it sloped to one side, it was the best chair in the world. People were spreadeagled on the floor, sticking Elastoplast on to butchered feet. The hut smelt of antiseptic, gravy and wet clothes. Midnight struck.

I snoozed for a while, then claimed my hot meal. This consisted of watery stew, disintegrating peas and over-boiled potatoes, followed by Swiss roll with cold custard and right at that minute it was as deeply wonderful as lobster and champagne. It's got to be said, though, that the pale, bloated Swiss roll seemed oddly familiar and indeed when I had a closer look I realized it was a clone of my right ankle. I could just about stand up, but putting one foot in front of the other was a step too far. I had done 43 miles. There were only 21 to go, but I couldn't face another yard.

I was towed away through silent country roads back to Gilwell, dozing under a red check blanket in a car belonging to a kind and helpful stranger called Reg, who turned out to be Janet's husband. I got home at six on Sunday morning and slept where I fell. When I reported for maternal duties twelve hours later, my eleven-year-old asked why I was waddling. I told him why. My knees were sore. My ankles creaked. Every metatarsal was a throbbing beacon of pain, each toe, not to mention my fingers, scraped by every bramble in Hertfordshire. And then there was the self-reproach, because Bobby was right. When I packed it in, I had walked and jogged the length of one and a half marathons, a matter, I believed at the time, for quiet self-congratulation. Now I knew I was just a wimp.

A rational wimp, I grant you. The decision I'd made to terminate the walk was based on the perfectly reason-able conclusion that I had already suffered quite severe muscle damage. It was to be four days before I stopped walking like a performing seal and a week before the swelling in my ankle went down. My job depended on being able to function physically. It was another month before I could train properly again. I hadn't even needed to go any further. I'd been there as a journalist and I'd got my story already. And it was all utter shit. I was *haunted* by those unwalked miles. Asking myself whether if I had hung on till the next checkpoint I would have made it home despite the pain and exhaustion, I was back in the land of Not Finishing Things. I thought I'd left it for ever, but I was wrong and I didn't like it one bit.

UNFINISHED BUSINESS

Runner's World Training Log.
Day: Thursday. **Distance:** 4 m. **Time:** 40 min.
Weather: Wet and cold. **Course/notes:** Lee Green
station and back. Car horns sounding and a cyclist
shouting at a driver. At Lee Green people in work clothes
stream away like migrating birds. I dodge round them,
up the drive, padding alongside the grey, humming
railway. 'I am not a number, I am a free woman.'

I'd always had trouble finishing things. My cupboards
were full of projects – novels, needlepoint cushions, pro-
posals for TV series, knitting kits – which had been
embarked on with optimism and élan and then surrendered at the moment about a quarter of the way in when
a small voice in my head murmured, 'Your tent stitch is
crap,' or 'You're not going to write *that*, are you?'
    The only time I ever showed tenacity was in the
relationship I had with a married man all through the
seventies and early eighties. When it came to being
miserable, I really stuck with it, though you never would
have known because another trouble with me was that in
company I smiled and told jokes a lot so no one could see
how much I was hurting. Even now I've got a breezy
manner which masks great stagnant lakes of despondency
and pessimism. I blame the Scandinavians myself. They're
the gloomiest buggers alive and centuries ago they got in

their boats, fetched up in East Anglia and passed the Eeyore gene on to some of my ancestors.

There I go again, making jokes. Depression is one of the worst feelings in the world. Mine wasn't even a feeling. I'd go around within a kind of paralysed nothingness for months, years sometimes. It was the life equivalent of being in a plane stacked in dense cloud above Heathrow airport. Endless greyness, greyness.

About the only nice thing I can say about my depressions is that they never made me want to kill myself. Except once when the Married Man left his wife to move in with me, stayed a week then moved out again. Around that time I just happened to be walking over the Thames at Blackfriars Bridge. It was November. I looked down into those black swirling depths and thought, 'I wonder . . .'

Fortunately, I remembered that many years previously my older sister, at the culmination of an extremely successful career (head girl, captain of hockey, place at blue chip university) at the school at which I later turned into a dolt, had stood on this very spot and flung her panama hat into the river. It was an annual school tradition, the Ceremonial Discarding Of The Panamas, performed by all those girls who were leaving. I think Big Sis and her chums had had their photographs taken for a newspaper. Anyway, my mum was very proud that my sister had been to the sort of school where they had traditions, especially such a mildly daredevil one as this. So I stepped away from the parapet and walked on, having decided that it wouldn't be very nice for Mum to have a second daughter who, Thames-wise, didn't just stop at her hat.

Ever since I'd started running and walking and cycling for a living I didn't get the really horrible depressions any more. But once I didn't have depression blocking the way into my head I felt duty bound to go in there and sift through the accumulated mental lumber and, goodness me, what a lot of interesting items I discovered. Trunks full of things I was fond of which I thought I'd lost for ever – memories, feelings, jokes. And stuff which I really didn't want at all and was rather put out to discover was mine.

For instance, I just realized that part of the reason I never finished things was not through being a headcase but because I was a rather lazy person. I liked to let somebody else do the difficult work: deciphering the route maps, nailing down the managers for the post-match quotes.

This was brought home especially clearly to me when I received my LDWA certificate stating that I had taken part in the Three Forests Challenge Walk. But I *did not complete.*

When you go to a big time darts competition (if there is such a thing) one of the things you notice is the chips-trodden-into-the-carpet decor compared to the grandeur of the emcee's terminology, the original gap between aspiration and accomplishment. A darts player doesn't need or want 21 to clinch the frame, he *requires.* And walkers don't finish, or arrive back at base, or crack it. They complete.

At first I'd thought, How quaint. It was one of those things that in the past I might have written something smart-alecky about. But once I did one of the walks I understood the significance of the word. It was resonant with wholeness, satisfaction, dues paid, nothing owing. A journey had been undertaken, not lightly but with due diligence and seriousness. I'd gone into the Three Forests at half cock almost, shrieking about how funny it would be to blunder around the woods with a load of geeky people in anoraks. I'd gushed about my childhood haunts, and done some rather showy jogging and moaned about my feet, and while I was doing that, other people were stubbornly plodding on through the night to reach their goal.

What did they get out of it? On the face of it, not much. A very fine breakfast, I'll give you that – sausage, beans and enough squares of toast to tile the floor of a medium-sized bathroom – and, a few weeks later, a certificate. But no trophies, no money, no mentions on the news. Then again, it wasn't about that anyway. It was something to do with yourself – how you did things.

MY DAD

Runner's World Training Log.
Day: Saturday. **Distance:** 3 m. **Time:** 40 min.
Course/notes: Ran to The Valley for Charlton match.
Boasted to everyone about it on the sports desk, which
was a mistake. Won't be able to claim taxi fares on
expenses now because they'll know it isn't true. Place
confirmed in the London Marathon.

Six of my favourite names of challenge walks (from
Strider, the Journal of the Long Distance Walkers
Association)

1) The Tulketh Trundle
2) The Stanage Stumble
3) The Purbeck Plod
4) The Gifford Gongoozler
5) Where Eagles Fly
6) The Finished Business (I invented that one)

In what a certain kind of author would call the cold
light of day, the towpath alongside the River Stort
turned out to be a wonderfully pretty place. Even in
winter it was leafy and sweet-smelling, with little white-
painted boats bobbing on the pewter-coloured water
and the banks busy with moorhen and ducks. They
looked peaceful and well wrapped up, as though wearing
greatcoats.

Sawbridgeworth Scout Group HQ, towards which I had lunged so painfully in the dead of a November night, was shuttered and padlocked. Not even a discarded blister plaster remained as testimony to the heroic efforts of my walking companions of two weeks back. I stood around for a while, listening to the din of hibernating squirrels and assessing my palm for raindrops, then checked my rucksack for the small Tupperware box which contained my Refreshments. These were a packet of bourbon biscuits, a bottle of lemonade and a special Long Distance Walker's Cheese Sandwich based on the original recipe, which I give here (I have made one or two adaptations which, I trust, will find favour with even the stubbornest traditionalist):

2 slices Mother's Pride
1 slice processed cheese
Blue Band margarine to taste
4 oz goat's Cheddar
4 anchoas de Escala
1 piccolo ciabatta or similar
1 large clove garlic, peeled
1 juicy vine tomato, halved
olive oil
sea salt and freshly ground pepper

Method: Throw away the Mother's Pride, processed cheese and margarine. Cut the ciabatta in half lengthwise and rub both halves with garlic and the half of tomato. Drizzle olive oil on one half then place on top the thinly sliced goat's Cheddar and anchoas. Season to taste and cover with the other half. Wrap in clingfilm and either place in Tupperware box or, to make it really authentic, squash between two OS maps and a head torch and allow orangeade to leak over it for five hours.

I felt in the pockets of my anorak for blister plasters then got out my Three Forests Route map. It seemed rather odd to be setting out on my own, early on a mid-week morning, without the cheerful jabber of other walkers. I wondered fleetingly where the nearest minicab company might be, but then I pulled my rainhood down over my forehead and started trudging up FP opposite through KG.

*

When I became a football reporter in August 1973 I suppose I thought I'd do it for a couple of years. Then I'd publish a novel or have a play shown on television and then I'd do what I originally set out to do at six and a half, which was to be a writer.

Instead seasons ended and I spent my summers screwing up pieces of paper and throwing them into waste-paper baskets and then a new season would start and I'd find myself clambering into the press box again. Then my first marriage broke up. I won't dwell here on this unhappy period except to say that every single TV play and novel I embarked on and failed to complete around that time was based around the theme Flaky Twentysome-thing Throws Herself Into Football As Substitute For Having A Love Life.

But it wasn't only that. Being a football reporter was to do with looking for my father. Not the portly gentleman in his sixties which he'd become, but the one of my childhood and before. Who was he, what had been his experience, what had it been like to be him?

When I was little, he was away a lot. He was a sentence, uttered as he left with his briefcase: 'I'll be at the Imperial, Newcastle upon Tyne.' This, along with the

George at Alfreton, and dozens of other modestly comfortable hotels in the North and Midlands – South Shields, North Shields, Sheffield, Mansfield, Nottingham – was where he based himself while doing business. His company traded in light plant: blocks and tackle, pit props, jacks. (My first husband was called Jack. I do sometimes wonder.)

I recreated my father in my imagination, taking myself off to the football towns and cities in whose pubs and working men's clubs this navy-suited, maroon-tied, apple-cheeked God had smoked Players Navy Cut, eaten pickled onions and told risqué jokes with beefy men from the Coal Board and colliery workers. Dad liked these people very much, even though they were quite unlike the sort of person he appeared to us at home; then again, I always liked footballers and managers very much. When I was four I sat on the carpet with him, helping to pack Christmas boxes for these men whose value ranged from a gift pack of fifty cigarettes to a rough wooden crate of Scotch. Even now I can be made happy and nostalgic by the smell of tobacco and wood shavings.

Later as he became richer and more important I thought he grew away from us. The widening space between him and us was literally expressed in our big new house, where we moved when I was six years old: the office on the first floor where he shuffled papers at his desk while Mum banged pots and pans in the kitchen. Sometimes I was sent up as an emissary, an object dangled in front of him to catch his attention, a glove puppet, a carrot on a string. I stood at his shoulder waiting for him to look up from his papers, at which I repeated in a monotone what Mum had told me to say. When my voiceover finished he would say, 'Ah yes. Very good.

Rightio.' I'd stand there for a bit and then drift off downstairs again. Maybe it was a harbinger of things to come: my supreme uselessness at getting the quotes.

Actually, I don't suppose my parents' marriage was any worse than a lot of couples'. It certainly lasted a long time. They married in 1937 and their walk together only ended with my father's death. They raised two children, moved house three times, built up a business empire which at its height had Dad's name emblazoned on the sides of several large lorries thundering the length and breadth of the kingdom. Like I've said, Dad was also a big wheel in local politics and in his pomp was pictured in many Gazettes, Independents and Advertisers of the day, his rubicund features suffused with civic pride, various chains of office on his breast, as he inaugurated the planting of memorial trees or attended the opening of municipal amenities. We were host to many Conservative gatherings; at one stage I seem to remember Mum was never without a platter of sausage rolls and prawn vol-au-vents in her hands, though these may have been a blockade against the local Conservative sex fiend who only needed half an hour of canasta and a gin and tonic before he'd steam in on any Tory lady who still had a heartbeat and slam his dentures against her puckered lips.

My memories, in that they are subjective, are of course no different from anyone else's. Recently Mum was reflecting on her marriage. 'We never', she said, 'had a cross word.'

I murmured that in my recollection their relationship crackled with a certain amount of mutual vexation.

'Oh no,' she said. After a pause: 'We agreed to differ.' Another pause. 'We were good pals.'

And oh Lord, could these good pals agree to differ. The odd thing was that they seemed to enjoy having an audience for their skirmishes. A case in point was one day trip they took with the Conservative Association to Brussels.

Sometimes I think Dad should have become a vicar. The fact he didn't was, I suppose, due to Mammon winning out over God: he liked money, doing deals, pickled onions and Scotch. But he shared certain attributes of a man of the cloth: the delight in helping people, a tendency to be the focus of interest of the widowed, the divorced and the never married. As the years went on Mum often found her travels with Dad involved a retinue of unattached Tory ladies.

While in Brussels, Dad wanted to buy some black pudding to bring home. Mum vetoed the idea. They argued at the ferry terminal. Dad went off for a recce. When he returned to his seat he had something wrapped in waxed paper, half-concealed under his jacket. For a while twitters of conversation continued among the Tory ladies. But one by one they fell silent as Dad, first slyly then with increasing brazenness, unsheathed a large blood sausage and without comment slapped it on the table in front of them.

My dad had been born by the Forest and that was where, despite all his journeys, he stayed. I might have broken away in my wild times but I'd always come back to find him exactly where I left him. Preoccupied, stubborn, absent-mindedly loving, he was still there, never shifting from his position, like an old tree. 'Ah yes. Very good. Rightio.'

At the end of his life, all his capabilities seemed to go, one by one. His sight faded dreadfully though if he caught my gaze his eyes would still glint with mischief and conspiracy. His stubby hands, the ones that had once wrapped Christmas boxes for Coal Board cronies, shook and shrivelled and needed gloves indoors to protect him from the cold. He'd had an operation and started fretting about whether he'd be able to get to the loo in time. But he still plodded on, delivering Conservative Party leaflets, sitting on boards of governors, rattling collecting tins: a very thin, frail old man, trudging down a road and ringing on people's doorbells, keeping his head warm with a cap and his legs steady with a stick.

I knew he was slowly dying and was sad, and my friend Lucy, who was twenty-one when her mother had died and knew about these things, told me the best thing was to see as much of him as possible. But I'd got so used to him being rushed off to hospital, then coming out again after a few days or weeks baying for a Carlsberg special brew and his walking stick, and anyway I was too cowardly to see him so dim and powerless and bolshie. And I hated it when my mum, frazzled by caring for him day after day, in fragile health herself, shouted at him and bewailed her lot in front of him, so a lot of the time I stayed away.

Some weeks before he died, Mum went suddenly into Harlow hospital for an emergency operation. All her carefully constructed plans for his care – he was to spend two days in a Home near by – went out of the window when he absolutely refused to go, despite the best efforts of Jo, the diminutive, very efficient GP. He was determined to stay in his own house and was adamant that he could look after himself. While we made jokes that he was probably already organizing himself a taxi down to the off-licence for his stash of Carlsberg even as the ambulance headed off, it was clear that everyone would feel happier if we knew he couldn't fall downstairs or burn down the house. So I became his temporary minder.

On the second day of my duties we went hospital

visiting. Mum was in a mixed ward and excitedly introduced me to the occupant of the bed opposite. He was the father of the man who wrote about racing in the *Daily Telegraph*. What a delightful coincidence! Then she and my father had a loud, brisk row, which centred on his intransigence about entering the Home. 'He wanted to be near his lavatory!' cried Mum to the listening world. 'It's all he cares about, his lavatory!'

Afterwards Dad and I had lunch in Epping where he consumed prawns, brown bread and two glasses of white wine with a sort of deft clumsiness and said plaintively that my mother was kindness personified but he did wish she didn't shout at him so. Then we went home and watched *Grandstand* together, which was what we had done on Saturday afternoons when I was growing up.

Around six weeks later I'd come back from a BBC press conference – to do with *Grandstand*, as it happened – to find a phone message that he'd been taken to hospital again. When I spoke to my mother she said the crisis was over but an hour later I got a call from the hospital. They asked me to hurry; he wouldn't last the hour.

The roads were busy, and the hospital buildings all joined together by long, poorly signposted corridors, so I missed his dying by a few minutes. But he was still warm and it seemed as if some bit of him that no longer belonged to his body was still in the room.

I cried and cried in Mum's arms. 'Now, we've all got to be very brave,' she said, and we sat with him for a while. She held his hand all the time, and told me that he'd died after making one last joke. When he was wheeled into the ward, a nurse asked if he would like a drink and he said, 'Yes! Mine's a Carlsberg.'

I kissed him and said goodbye. Then I left Mum to have her last conversation with him. She was tucking the covers round him; she kissed his forehead. 'Night night,' she murmured. Afterwards, I drove behind her to her house so she could pack a case and come home with me. Watching her battle through the traffic I couldn't help thinking what a brave old girl she was, and reflecting that when I'd fallen into her arms it was the first time I'd allowed her to comfort me since 23 April 1966, when Jug-Eared Richard told me he didn't love me any more.

We held Dad's funeral service at Parndon crematorium, on the edge of the Three Forests Way where it runs past Harlow and through Epping Long Green. It was mid-morning when I walked by, though I couldn't see it through the woods. What would have been the point? He wasn't there and anyway, it was raining. I walked on, for a while imagining him as part of the communion of souls, of which he would no doubt have been elected chairman already, banging his gavel and lacing the water carafes with gin. Around lunchtime I happened on the King's Oak, a vast brown-varnished Edwardian pub at High Beach. Forty years back it had been a hotel, and I wandered down past the car park to see if it still boasted the swimming pool where as an eight-year-old I had clung to the hand of diminutive, very efficient Jo and jumped with her off the top board of the diving platform. A cobwebby fence was all that remained. I sat on a log and ate my Refreshments looking down over the wet grass and wintry forest.

It was raining even harder now. I felt tired and a bit lonely and there were still another six miles to walk to Gilwell. But I was glad I'd been able to say goodbye to Dad, and that we'd spent that last Saturday together which we both enjoyed and which had given me one final opportunity to be his daughter. And just as on that Grandstand Saturday my father and I completed our forty-seven years together, I now completed the Three Forests Way.

ON MERTHYR MAWR

Runner's World Training Log.
Day: Wednesday. **Distance:** 7 m. **Time:** 1 h. 20 min.
Weather: Fog and ice. **Course/notes:** Ran with the
Blackheath Harriers. Someone gave us a lift to the Rose
and Crown, Locksbottom, and left us there without any
money so I couldn't have copped out even if I'd wanted
to. My longest road run ever. Might make 35 miles this
week.

The first race I ever ran was on a Sunday morning
three days short of Christmas, 182 miles from home. For
an hour before the start of the 1996 Merthyr Mawr
Christmas Pudding 10k the wind-blasted dunes of Swan-
sea Bay buzzed with life as men dressed as fairies pinned
numbers on their fronts, women stretched their quadri-
ceps against trees and an apprehensive line formed at
the pungent Portaloo known in running circles as a
NURD (Not Unless Really Desperate). I had the hot
forehead and heavy legs of flu but all the same I felt
greatly privileged to be able to don my thermal vest and
tights, fill every available pocket with Kleenex and cold
remedies and join this knee-flexing, steamy-breathed
throng. Just think, I could have been with my unlucky
colleagues in Canary Wharf, who even now were probably
dragging themselves from hostelry to hostelry, downing
champagne, pulling crackers and performing all the other

back-breaking chores of bringing out a sports section at Christmas.

The only cloud on the horizon was that at some moment in the none too distant future I would have to cover six miles of some of the bleakest, most hostile terrain in Britain, and I speak as one who has in her time walked from Wootton station to Villa Park with 2,000 Leeds supporters. Of all the races that no one outside Runner's World has ever heard of, the Merthyr Mawr Christmas Pudding 10k is one of the most famous and most sadistic. It was the brainchild of a former Olympic marathon runner called Steve Brace, who lives close by and used the leaf-carpeted forest and yielding dunes as his summer training route. It is run a few miles inland from Porthcawl, where my family sometimes took holidays when I was a child. In those days only half Porthcawl's beach was available to the public. The rest was taken up with the rusting, gullshit-splattered hulk of a wrecked ship, which people made special journeys from all points of the country to view (and you ask what we did before Sky Sports).

We stayed in a nearby village. One night the sweet shop caught fire. When the fire brigade washed their hands of it, my dad donned cricket flannels over his pyjamas, appropriated a ladder and climbed in through an upper window. At great personal risk he brought six jars of boiled sweets to safety. I had free pear drops and aniseed balls for a year, some fused into delicious clusters.

Yes, I had very happy memories of Porthcawl and Merthyr Mawr. Even in winter, when frost hung from the trees just like it did on Christmas cards, this part of South Wales could be unutterably lovely and, seduced by the promise of Christmas pud, bread, soup and spot prize draw for all finishers, I had rushed to post off my £4 entry fee to the Bridgend Athletic Club. It was only when I got to the start of the race that I realized I had paid £4 to run up a vertical beach.

Eight hundred and eight foot high, sprouting whiskers of grass and gouged out with frosty footprints, the Big Dipper is the biggest sand dune in Europe, and it was twenty strides from the start line. As I jostled for position I looked around at my fellow competitors and realized that what separated me from them was not so much my stupendous lack of athletic talent but the fact that they were smiling eagerly at the prospect of shinning up this gruesome wall of sand while I was worrying that I hadn't made a will.

Halfway up I glimpsed Mike King, cameras hanging from his shoulders. As I staggered towards him, what I meant to say was, 'That's it, I'm going home,' but what came out was a death rattle. 'All downhill after this,' said Mike comfortingly, turning me to face the right direction and giving me an encouraging shove. (I like to regard that as a touching example of Mike's kindness and am positive that it had absolutely nothing to do with the fact that I was about to throw up over his telephoto lens.)

I soon manoeuvred myself smoothly into position two miles behind the leaders and when I say that the next thousand yards or so, a stretch of tarmac road stippled with frozen cow dung, was by far the most entertaining part of the race you will understand just how seriously hellish the rest of it was: mile upon mile of bleak moorland, pockmarked track, lumpy mud and matted grass, strafed by crosswinds and dotted with sheep whose coats were iced solid. I emerged at the foot of a rock-strewn hill and embarked upon the final challenge, which was to run through a stream. I felt extremely sorry for myself, and even sorrier for the marshal who had been spending the last twenty minutes ankle deep in sub-zero water waiting for me to finish.

I shook hands with him gratefully and congratulated him on the Bridgend Athletic Club's masterly organization of the event, its unique charm and festive nature, and then I said, 'Well, that's it, then. I expect you'll be glad to get into the warm.'

'Oh, can't do that. There's a few out there yet.'

I looked back the way I'd come and was absolutely flabbergasted. At least three more mist-shrouded figures were lurching down the hillside towards us. And as I crossed the finishing line and stood shivering in the queue for bread, soup and spot prize draw I cheered myself with the following thoughts:

1) I had run up the Big Dipper and lived.
2) I had won a Christmas pudding.
3) There were three runners in the world who were even more useless than me.

A few days later, the editor of 'Active' called. 'How did it go on Merthyr Mawr?'

'I hope you realize I put my health at risk,' I snapped. 'You're not meant to run with a temperature. I could have damaged my heart.'

'Oh dear. I hope you'll be better soon—'

'Thank you.'

'—because we'd like you to camp out on the Brecon Beacons tomorrow night.'

'You bastards. I hate the lot of you. I wish I'd never taken this job.'

It was the last time for a long few months that I would be so happy.

NO LONGER ACTIVE

Runner's World Training Log.
Day: Monday. **Distance:** 7 m. **Time:** 1 h. 5 min.
Weather: Rain. **Course/notes:** Through Blackheath
Village and Lee to the South Circular, back through
Kidbrooke. It was runner's time: five or six of us padding
along the pavements, in that special state known as
runner's trance. A cold night and you could hear the
station announcements from Greenwich, floating up the
hill and across the heath.

Towards the end of my dad's life I had to take him to the
chiropodist. A lady in a Thatcher-blue overall clipped his
toenails and made the sort of small talk which arises in
circumstances more intimate than at the greengrocer's but
less than chez, say, the urologist. Personal details stopping
short of outright self-revelation and body function. 'And
what did you used to do?' she asked.

My dad drew himself up a little bit straighter and said,
'Soldier.'

He had lived for eighty-seven years and had been a
soldier for approximately five of them, during the Second
World War. Already over the age for call-up, he nevertheless volunteered and quickly rose to the rank of captain.
The nearest he got to the front was Essex. But though he
had spent much more of his life doing other things,
defending Chelmsford and Frinton-on-Sea from the Hun

was in some way the most fulfilling period of his life, the time when he was a patriot, a leader and defender of his family and community. Being a soldier was his personal myth.

Mine came about over an even shorter length of time. Eight months on 'Active' was all it had taken, plus the encouragement of sweet-natured, though possibly sight-impaired, colleagues like Alice, who on my return from some particularly hideous bout of fell-running or kick-boxing would smile on my wind-battered face and creaking knees and declare, 'You are an inspiration to us all.'

The myth was that I was this fantastic, ageless, energetic creature who every week disappeared to perform some new feat of athleticism and daring before returning to carry out the supermarket trip and scrub algae off the sides of the fish tank. Thus were nourished two aspects of my character which I'd always felt were rather iffy, namely personal valour and domestic competence.

Looking back now on those days with 'Active', I remember thinking that for the first time in my life, I'd found something that was completely, utterly me. During those eight months I had played the heroine: roaming, battling against the elements and myself, enduring, risk-taking, often being humbled and humiliated, but very occasionally succeeding; for life, my life anyway, it was a pretty fair metaphor. Getting my photo in the paper most weeks wasn't all that bad either, and after years of my having to scrape up the membership fees, people were actually paying *me* for going to the gym. I was on the brink of a £10,000 a year salary increase. The new Mercedes was almost parked in the street, a new computer as good as on my desk, the top floor bathroom already stripped out and redecorated in my head. But more than anything, I felt realized. I was at last in touch with a central, undeniable self, what the psychologists call the fully-who-I-am.

'Active' was launched in April 1996. By then I had been at the *Sunday Telegraph* for six months, routinely covering football and snooker as I had done for eighteen years and five papers while wondering how many more papers and years it would be before I found It. I even knew what It was. It was all there, all in my brain already, like a limbo file I just had to get back. I wanted my paper to start a fitness section. I was an evangelist for aerobics. I wanted to tell every fat, depressed, forty-year-old woman in the country how to be able to get back into her size 10 jeans.

One of my favourite bits in *Fried Green Tomatoes at the Whistlestop Café* is at the beginning, when Mrs Cleo Threadgoode remarks wistfully that she 'cain't tell you when it was I got to be so old. It just sorta slipped up on me.' Well, six years previously I had no idea how I got to be such a pink-faced, slowed-down, exhausted, jumbo-sized blob.

Actually, I did really. What just sorta slipped up on me was a decade of solid munching and glugging and the tendency to drive everywhere when in leaner days I might have walked. After a colleague of mine was killed while cycling to work, I even presented my idleness as common sense. To this was added the renunciation of a two packs a day smoking habit that had me plundering the sweetie tin and cheese board every time I felt the pangs of withdrawal. Already a testament to the body-building powers of Beaujolais, Fromage de Chevre, Bendick's Bittermints and a little red Peugeot 205 Gti, I had also had three babies, two at an age when you steal a look at your antenatal notes and are aghast to see yourself described as an Elderly Multigravida. In laywoman's terms, this meant that my body resolutely declined to snap back into shape the way it did when I was twenty.

And it was worse than that. When the second of my children was born, I gave up my job as a football reporter. I was going to be a major scriptwriter. And after three years I wasn't. Nothing I wrote got made. Producers stopped asking me to write things. I felt I didn't exist. Maybe that's why I ate so much. I had to add bulk manually, literally to restore my sense of myself as a person of substance.

It wasn't all grim. My babies were beautiful and my new husband was not only the sexiest, most interesting man in the world but also put the dustbins out. One year I managed to heave myself off the floor long enough to flop back in a chair and write a novel which somebody wanted to publish. Then, when the time came to look at the publicity photos, a shapelessly clothed creature with three chins and bad hair leered from the dust jacket. I realized it was me. Inside I might still have been a little slip of a thing but what the world saw was the winner of first prize in the Luciano Pavarotti lookalike contest.

I dealt with it like I dealt with everything awful: I made it into a joke. No one ever told Virginia Woolf to get her teeth fixed, I said. George Eliot never lost sales through being a frump. Even so, I was unhappy enough about what I'd become to want to do something about it. The trouble was, what? It seems strange to think of it now, but even six years ago the gym was still alien territory for most women; a place smelling of socks and reputedly inhabited by headbangers on steroids. Aerobics classes? You had to wear a spangly leotard before they'd let you through the door and I couldn't get a leotard past my knees.

I fetched up at an exercise class the way I usually fetch up at things I don't really want to do but can't think of a good enough excuse for getting out of. A neighbour was offering fitness courses in her own home and I was too cowardly to say I'd rather have rabies. I had sampled one of these ladies-who-lunch stretch-and-tonefests before. I had waved my arms around for five minutes before the instructor switched off the music and said, 'Will whoever has been eating garlic please open the window.' So I opened the door instead and went out, never to return. No I didn't, I was far too craven to do any such thing. I just stumbled through the rest of the class, odorous and humiliated, but what's true is that I didn't go back.

This new class turned out to be an exclusive affair held in the swishest house in our area and run by a whip-thin, gimlet-eyed young woman who made us do excruciating things to our muscles to the sound of Mozart and prodded our leotards to check whether there had been any back-sliding in the matter of Danish pastries. The regulars were all friends and neighbours. Never underestimate social guilt as a motivator. If you stop turning up, you will feel embarrassed and start hiding behind the Bathroom Tissues shelves when you spot your former classmates in Sainsbury's. Your lie that you have not been well or are under a bit of pressure at work goes round in the form of rumours involving divorce, cancer or bankruptcy. And anyway, around that time two things happened which seemed rather extrordinary. The first was that I got thinner, and the second was that I actually started to enjoy myself.

That was something I'd forgotten how to do. By enjoyment I don't mean the kind of waves-crashing, bells-ringing, bluebirds-swooping occasions to do with men or babies, but ordinary having yourself a good time, the sort you have when you're about five with a few friends. I was *playing*.

Fitness crept up on me by stealth. The decorous strains of Wolfgang Amadeus were no longer enough. My new-found strength and suppleness had me longing to leap around and take on something less languid. One Sunday afternoon, I sneaked into the step aerobics class at our local leisure centre. I was frightened that it would be full of lithe young women in crop tops who would eye me with contempt and pity. There were a few of those but more, many more, were people rather like me, shrouded in old T-shirts to hide the bulbous bits and cowering in the back row where we could trip over our steps in obscurity.

So, in the ensuing six years I stepped, I stormed the bastion of the gym, got the tennis rackets out of the garden shed for the first time in ages and bought a pair of running shoes. *Running*. An activity which I had last, reluctantly, performed at school, at which I sometimes made the C team if I was unlucky, which I associated with cold foggy afternoons and wet Aertex. If you'd told me when I was fourteen that running would one day give me adventure, confidence, pride, calm and even, maybe, sometimes, a reason to go on, that it would work on me far more magically than any mind drug, that through running I would learn far more about myself than I ever did in any psychiatrist's chair, I would have just laughed. But some thirty years on, it was true. And, as we used to say on radio when we were stuck for a better link, then *this*.

This was ... what? Well, on 8 January 1997, late in the evening, just after the last swallow of the last glass of Marques de Grinon 94, the editor of 'Active' called to say I'd lost my job.

Snow was falling. I had just got home from the assign-ment in the Brecon Beacons, backpacking with a group of women who were leaving shortly afterwards for the North Pole. I was not going with them, but yomped up and down Pen y Fan till dusk and came to discover the immense psychological satisfaction gained from carrying a burden on your back all day then successfully laying it down.

(I had also discovered a wonderful pub in Talybont-on-Usk, which dispenses game soup in bowls the size of reservoirs. It is called The Traveller's Friend and I can also recommend the steaks. You may find that they too are a bit on the large side to manage at one sitting but you can always take the leftovers home to feed your pack of lions.)

If memory serves me right, the editor began by telling me how well I had done on 'Active'. This is the conversational equivalent of the loss-leader, a ploy in which supermarkets display baked beans at 5p per can just inside the entrance to lure you in. With the 34p you have saved on baked beans, you then buy truffle oil, fresh Japanese seaweed, 2lbs of cepes and a whole tuna. When the editor told me how well I had done, I responded by argumentatively nodding in agreement and then as he went on to say that 'Active' was being axed in April in favour of a stand-alone health section called something else – I now forget – like 'The Good Piles Guide', and that it was going to be staffed by young men in red braces and girls called Fiona and that we were all doomed, doomed, I just couldn't bloody *stop* nodding and saying, 'Yes . . . Yes . . . Absolutely,' until the very end of the phone call, when he said, 'Please don't take it personally,' and with a last quarrelsome, 'No . . . No . . . Absolutely . . .' I shook my head instead.

But of course I took it personally. At the height of my misery and paranoia, I may even have thought that someone – the editor of the *Sunday Telegraph*, Ann Widde-combe, possibly God – had spotted me having too good a time. Maybe it was my come-uppance for spending the last few months boasting about my wonderful job when everyone else was working for the National Health or teaching in state schools or getting down-sized. Maybe I had the wrong feng-shui in my house or I hadn't watched out for Uranus transiting my natal Moon or whatever. But then I decided it was just that you can't ever legislate for the sheer bloody-mindedness of life, the force majeure and acts of God, the lamp-posts that you walk into because you're too busy concentrating on not falling down manholes. It's like dying really. You do everything to stave off the moment, keep fit, eat the right things, give up bungee-jumping or drinking a bottle of rioja a night, but one day it just happens to you anyway.

NOT TOUGH GUY '97

Runner's World Training Log.
Day: Tuesday. **Distance:** 5.5 m. **Time:** 1 h.
Weather: Slush. **Course/notes:** Blackheath village to
Lewisham via Lee Park. Yellow lights, empty shops,
fathers dismantling Christmas trees behind steamed-up
windows.

I'm quite used to getting sacked by now. Everyone is who
works in newspapers or television or broadcasting, and I
strut my stuff in all three. OK, it's never really the sack –
people like me don't have to scrabble about for our P45s
because we all operate on short-term contracts, or even
no contract at all but carefully worded letters of appointment which make you feel wanted but would be toast in a
court of law. But the result's always the same – no four
figure sum in your bank account next month and you
cancel your order from the latest Racing Green catalogue
and at the supermarket your hand hovers over the Economy biscuits.

Usually I start off feeling sorry for whoever has to
deliver the news. This is almost never the person respon-
sible for rendering me homeless/bankrupt at one stroke
but someone I like very much who is in an agony of
embarrassment because s/he's got to fire the bullet. I
know that however horrible it is for them it's nowhere
near as horrible as it is for me, but this still doesn't stop

me spending the next five minutes trying to make them feel better. Heartened by my sympathy, s/he then starts going on about all the other ones who've got the chop, and how these people are even worse off than me, so I put the phone down thinking, Tch, poor Amanda/Trevor/Rick. Then in the night I think, Hang on. They haven't got to pay school fees. They aren't forty-eight. They hadn't just been promised an extra ten grand a year. Their cars aren't rusting heaps of crap.

When a job ends that you've particularly liked, you go through a process akin to the four stages of mourning. First you're numb. Then you're angry. Then you realize the job isn't going to come back any more whatever you do by way of sticking pins into voodoo dolls of your replacement, so you move on to grieving for your lost picture byline or whatever. Then what's meant to happen is serene acceptance, which means that you shelve your plan to waylay the guilty editor/producer with a machete and curt greeting on the lines of 'This time it's personal' because some time soon you and s/he are going to need each other again.

Because I've been given the bum's rush so many times by so many papers and radio stations and TV companies and shortly after been taken on by so many others, it doesn't usually take me long to pick up the broken crockery, work through a box of Kleenex and head onward and upward. But this time I seemed to get stuck on the angry stage, when all my conversation took on the quality of a Channel 4 themed night. 6.00 p.m.: Those Fuckers at the *Sunday Telegraph*. 7.50 p.m.: Middle-aged woman bangs on about those heartless bastards at the *Sunday Telegraph*. 9.00 p.m.: Why the *Sunday Telegraph* Are A Bunch Of Shits, by a sacked sportswriter. 1.00 a.m.:

Another chance to see Those Fuckers At The *Sunday Telegraph.*

It was in this spirit of *entente cordiale* that I set out for the Midlands on a crisp January Sunday to run Tough Guy '97.

*

Let's get one thing straight about Billy Wilson from the start. The promoter of Tough Guy is not far from being a saint. He rounds up kids from the meaner streets of Wolverhampton and gives them jobs on his farm as an alternative to pinching cars. He also runs a horse and donkey sanctuary and here we come to the nub of the matter. Providing a billet for surplus equines to live out their last days in peace and comfort requires regular injections of the folding stuff and Wilson has obviously cottoned on to the best way to cover its running costs. Roughly, it works like this. Devise a 14-mile cross-country race based on all your worst nightmares, prepare a disclaimer saying, 'I confirm that if I should die, it is my own bloody fault for coming,' and 2500 people will turn up from far and wide and hand over £30 to prove how manly they are.

When I say manly, I am of course using the word in a strictly non-gender specific sense. Around 10 per cent of Tough Guy's entrants are allegedly women though by the time they have swum underwater through tunnels, dived into trenches filled with floating ice, slithered beneath twenty feet of barbed wire and been electrocuted, it's hard to tell since all you can see of anybody is the whites of their eyes. But mainly Tough Guy is run by men. Men emerging from the undergrowth with blood pouring from gashed legs. Men going 'Aaargh!' as sub-zero water hits their nuts. Men scraping bits of barbed wire out of their ears. Men sobbing, 'I can't go on.'

Aren't people extraordinary? Show them an experience which will cause them extreme discomfort and humiliation, leave them out of pocket and with no chance of redress should anything go wrong and they'll sign up in droves. Just look at how, in 1992, they voted the Tories back in for a fourth term of government.

The first few miles of Tough Guy looked merely awful, the sort of stuff you meet in every cross-country race taking place in Britain between November and February: running up and down hills in shoes clogged with sludge, slipping on damp leaves, barking your shins on logs, a bit of hypothermia here, a broken ankle or two there. After that, the fun really started: so much fun that when I spotted that between two oak trees, high in the air, was a rope, and when I was given to understand that in due course I would be suspended from it as I made my way from one oak to another, the most astonishing thing happened. I pulled my hamstring just by looking at it. With great regret, I withdrew from the event.

Mind you, right up till the last moment I wavered. I might have been in a bit of a huff with the *Sunday Telegraph* but hey, listen, I'm as manly as the next woman. And besides, the race was in such a good cause. Then as my eyes swept over the Killing Fields, The Swamp, Dead Leg Marsh, Tunnel Terror and the wildly misnamed Paradise Climb a thought popped into my head. It was, 'Sod the donkeys.'

I didn't want to prove how tough I could be. I didn't feel tough. I felt dreadfully, dreadfully feeble. Moreover, I strongly didn't want Mike King to immortalize me on film waist deep in icy water with mud and, possibly, fish streaming from my nose. I didn't want to be the butt of my own joke, staggering round a hideous assault course for hour after hour, knowing all the decent people would be crossing the finish while I was still up to my nipples in a swamp alongside the grizzled old bloke in the London Marathon '84 T-shirt and someone dressed as Mr Blobby. I knew I couldn't win, and I didn't want to be seen beaten. I'd been humiliated once by the *Sunday Telegraph* when they took my job away from me and no way was I going to reciprocate the compliment by humiliating myself on their behalf.

Gosh, don't I get up on my hind legs sometimes? And because it got worse, because I whiled away the entire journey back to London with repeats of that well-loved classic Those Fuckers At The *Sunday Telegraph*, and because the minute I walked into the house I switched on two lights and both bulbs blew, and because on the following morning the clutch failed on my car, I shall close this unedifying episode by talking instead about women-only classes at health clubs.

Women-only classes are often called Tums and Bums, these being the places to which Belgian chocolates and deep-pan four-cheese pizza travel directly after entering the mouth. Most aerobics classes are in any case women-only without the need to spell it out, males being far too terrified or repelled to brave the wobbling, pounding maelstrom of female flesh that is called Fatbusters on the club brochure but is widely known among instructors as Vile Bodies. Other classes are given special, womany names on purpose to keep men out. These include Soft and Gentle and Aqua Motion, and anything else which evokes knitting wools and colonic irrigation.

Men-only classes are not prevalent, though if one were specially created for them it would probably be called Butts and Nuts. Classes designed to attract men are those which suggest urgent, dynamic male activity such as Pumping Iron or Hard and High, though not Roll Over And Start Snoring. A masculine tilt can be achieved by tacking on an exclamation mark. Aqua Motion! Post Natal Exercise Class!

Men will sign up for anything with Challenge in the title. This is because it is a challenge for them to get through the class without being arrested for indecent exposure, particularly during the leg extensions when the design of running briefs meets the law of gravity.

And that is why at health clubs you often see men in those baggy knee shorts last worn by thirties footballers and founders of the Scout movement. They are not making an ironically retro fashion statement, they are not South African white supremacists, they are merely keeping their trouser furniture under wraps.

THE JOY OF BEXLEY

Runner's World Training Log.
Day: Tuesday. **Distance:** 6 m. **Time:** 55 min.
Weather: Chilly. **Course/notes:** The Blackheath–
Kidbrooke Park trundle. Passed one grim-faced middle-
aged man running in the other direction. Another man in
front of me was just a disappearing arse. Knackered – 40
miles last week. Have to keep telling myself I can do it.

I spent a few more weeks brooding over everything to
which, now I had entered the world of the unwaged, I
could no longer aspire – the Queen Anne rectory with
staff annexe in Hampshire, the modest little weekend
chateau in the Medoc, a matching set of His and Hers
Maseratis, oh, and while we're about it, let's throw in
shoes for the children – and then I decided to look for
alternative employment. This took thirty-six hours, because after springing out of bed and saying to myself,
'Today I'm going to devote my time to seeking alternative
employment,' I spent the best part of an entire day and
much of the following one wondering which would be the
right moment to start ringing editors and how was I going
to pitch my request for work so that it didn't come out as
HELP ME I AM DESPERATE I'LL WRITE ANY-
THING AS LONG AS IT ISN'T FOOTBALL.

I'd grown to hate ringing up editors. My position was
that if an editor wanted you, minions would be dispatched

to track you down. Your phone would ring and presently you would be bandying around words and phrases like 'lunch', 'commission' and 'does £10,000 sound all right to you?' (or 'does £12.50 sound all right to you?' if s/he was from *Five Live*). If you didn't get one of these calls from an editor you could safely assume that s/he had no desire to speak to you whatsoever. To call an editor asking for work was to put yourself on the level of junk mail.

Believe me, I *know*. Many centuries ago when I was a gently-brought-up girl innocently starting out on her working life around those dens of vice collectively known as Fleet Street I was for a short while secretary to a sports editor, and every Tuesday morning I would hear the same roar down the phone. 'Pilkington here! Put me on to the editor!'

Henry Pilkington had once been Someone in football reporting, hence his lordly manner, but over the years his 800-word page lead with picture byline had dwindled into three paragraphs on the F.A. Vase with (writes G.B.H. Pilkington) tacked on the end of the opening sentence. Every season a new batch of keen-eyed, ambitious young men would crowd into the press boxes and he was just another tedious old bore with gravy-splattered tie and piss-stained trousers who had to make way for them. By the time our paths crossed, the sports editor had stopped paying Mr Pilkington his meagre but regular retainer but, in order to ensure he went quietly, told him, 'Call me every week and I'll find some work for you.'

And so every Tuesday morning I would put my hand over the mouthpiece and whisper, 'Mr Pilkington wants to know if you've got a match for him on Saturday. What shall I tell him?'

The sports editor briefly broke off from swigging

brandy from a hip flask and goosing the picture researcher with the big tits to say, 'Tell him fuck him.'

'Mr Pilkington, the sports editor is in conference at the moment but looking down our list of matches I can see they're more or less all assigned. Sorry.'

'All I can say is that it's come to a pretty pass when the secretary decides who is going to work for our newspaper. I don't like your telephone manner at all and I shall be speaking to the editor about it.' Mr Pilkington slammed down the phone and no doubt tottered off to tend to his sick wife, who deprived of the expensive treatment that had been funded by his match reports was expiring in ever-increasing agony. Oh hell, it didn't bear thinking about.

And, of course, I didn't think about it for long. I might not have been a man but I was young, ambitious and keen-eyed and within a few months I had Mr Pilkington's job.

And now, as a prelude to explaining why I never wanted to report a football match again, I will take you back to those sunny afternoons at the start of the '73–'74 season when main stands were built of wood and vibrated to the clatter of studs as the teams walked out through the tunnel, when football shirts were made of cotton, bore a number on the back and a badge at the front and were the same design year upon year, when at half time at Nottingham Forest you could buy a bowl of mushy peas and eat them with a spoon attached by a metal chain to a giant enamel jug and when an unsuspecting young football reporter could push open a door marked Press at White Hart Lane and find herself in a gentlemen's toilet with six pairs of eyes (and who knows what else?) turned accusingly upon her.

The most accusing of these belonged to Ronan Gold-blatt, Chief Football Correspondent for one of the quality broadsheets and by a long chalk the most terrifying-looking human being I had ever met. Goldblatt's eyes bulged like shelled hard-boiled eggs, his face was a sort of mottled salami colour, his mouth was full of large, diced potato teeth. He also wore a long black cloak, and it's hard to describe the overall effect; the closest I can get is a plate of hors-d'oeuvre crossed with Dracula.

Shit. I go through life trying to give the impression that I never think about Ronan Goldblatt from one day to the next, and he's there again, sitting right behind me, hissing, 'Women in the press box! So it's come to that.' He had two obsessions. The first just engendered a feeling of resigned irritation, like wearing wet shoes. He regarded himself as an authority on Brazilian football, and here, before we get on to Goldblatt's other obsession, I will digress if I may. In those days, top sportswriters were awarded not just a picture byline but a strap. In the tabloids, you would be invited to enjoy the aperçus of Dave Sleaze, The Man They Can't Gag. Populist broadsheets like the *Daily Express* would bring you the ravings of Campbell Mucky, a huge, vivacious Glaswegian who changed his clothes every two years and, judging by his breath, sustained himself on a diet of pondwater and raw liver. To those who sat within twenty feet of him, he was The Man Who Makes You Gag. Ronan Goldblatt, meanwhile, was The Man Who Wouldn't Fucking Shut Up.

Goldblatt wasn't the only football writer to give me a rough time. 'It's our last acre of sacred ground,' spat Campbell Mucky. (I can't do a Scottish accent so you'll simply have to imagine these words coming at you on a tide of dead heather and rotting neeps.) 'We don't interfere with your sewing and cooking. Why would you want to interfere with our football? Would you not prefer to meet us with a bottle of Dom Perignon and a dozen candles after a nice fragrant bath?'

'Campbell,' I said, 'that's the best idea you've had all year. I'll keep an eye on the game while you nip off and run yourself one.'

Sorry, I was fantasizing there. As I was saying, Goldblatt wasn't the sole scourge of female football reporters, but he was their Anne Elliott, hating longest, when existence or when hope was gone. Now of course I realize that I had barged in on a long-standing arrangement to have men-only group sex in the press box every Saturday afternoon but at the time I was deeply baffled that I could attract such odium simply by not being a man, and it made me very miserable. And actually there's no way I can write with affectionate nostalgia about people like Ronan Goldblatt because they are mad and horrible.

One night during the summer of 1981, when I had been a football reporter for eight years, and a single mother and girlfriend of the Married Man for rather longer than that, I suddenly became so utterly wet and weepy that I phoned the Samaritans, and that led me via various surgeries and outpatient departments to the consulting room of a kindly Hampstead shrink. I say 'suddenly' but of course it had been a long time building up, this feeling that I was a complete failure at everything that truly meant anything in life, at being accepted by my family, at finding someone to love me, at writing novels and television scripts that people actually wanted to read and make, but this will tell you how absolutely demented with unhappiness I was, how even my last meagre cache of marbles had rolled beyond my reach: what I cared about more than anything as I huddled sobbing in a comfortable chair in Hampstead was not this terrible feeling of not belonging anywhere but that Ronan Gold-blatt didn't like me, and the prospect of going through the rest of my working life with him hissing behind me in the press box and none of the other football reporters talking to me was unbearable.

But here's a strange thing. Around that time I was sent by my newspaper to interview James Fixx, who'd been a tall fat American till he took up running, when he became a tall, lean American. He was over in London to promote his *Complete Book of Running*, and the plan was for me to step out of the front door with him and go for a little jog.

So I bought myself a pair of cheap trainers, stubbed out my cigarette and lasted from his hotel at the top of Jermyn Street to the far edge of the park. Jim Fixx was nearing fifty and I was barely past thirty. That is an age when women like me can run sub-three-hour marathons, and I couldn't manage 500 yards without stopping to cough up great globs of two-packets-a-day yuck.

But it was lovely, almost magical, to be out running in the fresh air instead of lurching round the pubs and clubs of Fleet Street, and as we padded through the tranquil park my troubles were so far away they might have belonged to another person entirely. When we got back I had a glow to my cheeks that for once had not been induced by six double Bacardis followed by a swift grope in Temple car park with the Married Man, and after divesting myself of a few final batches of tar-streaked phlegm I croaked, 'I really enjoyed that and now I know how good it makes you feel I'm going to run on a regular basis.'

Jim Fixx smiled and said, 'I'm glad.' And when I got home I took off the trainers and studied them wonderingly for a long time. And then I threw them in the bin and went out for another box of cigarettes.

Well, life got better despite my best efforts. One day a few of the football reporters began speaking to me. In some cases it might only have been, 'Is this your phone or mine?' but it meant a lot, I can tell you. One day I wrote a script about how I became the first female football reporter, and it was made into a film. One morning I sat up in bed and light was shining through the gap in the curtains on to the dark, curly hair of a man who had not had to go home to his wife. In fact, as recollections of the previous day's celebrations began to come back to me piecemeal, it dawned on me that I *was* his wife.

I left football reporting to have a couple of babies. In the six years that I was away, all the wooden stands were pulled down and replaced, and football strips started looking as though they'd been designed by blind chimpanzees in a paint factory. New press boxes were built, to be filled by new generations of keen-eyed, ambitious young reporters, some of whom were women.

I never imagined I'd go back but of course from time to time I did, lured by the beautiful game and the horrifying bank statement. For the first few games it was always wonderful, as if I'd met my younger self coming up the stairs and then, oh I don't know, it just happened again. I'd walk into a press room and a gnarled old tosser called something like Reg Hiccup of *The Post* would greet me with, 'It's all your fault.'

'What is?'

'All these bloody women in the press box nowadays. You started it.' And I'd remind myself that it was his idea of friendly joshing and only one last feeble wave of a tired old willy and I'd come back with a cutting riposte like 'Ooh, you are a caution,' and we'd all go on our way rejoicing.

Which brings me back to the early days of 1997; the

days when 'Active' got the axe; the days when I never thought I'd work again. I knew that if I went back to football reporting there would still be moments when it would be wonderful, when I would find myself thinking, Mm, I could use this life. Let me relive Alan Shearer scoring three on a late summer day at Ewood Park. Show me a re-run of the first goal ever scored by John Jensen in ninety-eight games for Arsenal. Even give me another chance to see Julian Dicks getting sent off for the eleventh time in his career. But I also knew that if I walked into one more press room and another antiquated clot said, 'It's all your fault,' I would begin to say, 'Oh God, I know, I'm most dreadfully sorry,' and then something would snap. I would get out my Kalashnikov, line up the whole lot of them against the press room bar and riddle them with bullets, balls first.

Of course I wouldn't. I would just go on turning up at Selhurst Park, or White Hart Lane, or Stamford Bridge or Villa Park, season upon season, until one day I would *be* one of those dilapidated old fools, tripping people up with my stick, fretting about my incontinence pad and too deaf to hear the half time whistle. I would be the first female Pilkington.

These were sad and sobering thoughts and I dwelt on them self-pityingly, knowing that it would be but a short step from there to the stash of gin bottles behind the cistern, the prescription for the kind of pills that give you revolving eyes and eventually the locked ward of the NH hospital where I would rock back and forth all day dictating old match reports while a sadistic male nurse sat behind me, hissing, 'Women in the press box! So it's come to that.' Then I thought, Forget it, I'll go for a run instead.

*

I will leave it to the experts and their handbooks to expatiate upon the beneficial effects of running. All I will say is that I went on one of my favourite routes, the one which took me up and down Shooters Hill, past Oxleas Wood and along Bexley High Street. I saw crocuses, squirrels and the first green leaves. I saluted the Bexley-heath Formation Dog-walkers, a crack squad of middle-aged ladies with poodles whose disciplined four-abreast strut was famous for causing pedestrian tailbacks as far away as Erith. The pavements of Bexley were nicely cluttered even on a rainy day in March and I ticked off all my familiar landmarks – paint shops, old-fashioned ironmongers, second-hand car showrooms and the old lady who always timed her shuffle from the launderette to the Post Office to coincide with the moment I practised my one-minute sprints. We had never spoken but after colliding with her so many times I looked on her as an old friend.

And after an hour or so of contributing generously to the European sweat lake, filling up my mouth with dust and small flying insects and wiping off snot with my sleeve, I cut back across the heath and arrived home feeling taut, powerful and mysterious. The London Marathon was just three weeks away and I was as ready as I'd ever be.

ME AND STEVE CRAM

Runner's World Training Log.
Day: Monday. **Distance:** 13 m. **Time:** 2 h. 3 min.
Weather: 100% spring. **Course/notes:** Grove Park–
Bromley–Chislehurst. Warm pavements, rush hour.
Daffodils, almond blossom, people pulling down metal
shutters over shop windows. Last long run before the
marathon.

I went to Olympia and bought a pair of sorbothane
insoles. All I want to know is: *why?* Of all the necessities of
life – food, shelter, someone to love, a car with a gearbox
that doesn't go bust halfway up the M4 on a freezing
night – sorbothane insoles, and their travelling companions sorbothane heel pads, came a long way down my
list, along with heart-rate monitors, and entry forms for
the No More Mr Nice Guy 200-mile Cross-country Dash
or something, and air-conditioned singlets, and training
tights with fluorescent leg flash so that at night motorists
could see who they were knocking over. These too were
bulking out the white polythene bag, stamped with Flora
London Marathon and roughly the size needed to provide
a shroud for a dead alsatian, that I dragged through the
front door on my return from the National Exhibition
Hall. I say again, *why?*

Actually, I can tell you why. Running the London
Marathon itself – that is, turning up at the start in

Greenwich Park, puffing and blowing for 26.2 miles, then picking up a medal just up the road from Buck House – will take you anything from 2 hours 8 minutes to something more seven-ish in nature, depending on how fast your legs go round, but 'running the London Marathon' in its true, wide sense eats up six months of your life.

Believe me, that is no exaggeration. A short while back I appeared on a television programme with Steve Cram. For our younger readers, let me just explain that long, long ago, all of fifteen years or so, Steve Cram was a colossus of middle distance running. He won gold medals. He had legs that began at his ear lobes. So swiftly and uncatchably did he cover 1500 metres that his 1985 European record was only broken by Fermin Cacho on 13 August 1997. In short, had Steve Cram worn a skirt, I would have knelt and kissed the hem of it, but had to be content with asking longingly, 'What was it like to be a real runner?'

'The only way I can explain it,' said Cram, 'is that it was like being in love. Even when you weren't with them, whatever you did, wherever you were, you weren't able to stop thinking about that person. Running was the same. It dominated every other aspect of your life.'

And I looked at him helplessly, because he was talking about *me*.

Just to demonstrate the totally sad nature of my affliction, let me remind you that I no longer needed to lace up a pair of running shoes ever again, because, as the former editor of 'Active' said, with the tact and diplomacy for which he was noted, 'Look on the bright side. Now you won't have to do the London Marathon.' But it was too late. I was already hopelessly, irrevocably hooked. I fell asleep worrying whether I needed cushioned or stability shoes. I woke up wondering how to optimize my fluid intake. Between waking and sleeping my daily schedule in the last four weeks before London looked like this:

Run: 2 hours
Walk rest of way after left knee packs up: 1 hour
Scrape dogshit off shoes: 20 minutes
Repeatedly squeeze left knee and consult medical
    textbooks to find out if such a condition as iron
    filings in the patella: 3 hours
Consume training diet of pasta and fruit: 30 minutes
Fall foul of severe Proper Food deprivation and eat
    Roquefort sandwich, leftovers of venison stew, two
    hazelnut yogurts, helping of trifle and a cold
    chipolata: 3 minutes
Doze bloatedly: 2 hours
Wake 2 stone heavier and realize nothing for it but to
    work off effects of Roquefort sandwich etc., by going
    for a
Run: 2 hours

And so it went on until, some twenty-four hours before I was due to gather at the start, I found myself on a platform at Earls Court station with 39,000 souls all waiting, like me, to board the train to Olympia in order to pick up their race numbers.

As I've gone through life and settled in various communities – the more squalid streets of Bristol where I had the student flat, then my first London pad where I set out my hi-fi equipment and unrolled the futon in a damp-walled shoebox beyond the far end of the Northern Line, then my first married home and so on, I'd noticed one constant. Wherever I hung my hat there was always a harmless neighbourhood nutter who rode around on an ancient bicycle. One had an L-plate strung round his chest; another wore a fireman's helmet and tweed jacket;

like successive actors in a long-running West End production, each nutter would bring his own interpretation to the role. But they had one thing in common beyond a general benevolent doolalliness. Spring, summer, autumn, winter, the nutter always wore shorts. And as I stood on the platform at Earls Court, listening to a bunch of wizened men in green vests printed with Guildford Greyhounds singing, 'Oggy, oggy, oggy! Oy! Oy! Oy!' I couldn't help noticing that every person I saw was travelling to Olympia in shorts. When I looked down it dawned on me that I too was wearing shorts, had worn nothing but shorts for the last six weeks, was actually even then considering whether I had enough shorts or perhaps needed one more pair of running briefs with flame-retardant gusset and unique detachable rainhood (I think I have that right) to be on the safe side. At that moment, the tube train drew up. I boarded it and whiled away the crowded ride to Olympia by pondering where on a Saturday morning in Kensington I could pick myself up an L-plate.

But it was a fine thing, all the same, to be part of this happy band of running men and women. I strolled limberly up to a desk, signed for my race number and, pausing only for a few nonchalant quad stretches that quite clearly said, 'No fun runner, me!', reached a line of benignly smiling young people whose sole purpose for being there seemed to be to hand me all sorts of booty. Before I was out of the registration area I was the proud possessor of not only the alsatian's body bag but a giant blue plastic carrier (empty except for three leaflets), a packet of crisps and bottle of water, a blister plaster, a tub of Vaseline, a deodorant and something squishy in a sachet which burst before I could decide whether to rub it on my knee or mix it into a stimulating drink.

Downstairs from the registration area an exhibition was taking place, an exhibition laid on solely for the benefit of people who liked promenading round Kensington on a nippy April morning in shorts. It was full of stalls called Runners' Things, and More Runners' Things Than They've Got, and If You Think They've Got Lots Of Runners' Things, Wait Till You See The Runners' Things We've Got Here. In fact, it was runners' heaven and I'm afraid it went to my head. I passed near on half an hour at a bookstall, thumbing through titles like *100 Things You Didn't Know About Ilio-Tibial Band Friction Syndrome*, and *Fartlek Made Simple*. I rummaged through baskets of half-price vests which were, alas, all leftovers from the World's Tallest Man competition. I queued for my free sample of something called a Power Bar, which was virtually indescribable, though if you like snacking off bathroom tiles it might be just your kind of thing. In a state of happy absorption, and still picking pieces of grouting out of my teeth, I fetched up at a stall called something like Run To Seed where a group of grey-haired men in purple vests printed with Ramsgate Roadhogs were baying in loud, runners' voices. 'Colin's going to turn round as soon as he gets to the finish and run back to Greenwich,' I heard one say.

'Only back to Greenwich?' said another of them, rolling his eyes in scorn at such a pantywaisted project. 'Roger's going to get to the finish, turn round, run all the way back and then do a circuit of the M25 before he goes home.'

'That's nothing,' said someone else. 'Dick here, he's going to get to the finish, turn round, run all the way back, do a circuit of the M25 then keep running round England till this time next year when he'll start all over again at Greenwich.'

I poked around a box of weird-looking plasticky arte-facts and was thinking idly that these were exactly what you'd get if Tupperware and the Ann Summers catalogue ever colluded on a joint venture when a voice said, 'Need any help?'

I looked up to find Dick grinning at me dementedly. He was long, weathered and thin, like two sticks of salsify held together by shorts. 'Uh, no thanks,' I said.

But Dick had clearly decided to dazzle me with his expertise. 'Water bottles,' he said. 'You drink from them.'

'Gosh, I thought you hung it round your ear.' I grabbed a pair of sorbothane insoles and took them up to the counter. At least they were a recognizable shape and I would know not to stick them on my nose.

Dick – I never got around to finding out his surname but I fancy his parents had been called Mr and Mrs Head – said, 'Ever used those before?'

'Sorry?'

'You don't want to run in anything you haven't used for at least sixty years, seventy if you're really after a fast time. Chap next to me in the Timor To Tibet 800-mile Trail Trial picked up a nasty blister 522 miles short of Llasa. Tried out a plaster he'd only had in his bumbag for four years and' – he made a throat-slitting gesture – 'had to leave his foot at the bottom of Kinchingunga. Cost him two seconds off his finishing time.'

'As a matter of fact,' I snapped, 'I get through six pairs of these a month. More if I go over 150 miles a week.'

Back home I grumpily emptied all my shopping on to the bed and it was, of course, like coming round from a sleepwalk. I was the owner of three bottles of special carbohydrate drink which I seriously could not remember buying – a sticky, dreadfully sweet special drink which coated the inside of my mouth like bubblegum-flavoured wallpaper paste. The tights with the fluorescent flashes were more than a foot too long. If I wanted to get any wear out of them, I would have to train in stilts. Resignedly, I set about butchering the sorbothane insoles till they fitted my shoes. I walked around on them. They were very comfortable. After half an hour, they also made my calves feel as though someone had stuck a rolled-up newspaper down them. Eventually, feeling very silly and rather sick (I could *not* get that bloody taste of bubblegum out of my mouth) I sat down and gave in to a good old fret, about whether or not I'd make it to the finish, about the sheer enormity of going for a run IN PUBLIC, about hundreds and hundreds of people lining the pavements to watch me dribble and get my sleeves covered in snot, and by the time darkness fell I was actually wondering whether I could pull out of the race on the grounds of severe bubblegum poisoning.

But the mood passed, and not all of my purchases were catastrophic. During my visit to the Exhibition Hall my eyes had been drawn to a pile of merchandise labelled 1000 Mile socks. Naturally my first thought was that they were the footwear of choice for people called Dick but no. They were simply guaranteed to accompany your feet along an accumulated 1000 miles of pavement without wearing out. And at £4.99 what a bargain they turned out to be. I wore them for the first time during the next day's race and they remained springy and sweet-smelling to the last, which was more than I could claim for their owner. Since then, they have run Le Touquet with me, and Galway and Munich and the seafronts of the Costa Brava, and they have been all round Inverness, not to mention up and down Snowdon and Scafell Pike. They are now approaching their 999th mile, but it will be with a heavy heart and a tear in my eye that I say, 'Goodbye, faithful friends,' as I dispatch them to the great laundry basket in the sky.

I have not, of course, been paid a penny by the manufacturers for mentioning 1000 Mile socks, and it goes without saying that were a van containing a lifetime's supply of this wondrous hosiery to draw up outside my house as a mark of acknowledgement from a grateful manufacturer I would naturally send them right back where they came from. The very thought!

P.S. That goes for Animal watches, too.

P.P.S. And, of course, anything supplied by Field & Trek.

THE LONG RUN

Runner's World Training Log.
Day: Sunday. **Distance:** 3 m. **Time:** 30 min.
Weather: April sun. **Course/notes:** Gave sorbothane
insoles a last chance. Jogged across the heath to
Greenwich Park to look at the start. Crash barriers,
NURDS, baggage vans, start lines. Enjoyed busy scene.
Massaged calves. Binned sorbothane insoles.

Dream: I come home eighth in the London Marathon.
My friends from the *Sunday Telegraph* are there. I am
surprised I have done so well but modestly rise to the
occasion and acknowledge my feat.

Because I was small and middle-aged and had short legs
and an unquenchable thirst for an Italian wine called Uva
di Troia of which we had recently been able to obtain three
cases at preferential prices, I did not cherish any very great
hopes of fighting it out for the winner's medal along the
Embankment just after eleven that Sunday morning. So it
turned out, but what the hell. As Baron de Coubertin often
said to me, It is not the winning that counts, it is the taking
ten minutes just to work your way up to the start line, and
the battling it out to the death with men dressed as Pot
Noodles, and the surviving of the cobbled stretch at St
Katharine's Dock, and the way your toenails turn to the
colour of Ribena, and the free cheese and tomato sandwich
and bag of crisps they give you at the end.

No, I'll admit I wasn't a very good runner, but neither were most of the people whose journey I was sharing. We'd all spent six months in shorts. We'd all put on the woolly hats and stupid tights and struggled over the parks and heaths of Britain in any weather that wasn't actually a typhoon. Some were nearly very good. They probably ran London in 2 hours 29 minutes, which made them about the length of Birdcage Walk away from greatness and must have been rather frustrating. Others, like me, were set apart by a rather longer slog. If you want to know just how long a slog it was in my case, I can only put it like this. When Joyce Chepchumba and Liz Mc-Colgan were neck and neck in the Mall, I had just crossed Tower Bridge.

But this is the way I look at it. There are billions of people in the world and out of all of them only a very small number, a minimicrodot of humanity, are con-structed in such a way that they can run 26.2 miles in 2 hours and a few minutes. A couple of dozen of them turn up every year for the London Marathon. They run towards you. They run past you. They're gone. Would you get your jazzband out and play on the pavement just for that?

It was in this feisty frame of mind that I left Tower Bridge behind me and trundled on with all the other people who were prepared to run halfway across London for a cheese and tomato sandwich. I ran in a bloc which included three elves, the Pot Noodles and a fine cross-section of styles. I was with jaunty bouncers, flailers, lumberers, skitterers and a man who held his arms very high on his chest, like a child riding an imaginary horse. Indeed, if you were one of the good and kindly people who stayed on to watch, cheer and encourage long after the real runners had gone home to put their feet up, you may have glimpsed a beetroot-cheeked, sweat-stained creature leaning forward, pumping her right arm and staring at the ground as though she was pushing an imaginary hoover. If you did, and especially if you had the decency and compassion not to laugh out loud, I'd just like to say a belated, 'Hi.'

Roads unravelled in front of us, sticky with spat-out special carbohydrate drink. Water bottles crunched and exploded under pounding feet. Around the 18th mile I started feeling awful. I'd been running since the dawn of time and there was still so far to go. Eight more miles – it was unimaginable. The mile markers played tricks on me. As I staggered towards them they moved backwards.

Over the next two miles the lower half of my body began transmitting a series of messages, all of them out-raged. My legs were running on empty, I had lost radio contact with my shins, and a woodpecker seemed to be lodging in my knee. Around me runners winced and fussed and gritted their teeth. In front, a man emptied a bottle of cold water over his bottom. Time passed, slower than I could imagine. We reached St Katharine's Dock, where the tarmac road surface abruptly turned to cobbles because, I think, the organizers of the London Marathon genuinely believed that after running twenty-odd miles what we wanted was to have our feet beaten into throb-bing lumps of hamburger. But as the first jolt of pain shot up my legs, I noticed something spooky, something that even now I can't quite find an explanation for. Each cobblestone bore the facial imprint of a certain person I never think about from one day to the next. It was enormously cheering, stomping over a hundred yards of cobbles while yelling, 'Ronan Goldblatt, fuck you.'

And that was about it, really. I staggered and yawed

along Queen Victoria Street, walked the longest half mile of my life up the Embankment, and was overtaken by a man dressed as a rhino. That hurt, I can tell you. I chased after him and left him for dead. At the entrance to Birdcage Walk, Mike King and his girlfriend Cathy sat in the sun like two rather serious children at a rock pool. My two friends. As long as I live, I will never forget seeing them there, specs glinting earnestly. Mike took pictures of me, then discovered that he didn't have any film in that camera. The rhino ran past. I didn't mind. I was so happy.

Of the last mile and a half I remember little, apart from a distance marker partially obscured by branches. Tantalizingly, it read '00 metres to go'. I hoped the missing digit was a four. It turned out to be an eight. But I did it. I ran and ran and I made it to the finish. It had taken me 4 hours, 45 minutes and 0.4 of a second.

I'd like to say I knelt and kissed the ground, weeping tears of pride and gratitude for my safe deliverance but actually I was just frightfully glad not to be running any more. It was like laying down a colossal burden. A woman with tawny hair swept back in a pony tail smiled and hung a medal round my neck. I stared down at it. Even then, I didn't start blubbing. I just thought, 'This is mine. I've trained for it and I fully deserve it.'

Then I wrapped myself in my silver foil blanket and walked around very slowly looking like a Christmas cracker. I ate my cheese and tomato sandwich, felt the sun on my face and listened to runners all around me make tired but happy runner's noise. 'I haven't felt any sensation in my foot since the Blackfriars underpass.'

'Well, I haven't been able to bend my knee since the Cutty Sark.'

'That's nothing. Bloke next to me, his leg dropped off at Canary Wharf. He's just gone running back to look for it.'

I reflected quietly how marathons mimicked life, with their illusions of glory and savage pratfalls and sheer grinding miseries and very occasional raptures. And then I thought, 'That's *quite* enough of that,' and I drank and drank till the water ran down my chin, and gazed upon Admiralty Arch, imagining that on it was a giant scoreboard which flashed my name over and over again in golden lights.

A FEW OF LIFE'S MYSTERIES

Runner's World Training Log.
Day: Saturday. **Distance:** 10 m. **Time:** 1 h. 35 min.
Weather: Showery. **Course/notes:** The Bromley
Loop. Hawthorns in blossom, yellow and green laurels,
dripping chestnut trees. A barking black and white dog
following me along the heath, old girls spilling out of a
jumble sale onto the pavement, and a couple having a
row in a parked car on Hare and Billet Road.

I dressed up for my father: flowered chiffon skirt, chalk
white jersey, tan shoes, my favourite hat. It was two weeks
after the marathon, a few days before the General Election, and the gently breezy morning that had dawned
would have been his eighty-ninth birthday. This time last
year he had been four weeks away from death. I had a
snapshot of him, taken at his birthday tea: his head was
tilted back in laughter and his gloved hands clasped. Mum
said two of his friends had arrived unexpectedly to see
him, and I liked very much how he appeared in the
snapshot; he didn't look old, but had a lightness about
him, as if his burdens had already been laid down. Here
was a human being near the end of his journey, full of joy
at being with his friends. Now I was going with my mum
to visit his grave.

I drove through the clotted Blackwall Tunnel and then Leyton, an unalterably ugly jumble of back streets, faded shops and railway arches where many years ago Dad presided over the London branch of his business empire. Even on a fine day it is a slow and dismal way to leave the city but it has one saving charm, and that is the abruptness with which it ends. One minute I was in the vortex which was the Green Man roundabout and the next I was pootling along Whipps Cross Road with Epping Forest lapping at my wheels to the right and on my left the Sir Alfred Hitchcock Hotel. This was a gauntly handsome edifice which in all the years and at all the times of day and night I had driven past had never once appeared open to the public. The paintwork, however, was always spruce and the windows dark but freshly cleaned. I could only conjecture at what horrific activities were taking place within.

The Sir Alfred Hitchcock and the first green lozenge of forest signalled the outskirts of old-fashioned leafy suburbia. Until twenty years previously, just before the road swung right towards Woodford, a sign boasting 'Open Air Bathing Pool For 2000 People' had stood among the surrounding oaks. Once again, this had been a source of mystery. In all the years I was growing up in the area, I never did manage to find the pool, let alone the 2000 People. Perhaps ... no, surely not ... but could they have been sitting in the Sir Alfred Hitchcock in their bathing costumes all along?

Mum and I walked from her house to the graveyard to put bluebells on Dad's memorial stone. I blush to say this, but it was right by the very place where I had snogged Jug-Eared Richard on Youth Club nights. It also over-looked the cul-de-sac of modest but pretty houses where my parents had begun married life. Mum recalled me as a baby who woke up in the night a lot. 'Not crying, but playing,' she said. Dad had always leapt out of bed to attend to me. 'You were a novelty, I suppose.'

On the wall above the cranny where his ashes lay, a terracotta trough bulged with pansies. To mark the specialness of the day, Mum had also stuck in four red roses by their stems. They looked like corner flags. Underneath, Mum had wanted to put up a plaque saying 'Gone from my sight, but not from my heart,' but I had persuaded her to tone it down a bit. She had settled on, 'Forever with me, dear.'

After our solemn task had been completed and I had finished drying my eyes, we had lunch in Epping. We sat on damson-coloured sofas by a window, wavering between Chargrilled Chicken And Bacon Salad, Fan Of Avocado With Chef's Prawn Mousse and Fresh Salmon With Pasta And Selected Fresh Leaves, which offered Grilled Potato Farl as an added incitement, and over a glass or two of Chardonnay we discussed my dad.

He was, as I've said before, an attractive man, though the soul of propriety. During the war when he was on home leave, all he had to do was walk around in his captain's uniform, with, as Mum smiled reminiscently, 'his little stick at his side', for all the wives in the street to fall for him. Later, he and Mum welcomed into their hearts a magnificent divorced redhead called Jane and embarked on an interestingly triangular friendship which even now I don't think I've quite got to grips with.

Mum liked Jane very much, and so did I – she was witty, cultivated and easygoing – and Dad liked her best of all. She holidayed with us and we shared Christmas, as well as many ordinary family evenings. She became a director of Dad's company. During my teens, when Mum and I were having all our fights, she was my confidante and source of wisdom. She was a lot taller than all of us, and seemed to spread herself over us like an oak. She was always there. When she wasn't, everyone twiddled their thumbs a bit and shut themselves away in rooms.

'Of course,' said Mum, sipping on her Chardonnay, 'there was a lot of talk about how Dad was carrying on with Jane.'

I thought for a moment of the discrepancy in size, and the rectitude of the parties concerned, and said, 'Unimaginable, I would have thought.'

Mum nodded, then said, 'I only doubted him the once.'

She had been on one of her trips to Australia, where my big sister was living at the time. On her return, Dad and Jane met her at Heathrow. Later, a credit card bill dropped on our doormat. It was in Mum's name: a hotel bill for two people, dated the night before she arrived home.

Into Dad's business empire in Leyton marched Mum, and threw the bill onto his desk. 'I think you owe me an explanation for this,' she said, sailing out.

'Of course,' said Mum, taking another sip of Chardonnay, 'he came up with all sorts of explanations – they'd gone to a function in town and decided to stay overnight there rather than drive home, then all the way back to Heathrow in the morning – and there were separate rooms. He tried to make it up to me for a long time. I gave him the benefit of the doubt in the end. What do you think?'

I said I thought in the circumstances I would have done as she did, though for a while would probably have withdrawn certain privileges.

Her eyes gleamed. 'Oh – like sex.'

Actually, I hadn't meant sex so much as shepherd's pie and other favourite dinners. I wasn't sure what this said about my marriage. We were quiet for a while and then she said, 'But he was a dear.'

Two Fans of Avocado arrived and we set to eating and a little light bickering about the General Election, while I ruminated some more on Mum, Dad and Jane. Even as they grew old and as close of play approached, they were still a threesome, feet up in the living room, a plate of ham sandwiches on the table, playing Scrabble and collaborating on the *Telegraph* crossword. The last time I saw her was on a January day a year after my youngest son was born. When it was time for us to leave, Mum and Dad walked down the drive to see us out but for the first time Jane did not. Suddenly I saw her at the window. The light played tricks; her face was illuminated, the room behind her dark. She waved and smiled. I knew right away it was the final goodbye from my older friend and guardian, for whom I felt both huge affection and wistful ambivalence, and that this signified, long after it had physically finished, the end of my childhood. So it turned out; she died three days later. When Mum couldn't get Jane to answer her phone calls, she broke into her flat and found her body. She washed Jane's face and hands and prepared the bed for Jane to lie on. I still think how good and courageous Mum was, and I also feel a quiet triumph on her behalf that she had lasted longer.

What *did* I think, really? Well, when I was growing up it was sometimes like being stuck in a gigantic board game, the rules of which I couldn't quite get the hang of, and even now I'm not sure if I've got them right. But I do know that betrayal in a marriage doesn't have to be sexual, or even conscious. My father felt an emotional fellowship for Jane, however he tried to disguise it, however much Jane spread her branches to cover us all. It was the way he'd light up like a bulb when he saw her, and the stubborn inclusion of her in our plans even when my mother would have preferred her not to be there. And I know, too, all about how unbearable it is when the person you want to be yours and yours alone shares out their world between you and someone else.

Heigh-ho. I suppose all marriages are mysteries to the people outside them, even the children of the marriage. It was a mysterious day all round. When Mum and I returned to her house after lunch, we gasped. Dame Nature had waved her wand and all around the garden tall posts had sprung up and flowered with blue banners saying VOTE CONSERVATIVE.

I left her wondering who had put them there and drove home past the Sir Alfred Hitchcock Hotel where, for a second, I could have sworn I saw a ghostly figure in a bathing costume flit across an upstairs window, but it was only the moving shadow cast by oak branches in the breeze. 'And another thing,' I thought to myself, plunging into the whirl of the Green Man roundabout, 'what *was* a Grilled Potato Farl?'

POST-MARATHON DEPRESSION

Runner's World Training Log.
Day: Saturday. **Distance:** 15 m. **Time:** 2 h. 55 min.
Weather: Chilly. **Course/notes:** The first long road run after the marathon. Had to walk after 10 miles – rogue knee. Amazing moment on the way back through Blackheath. Teenage boy and girl sitting on the pavement, laughing their heads off as I ran towards them. Realized my T-shirt was longer than my shorts and they were trying to see if I was wearing anything under it.

I'm being serious now. I've noticed that my running seems to reflect what's going on in the rest of my life and around that time, in the weeks after the marathon, I became very anxious about being able to get myself home.

I won't bore you with details of my injury (oh, all right, if you insist – Ilio Tibial Band Friction Syndrome) but after running for anything between two and ten miles my knee would abruptly turn into a ball of wool with a pair of knitting needles stuck through it. That is, it felt both extremely painful and very weak, and I would be reduced to an embarrassing Quasimodo-style shuffling along the pavement until my agonies abated, and there was something not very dashing, if you like, about doing that in a sweaty T-shirt and not-quite-long-enough shorts with motorists winding down their windows and having a good old laugh.

And what did that have to do with the rest of my life, pray? Well, this, really. Ron was quite a lot older than me and so we'd sometimes discuss what would happen when he retired, which was that I would become the main breadwinner (he had such touching faith in my powers), leaving him free to concentrate on the truly important activities such as opening bottles of Uva di Troia, falling asleep on the sofa with the Test Match on and occasionally tossing off a little light autobiographical account of walking in Catalonia. And it all sounded fine to me, on those summery nights when we talked about it, sitting in our garden with a glass in our hands watching bees fight it out for tenancy of the best hollyhock and listening to the evening chorus of birdsong and sirens. And the time when he was due to retire got closer but still seemed a long way away, and besides, he was so good at making money anyway, so I didn't think about it very often; in fact, hardly at all. And then he, too, lost his job.

Well, nothing much changed because unlike certain people I could mention, Ron didn't slump around the house banging on about Those Fuckers At The *Sunday Telegraph*, but went straight out and got himself more work. But it was still deeply shocking and quite scary for both of us suddenly to be dog-paddling around in the shark-filled ocean that is life for the freelance and in the same way that I was anxious about getting myself home, I fretted and fussed about how I was going to provide for my family and keep us going when Ron retired. And that was how it came to pass, a few weeks after the marathon finished, that I sat in a line of traffic outside Sainsbury's, nursed my sore knee and logged on to one of those dreary, self-hating depressions which always seem to be loafing around my head waiting to be let in.

The awful thing was that someone had actually died during the marathon. A colleague, Paul, had been at the finishing line in his tinfoil blanket when the news came in. He'd watched the man's wife and kids standing there, grieving, while around them people in silly costumes were being congratulated by friends and family. How shitty can life get? When I thought about that, of course, it made no difference at all to my mood, apart from a vague sense of shame that after coming safely and reasonably enjoyably through one of the few rites of passage available to a woman in her late forties all I could do was sit moping in a traffic jam.

It is essential at times like these to retain a sense of perspective and normally it is enough simply to remind myself that my husband is lovely, I live in a house without dry rot and my children are beautiful, healthy and quite exceptionally intelligent (I speak, of course, from a position of scrupulous detachment quite unconnected with my status as their mother). Even more delightful was the notion that now the General Election was over I would never have to look at John Major's grin ever again, nor Michael Portillo's hair, nor the gap between David Mellor's front teeth. But it was no good. My job was over. The marathon was over. I just couldn't *see* anything out there. And it was then, as I glumly considered the prospect before me, with its absolute featurelessness and vast grey flatness, that I remembered the Bassin d'Arcachon.

*

These days my mum and I rub along pretty well. I think she is a sweet and admirable old bird and she is flatteringly delighted when I allow her to take a £20 cab ride to my house, sit down on a hard kitchen chair and sew name tapes on two separate sets of school uniform in return for a glass of Chardonnay. ('Just a small one, dear – you know I never touch the stuff.') Be that as it may, there is one topic which is guaranteed to rend apart this exemplar of mother–daughter relationships, a topic far more fraught and contentious than those political differences which in the run-up to the General Election led me at one point to consider strangling her over a family dinner in Pizza Hut. That topic is The Trip To France.

I've hated flying almost as far back as I can remember. (Bear with me, if you will – there is a point to this rant.) Flying combines two of the things I most dislike – noise and being cooped up. But this is not the whole story. The truth, of course, is that aeroplanes terrify me. I am so terrified I won't even take one of those courses that teach you not to be terrified, because then I'd fly, and the moment I do that I'll be in a plane crash. I know I'll be in a crash the first time I step back on to a plane because that's the sort of stupid unlucky joke that happens to me, like losing my job.

It wasn't always thus. The first time I ever flew in a plane was when I travelled to France, aged 10. I was on my own, and I thought it was absolutely wonderful to be thousands of feet in the air and not have to be perched between my parents, lying that I'd packed my toothbrush. We took off from Heathrow and after a thrilling hour and a half of watching propellers go round, gazing down on fields like snooker tables and the shirred waters of the Channel and consuming every single component of my in-flight meal down to the triangle of Dairylea I landed at Paris Orly.

I was going to stay with a family called Castaing. They

were acquaintances of my Big Sis, who was ten years older than me and had just got back from a year at the Sorbonne. For some reason lost in the mists of my memory an invitation had been extended to me to spend most of August with Monsieur, Madame and the *enfants* in their holiday villa at Cap Ferret on the Atlantic coast. I pestered my mum to let me go. It was to be my treat for having won a scholarship to the London public school.

At Orly I was met by Madame, who had casual blonde glamour and bosoms the likes of which I had never encountered among the mummies in our little corner of Essex. Monsieur was a hospital consultant. They lived in Tours, in a tall beige house in the rue Traversière, set back from the street by iron gates painted dark green. After a visit to the Eiffel Tower, we went there by train, in the dining car of which I ate my first French food, *frites* as golden and slim as straw and a steak seared with the criss-cross pattern of the griddle. To someone from a household where an added Oxo cube was as *haute* as the *cuisine* got, it was an epiphany. It also turned out to be the high point of my trip.

That evening in Tours I met the *enfants*. Benedicte was thirteen and had the beginnings of Madame's languid chic, bosoms included. Denis, the eleven-year-old, was unremarkable, just a French boy. Veronique, a year younger than me, was dark, sturdy and wore her hair in a glossy bob. Sophie, *la petite*, was chubby and cherubically pretty and later burgled my stash of chocolate. They spoke with beautiful incomprehensibility, in voices like razors dipped in honey.

Benedicte had a smattering of English and was supposed to be my minder for the holiday but, alas, it was not to be. Also invited to Cap Ferret was Janie, Benedicte's school friend, and once I set eyes on Janie I knew the project was doomed, because Janie was the most sophisticated thirteen-year-old I had ever seen. She had sunglasses *and a bikini*. How could I compete for Benedicte's regard when all I could bring to the feast was a modest blue one-piece with a crutch that filled with sea water and ballooned to my knees?

We sat down to a supper of weird pungent vegetables, served by Paulette the nanny from a boiling vat. Some, I was appalled to see, were black. (Aubergines, like Madame Castaing bosoms, had not at that time swept Essex.) Pallid white fish joined the pile of swarthy pap on my plate. Well, I just refused to eat it, of course. And I do believe that if Madame had been there she would have taken pity on me and rustled up something a little less foreign and leguminous (steak *à point* with *frites* would have been perfectly adequate) but Madame had obviously hightailed it with Monsieur round to the nearest Michelin-starred and was washing down her foie gras with Chateau Mouton Rothschild even as Paulette propped her huge French arse on the table next to my plate and persuaded the food into my mouth.

Oh, I had my revenge. Travelling south-west to Cap Ferret the next day in the Castaing family's Citroën, with its dung-beetle shape and strange hissing suspension, I was copiously car sick, covering Paulette with shrapnel of regurgitated mackerel and ratatouille. But it wasn't much of a way to kick off the holiday. The family had rented Villa Kikinette, a four-bedroom bungalow hidden from the road by sand-blasted pines. It had a huge living room, dominated by the dining table, on which Paulette changed the foul nappy of a visiting baby one evening. Benedicte and Janie shared a double bed and I slept on a temporary structure against a far wall.

On the first Sunday we went to church, sitting on

benches in the open air, kneeling down to pray with pine needles sticking in our knees. The church service went on for ever. Everything went on for ever – swimming in the seaweedy ocean, forlornly swinging on the climbing frames at Club Mickey, silently playing ball with beetle-browed Veronique, trying to make sense of oyster beds. On the fourth day, turning bored and lonely somersaults on the sand where Benedicte and Janie had left me, I discovered that every time I thought of my mum and dad my eyes filled with tears. At first it seemed quite an interesting trick but soon it was just another dull way of whiling away my holiday of a lifetime: alone on the edge of the Bassin d'Arcachon, acrobatically blubbing.

Cap Ferret is on a piece of land that's no more than a little finger crooked towards the ocean. On one side of it, the Atlantic pounds and roars. In 1959 it had a giant lighthouse, to which I would make solitary treks in order to pass the time, pausing only at the gift shop to assess badly made dolls in French national dress to bring back to my friends, should the day ever dawn when I was permitted to leave. (As you can gather, I felt *very* sorry for myself.) On the other side of Cap Ferret you have the aforesaid Bassin d'Arcachon, flat, still, giving no hint that beyond it is the busy gaiety of the town from which it gets its name. It was true; I really couldn't see anything out there. I had no escape.

I wrote to Mum and Dad on paper mottled with tears, begging them to let me come home. They never acknowledged the contents of my letter, though every day I received a copy of the *Daily Telegraph*, posted by my dad in some unspoken sympathy. Benedicte and Janie soon decided what an utterly damp squib I was and abandoned me. I shut myself in the vile-smelling lavatory, the ceiling of which was a rendezvous for every fly on the Atlantic coast, and read and re-read the four books I had brought with me, tied together with a brown leather strap. They were *What Katy Did, Little Women, The Reader's Digest Book of Laughter* and its companion volume, *The Reader's Digest Book of Life*, with 'How to Increase Your Word Power' by Wilfred Something-or-other.

Janie found a boyfriend, Joel, a plump hoarse-voiced boy with glasses. One night we joined in a religious procession which involved large numbers of white-clothed children and votive candles. Joel accompanied us and used our candles to light Gauloises for us. It was my first cigarette, but, though I say it myself, I acquitted myself well. Joel also offered to kiss me, but I said no; he was just *too* bespectacled.

At the end of August I skipped lightly off the plane at Heathrow clutching two rock-hard baguettes and talking everybody's ears off, and on the face of it I forgot all about The Trip To France but actually I must have been utterly traumatized. Two weeks later I started my first term at my new school, the one where I turned into a dolt. And yes, it's far too neat to explain everything away thus, but in my memory my childhood has always been divided into the years before I went to France, when I was lively and curious, and the years that followed when I was a lost, rebellious, intractable disappointment.

These days, if my mother and I are with any group of people, anywhere, it only needs the conversation to turn to such subjects as 'France', 'trip' and 'daughter' for an exchange to ensue that will thoroughly mystify the other parties present.

'You wanted to go,' Mum hisses. 'You pestered me.'

'You should have forbidden me to go.'

'Ho! And just how did you propose I did that, Little Miss Tantrum?'

At this point, Mum and I will find ourselves debating the issue to the sound of chairs being scraped back and hurriedly departing footsteps, as friends withdraw quietly rather than listen to a middle-aged woman bellyaching about three weeks in France in 1959 to a frail little widow of eighty-three.

Aren't children ungrateful? I can just imagine Mum happily planning that trip for me, sewing name tapes on my clothes, thinking how exciting it would be, how good to give me an opportunity she'd never had in her blighted childhood. Now I have my own children I can see how much she must have cherished the idea of some time to herself, without the demands of a prattling and boisterous ten-year-old. Perhaps she even dreamed of dinners *à deux* with my father, a little weekend trip or two, drawing up outside a good seaside hotel and lifting from the boot a suitcase which didn't have to be filled with pony books and ankle socks.

The oddest thing about it all was that as soon as I'd left France I couldn't wait to go back. I was in love with this country where I'd not only had my first cigarette and decent chips but my first glass of wine and cornet of pistachio ice cream, my earliest inkling of the dangerous beauty of the Atlantic and the interesting possibilities of a snog. As I grew up France laid on other firsts – a marriage proposal, a honeymoon, a Dorothee Bis dress. I loved the Routes Nationales lined with trees, the smell of Gauloises and pain au chocolat in the mornings, the roads that ran alongside sleepy rivers, the maverick plumbing and city houses set in courtyards, the Paris Metro and the crappy pop music and the way that when I stepped on French land I always felt that little bit more chic and interesting and somehow *bosomy*.

Since that first trip to France, too, I never suffered a

single further pang of homesickness. But every time after that when I had to go up in an aeroplane I'd feel worse and worse about the whole damn thing, even to the extent, on one shameful occasion, of asking to be taken off after the plane had closed its doors and begun taxiing towards the runway, because I never wanted to fly away from home again. And, if the truth be told, I still can't raise much of a cheer for ratatouille.

I've often tried to work out why I was so deeply affected by it all. Perhaps it was because I felt completely foolish. To think I had actually believed I could *do* it. How could I have not realized how long three weeks is to spend away from your bed and house and pets when you are ten years old and have never slept away for more than a night before? How could I not have foreseen what it would be like to be in a place where you have to eat black vegetables while people gabble at you in strange liquid voices?

Of course, I lost my blind trust in my parents, but that is something that comes to us all and is, after all, the key to growing up. Far worse was that I lost faith in myself and I've never completely regained it. I had got stuck out there because no one could come and get me and I had no way of getting back on my own. And ever since then, every time I've started to write a story and got stuck about a hundred pages in, I've had the same feeling of utter dejection, as though I'm ten years old, with no one to talk to and no way of getting back. It's just me at the lighthouse, marooned between the angry big ocean and quiet unfathomable bay, so far away from home.

PART TWO

BACK TO THE FUTURE

Runner's World Training Log.
Day: Sunday. **Distance:** 5 m. **Time:** 45 min.
Weather: Bleak midwinter. **Course/notes:** Last run before Cap Ferret. Trudged up to Ashwater Road and back past Lee Green station and the shop which sells the kind of front doors you'd never want to knock on. Three in the afternoon and already dark. Christmas lights over garage forecourts, frozen dog shit, empty buses. My rucksack is packed and waiting in the hall. Hate leaving home. Will I ever see it again? Et cetera.

I headed south-west on the autoroute from Calais, past Paris, Orléans, Blois, Tours and Poitiers. Nothing to say about them; they were just distant jumbles of roofs, high-rise blocks and hotels wearing their names up top like neon tiaras. It was a cold December morning with a dim sky, two weeks short of Christmas. Nothing to say about the journey, either – a forever of two lanes, three lanes, two lanes, stunted windbreaks and dented crash barriers. Lorry after lorry with the red and white livery of Norbert Dentressangle printed on the side. The usual question: 'Who exactly is Norbert Dentressangle anyway?'
　　I flipped the radio on and whiled away half an hour scanning for a station which wasn't playing the French Christmas Number One, on which three women sang, 'Tic tac, tic tac, disco, disco.' Bloody good idea that,

getting Noël Coward to write the lyrics. Sometimes in France, early in the day and quite how I don't know, you can get Tony Blackburn on Capital Gold. I thought I'd leave that till I was really desperate. I strayed in and out of several news broadcasts, a feature of each of which was that something dire seemed to be happening in Niort. Though, to be fair, that could have been because, like 'wormwood' and 'gall', it's impossible to say Niort and sound cheerful. I settled for Radio Trafic because I had a very immature sense of humour and enjoyed scoffing at French announcers who said, 'Take care. Drive coeshusly. Ze roads are damp zis morning.'

Indeed zey were. Zat's because it always pisses down in the middle of France. Stair rods bouncing off your car bonnet and geysers spouting from truck tyres to blind you at the overtaking point of no return. Even in July the sky suddenly breaks into a sweat. This is the stretch of motorway where I find myself contemplating becoming a better, more considerate person if allowed to survive. I will tape record a long, newsy letter for my old godmother, whose sight is failing; I should have done it before, but Mum's always on at me to keep in touch with her because she has no living relatives and may leave me her house; therefore if I keep in touch with her, she will suspect me of wanting her house. Fuck, shit, that lorry's going to swing out and staple us to the crash barrier. I will also take a postal course in Maths GCSE so I can help the boys with their homework. My marriage always breaks up on this bit, too.

'Pull over, I'll drive.'

'Don't be so fucking macho.'

'For fuck's sake, you're doing twenty miles an hour.'

'I'm trying not to get us killed.'

'A fucking hedgehog just sped past us.'

I'd journeyed the best part of the way to Cap Ferret before. In the summer of 1992 a friend, Clem Thomas, insisted we use his house in the Médoc for two weeks, no charge. Since Clem was a former Welsh rugby international and still built like a warehouse it seemed silly to offend him by turning down this insanely generous offer. The house was six miles inland from the Atlantic coast, fifty miles north of the Cap; I set off one day to show my family the source of my adolescent anomie but fetched up at a different Cap Ferret entirely, one with ten yards of seaweed where the beach should have been and a front lined with fancy shops and restaurants as though it had had cosmetic dentistry. It turned out I'd brought them to Cap Ferret Lege, the post bit which played Old Trafford to Cap Ferret's Maine Road. Did I happen to mention I wasn't much good with maps?

We had a lovely holiday at Clem's house. He's with the saints and angels now, toppled by a heart attack. The kindest, most benevolent man I ever knew, though of course I never faced him in the scrum. I still can't think of his part of France without pangs; it's my Gone Forever Place. When feeling especially masochistic, I exhume the holiday photos: my children pink-kneed and chunky like sugar mice, so small you could pick them up and hug them without end, so young they didn't want you to explain what the Always ad on Capital radio is about. God, they were beautiful. God, I was young. Younger.

Actually, the holiday was not entirely lovely because while we were there Ron was made redundant by his last newspaper but two. I can't believe one human being can do this to another: wait till you go on holiday, find out the number, ring it and say, 'Don't bother coming back next week, or indeed any other week.'

This sort of thing might go down well in Holland

where at Christmas it is considered high jinks indeed to present gift-wrapped turds to your loved ones, but it put a pretty dismal spin on our remaining days in the Médoc. It's to do with expectations, isn't it? I mean, on holiday. Are you ever going to throw your bucket and spade into the car boot with a light heart ever again? Well, I can't any more. You can say this for the *Sunday Telegraph*. At least they sack you at home, so you don't have to go to all the trouble beforehand of buying sunblock and finding your arse won't fit into last year's shorts.

A few miles up the road from Clem's house was a small town, Lesparre. It contained few uplifting buildings or tastebud-stimulating eateries of the sort hymned in guide books. Its most popular crowd-magnet seemed to be the Monsieur Bricolage on the way in. It also had a swimming pool which looked like a gigantic zit.

The pool was the kind of place which took a good hour or so to pinpoint because when, after following the Piscine signs helpfully dotted around the town you ended up in the middle of a field staring at a giant zit, the reaction was to say, 'This isn't it,' turn around and resume your search. But this was it: carmine red, the domed roof pocked with tiny windows, the blue water brimming over the sides of the pool and, during high tide caused by the arrival of the local schoolkids, flooding under the doors of the changing rooms. It looked so temporary, so accidental, a craft landed by aliens, and yet it was the purest and airiest pool in which I ever dipped a toe.

It also had a lodger. I took my children there every morning, and every time a bald German man was swimming up and down, cleaving his way through the water with fierce metronomic splashes, pate and goggles streaming, a polystyrene float between chin and chest. At poolside his immaculately dressed woman knelt with a stopwatch, baying encouragement, the swell darkening first her shoes, then hem, then lap until she looked as though she was suffering from rising damp. They're probably still there; by now the water will be up to her earrings.

Mind you, I expect she wonders what became of the miserable cow in the inadvisably ruched bathing costume, the one who hung around sullenly in the shallow end while her children splashed and cavorted. I was miserable even though my first novel had recently been published and I wasn't only miserable because Ron had just been made redundant, though not knowing how we would go on feeding, clothing and housing our little ones didn't help. I was miserable despite the fact I had been given a large sum of money to write my second because, in the months between the moolah hitting my bank account and our going on holiday, awful things had been happening to someone I loved very much and I couldn't do a damn thing to save him.

By the time we went to the Médoc it looked as though he was going to be OK after all but meanwhile I had lost three things which were 1) my feeling of invincibility, 2) my sense of maternal omnipotence and 3) most crucially, the plot of my second novel. Just as five years later I couldn't fix my bike saddle on the eve of Pedal to Paris, I could not fix that bloody book. I crossed out and rewrote and tore up and cut-and-pasted for month upon month and year after year and in the end the publisher gave up on it, and shot my novel like an old horse.

This was a bit of a blow, I can tell you, because ever since age six I'd planned to be An Authoress and when my first novel came out – my words and sentences and paragraphs and chapter headings all sandwiched between two delicious slices of hardback bearing my name – I honestly didn't mind the idea of dying so much. Not that

I intended to die for a very long time but at least when it happened I would have done what I set out to do, which was to be a proper writer.

The stupid thing was that I couldn't stop thinking of myself as An Authoress even when exposed to the bitter truth that I was not. I'd still get ideas for books and start writing, but then the small voice in my head, the one which said, 'Your tent stitch is crap,' would murmur, 'They won't publish this one either.' And I'd get stuck and have to pack up. Then I got the job on 'Active' and didn't have time for writing books I was never going to finish because I was too busy being myself, not An Authoress.

The summer that followed the closure of 'Active' was one of the scariest I can remember – not simply because I was losing a battle with a knee injury, although being unable to run reacquainted me with a raft of lost, slow, angry moods I had thought I was shot of for ever – but because I seemed to have forgotten how I did things successfully. A television company paid me an extraordinary sum of money to create a collection of flawed but interesting characters, set them in the glamorous world of big business, devise storylines for six one-hour episodes of prime time viewing, print everything out on A4 and bind the pages in a professional-looking document so they could put it in a cupboard in the producer's office and never refer to it again.

I did some freelance sports journalism. I don't know if I would have done it any better fifteen years back. I expect my copy would still have been hacked about by subs, or spiked. I would still have been bollocked by the sports editor for being late on deadline. I might still have had to listen to bullshit from the boss class about how keen they were to find a new role for me on the paper, and have been told when I asked for it that they were short of space at the moment. I don't suppose I would have felt so incompetent or acted so servile because fifteen years back I could afford to spend £400 at Joseph in one go, and my chin didn't sag.

And I started writing again, waiting for the voice in my head to say, 'This is crap,' but before it could speak, my knee injury healed and I was able to resume running. One evening I ran for a couple of hours. I ran beyond pain and tiredness to the state where I felt I could go on running for ever, and my spirit jumped out to greet me. It was a slow, dogged creature which wouldn't give up, and I felt very proud of it. That night I thought, 'I'm going back to Cap Ferret.'

The sack is an odd sort of gift but if I had not lost my job I would not have been on this French motorway now, heading back to the place where I had first experienced myself as stuck in an attempt to try and unstick myself once and for all. From Cap Ferret I was going to make my own way back home, as I wished I could have done at the age of ten. I was going to do it on foot for no other reason than that when I walked and ran for miles something happened in my head which was only possible to explain in a mundane way; things got clearer, I came to terms with them.

It might also be said that instead of being a bunch of callous, self-serving shits the bosses at the *Sunday Telegraph* were wise, far-sighted and humane. They had known intuitively that I needed the stimulus of redundancy to challenge and energize me. This new way of looking at the issue seemed quite promising. Gratitude and acceptance were far easier emotions than rage and bile. I gazed out of the window. We were getting close now, just north of Bordeaux where the road would bifurcate. The rain dried, the sun blinked and if I had stared hard at the sky I might even have seen a moon made of green cheese.

*

We took a thin scribble of road, never quite wide enough, that ran parallel to the Atlantic coast. On the dry hot day on which I first travelled there I probably heard the sea pounding on my right, the way I could hear it now in winter. The beach runs for nigh on sixty miles between Pointe de Grave on the mouth of the Gironde and Cap Ferret at the bottom. It is separated from the road by dunes, parched trees and flat plains of struggling grass. Cap Ferret is the southernmost point. After that, the options for the traveller are limited, though I suppose if you keep swimming long enough you will reach Nova Scotia.

Houdin, Carcans, Lacanau. Christmas lights strung across main streets, the bulbs in the form of shooting stars. They creaked in the wind. It was a little after ten in the morning, sunny and misty at the same time. Was this the road down which we had purred in Papa Castaing's Citroën, holding our noses after I had so inopportunely reacquainted Paulette with her ratatouille? There had been no white road markings or cycle paths then but the land was startlingly recognizable: the receding, salty, shimmering, marshy, spindle-pined, duned, bungalowed Aquitaine, held in my mind for more than thirty-eight years. I had glimpses of my feelings as a ten-year-old, like an old gate swinging and creaking in a gathering gale, faster and faster.

We were a few miles short of the Cap when we passed the graveyard. It was so familiar I felt shocked. It had been built on a steep slope. Wintry, crazily tiered, the stone crosses and circles and crowns spilling over the hillside, it looked as though a giant had been carrying it on a tray downstairs and tripped.

My eyes just welled up. The trouble with Christmas is that you know the whole story ends eventually in tears and as hard as I tried to drown it out with 'Tic tic, tic tac, disco, disco' I just couldn't get that verse from 'We Three Kings' out of my head, the one which goes:

> Myrrh is mine, its bitter perfume
> Breathes a life of gathering gloom.
> Sorrowing, sighing, bleeding, dying,
> Sealed in the stone-cold tomb.

And the whole damn thing just got to me, how I didn't have a job and would probably never get another one and how these days when I attempted to read the *Guardian* under anything less than floodlights the print was faint and blurred, and how I'd soon be wearing bifocals and sending off for beige windcheaters from those bottom-of-the-page ads in the *Daily Telegraph* (I always wondered what kind of sadsters bought them and now I knew) and how in no time at all our dear children would be grown up and gone, and after that there would be only the stone-cold tomb to look forward to, because I certainly wasn't going to take up line-dancing.

And it was in this morbid frame of mind that I bid my driver goodbye and set off on foot down the last kilometre of coastline. I was on my way to Cap Ferret, alone again.

FROM THE LIGHTHOUSE

Runner's World Training Log.
Day: Monday. **Distance:** 3 m. **Weather:** Cold
sunlight. **Course/notes:** Found the right Cap Ferret this
time. Possible good omen.

Contents of rucksack:

Runner's Medicine Chest (Travelling version:
Germolene, Voltaren Emulgel, Ibuprofen, emery
board, blister plasters, Band-Aids, antiseptic wipes,
nail scissors; also handy place to stash corkscrew)
Red hat
Wallet and credit cards
Power bars (2)
Water bottle
Notebook
Maps (Serie Verte 1:100000 55, 47, 40, 34, 26)
Several plastic bags for wet clothes
Fleece
Anorak
Quick-dry runner's tights with adjustable ankle zip
(from a well-wisher at *Runner's World*)
Waterproof mascara (from my friend Alice)
Plus a chorus of knickers, bras, long johns, ancient T-
shirts and 1000 Mile socks

I spent an hour poking around for Villa Kikinette in what
I gradually came to realize were the wrong streets entirely.

I wandered along roads that dipped up and down and criss-crossed like tangled pairs of tights in a drawer. I gave searching stares to sweetly crumbling old places with terracotta roofs; ducking beneath the pine trees, they seemed to be shrinking from the destruction that had been wrought on their contemporaries, wiped out to service the French preference for something modern and comfortable.

Kikinette could have been anywhere among those streets or nowhere. I began to think I had got the wrong holiday resort again. Perhaps I had got everything wrong: nothing significant or traumatic had happened here; I had made it all up to justify spending the rest of my childhood, my adolescence and early adulthood in a giant fuck-the-world strop. It was yet to dawn on me that what seems like miles to a kid of ten is probably only a schlepp of a few hundred yards and those long treks I made to a lighthouse in 1959 was a journey soon completed on adult legs.

I fetched up at Le Mirador, a restaurant which looked out over the cold, cold ocean from behind bristly dunes. Two men climbed out of a grimy blue truck and started to put up Christmas lights. I was at the place which put the Cap in Cap Ferret, that southernmost point, the very tip of the little finger. The sky was bright, almost silver. It was a blowy day and the sea was like blades.

I backtracked, turned a corner on impulse and found myself at La Poste, the inside of which had clearly not been licked with paint since stamps were sold in old francs. It was brown, dowdy and peaceful. Half of one wall was given over to ancient Poste Restante boxes. They had dusty padlocks. Behind the counter an elderly woman was selling stamps to an elderly man. They too looked brown, dowdy and peaceful. I asked if either knew of a

Villa Kikinette. They could not help, but directed me to the Mairie.

This was a new building, and bang opposite the lighthouse, which up till then, in my growing panic about Kikinette, I had not seen, and believe me, it must have taken some panic not to have noticed that lighthouse, red-topped, waisted, surrounded at the base by dark, bushy pines. Looking at it now, I was strongly reminded of a book called *Les semailles et les moissons* which I encountered while studying for French A Level. It had been recommended to us for light reading by Miss Sanford, the dark and mysteriously beautiful Head of Languages at the school for country Sloanes, and was a family saga set in rural France in the first half of the twentieth century. Proust it was not; in fact, all I can remember of it is that one chapter ended with a bonk which was signified by the heroine gazing at the hero and noting *son sexe avec son fourrure* (dot-dot-dot).

The odd thing was that the lighthouse (dot-dot-dot) was not the way I remembered it at all. The sturdy black railings and set of high gates which surrounded it looked venerable enough, but had surely not been in place in 1959. I felt indifferent to the building, and disappointed and a bit foolish, the way you feel when you rush up behind someone in the street to tap their shoulder because you think you know them. Then they turn round and you realize you have accosted a stranger.

But I plodded on into the Mairie, where I was greeted by an elegant lady of middle years who wore a short plaid skirt and black cashmere top over which a gilt necklace clinked quietly. She left her desk and went to a chipped metal cupboard. From a low shelf she pulled out a filing system and after some purposeful searching produced a dog-eared foolscap card. It said: Kikinette, 33 boulevard de la Plage. The owner was a Monsieur Jacques Sacchetti. I thanked her and left, armed with a town map on which she had traced my route in red biro. I was only a long spit away.

At rue de Goelands, where rue de la Mairie ended and boulevard de la Plage allegedly began, I stopped to consult the map. And that was when it happened. Turning to look back up the street, I saw it again: the lighthouse, 500 feet away, poking its red nose into the sky. I saw it from the angle that I had seen it at ten, plodding up the boulevard on those long ago afternoons, and immediately I was ten years old again. I couldn't believe it, how strong it was, how immediately recognizable, the overwhelming, profound, inadmissable, engulfing, despairing *loneliness* that swept over me as I stood on that street corner. At last I had a name for the pain I had been carrying around for more than thirty-eight years.

I wept intermittently all the way down the boulevard de la Plage, past rows of shuttered holiday homes, mopping my eyes and watching out for familiar buildings though to tell the truth I didn't much care now whether I ran Kikinette to earth or not. I had already found out what I wanted to know. A vaguely remembered two-storey house (its name, Etoile de Mer, was still on the gatepost, in white lettering on a blue enamel plaque) had been gutted and rebuilt. Where the living room had been, a motorcycle garage now jutted into the street. Only the terracotta pineapple on its roof had survived.

Back up the road stood Kikinette's twin, Marguerite. Its shutters were painted dark grey. An ancient Renault was parked round the side and a child's red and yellow bike had been left in the front garden. The house had double doors with four big glass panes; through these I could glimpse the cramped lobby, hung with empty coats like ghosts. Now I remembered Kikinette's walls and floors: the dingy cream paint and varnished woodwork, how the sandy tiles had felt under my bare feet. Veronique in a red sundress, spooning cold flageolets from a cut glass bowl. Janie with her sunglasses perched on her head. Benedicte with pink ribbons in her hair and ruching on her bathing costume. The smells and sounds from the kitchen, where Paulette stooped over her bubbling cauldrons of ratatouille, banging a wooden spoon against the side.

But I never did find Kikinette. It was another Gone Forever Place. Maybe M. Jacques Sacchetti's 33 was now the new shop called Day Co. It had *Listes de mariage* printed on the window, and inside that sort of tempting cornucopia the French assemble so well, convincing you that you cannot leave this spot until you have bought yourself a brass bedstead, white knitted rug, set of pale china dishes and gold candles covered with fake snow. Or Kikinette could have been the art gallery with apartments at the back and, in front, a display of sunsets as lividly coloured as an ulcerated stomach. The whole street was as jumbled up as a spilt jigsaw.

I think, though, that a white-walled house called Les Argonautes had been built where Kikinette fell. It was just to the left of the line of shops as I faced them, protected from nosey pilgrims like me by a set of high mahogany gates and a Défense de Stationner sign. I jumped up and clung to the top of the gatepost while I gazed around. The garden must have been recently returfed; the lawn was so green it looked synthetic. Here and there were giant, spiky-haired palms. One old tree remained, branches pared down to the trunk. It was roughly on the spot where I'd sat and blubbed, writing home.

I dropped down from the gatepost and crossed the

road to the beach. It was pitted with crisp footprints and strewn with seaweed, feathers, a shoe, like the floor of an untidy bedroom. Crushed shells glinted in the sand. This was where I had turned somersaults, dug holes with a bent spade at Club Mickey, played desultory volleyball, longed for my mother and father. How quiet the sea was in the little gullet of the bay. Beyond the bobbing boats and oyster beds, to my right, was a dark, bushy moustache of land. On the left, further out, surfacing above the water, was a little pleat of sand. And then – nothing. I still couldn't see Arcachon.

So I turned back and walked up the deserted boulevard, collecting house names: La Doucette, Côte Dargent, Dejeantina. The air smelled of woodsmoke and a corgi came charging past, claws pattering. Hemeli, Sapin Bleu, Les Mouettes. Outside Normandie the oldest Citroën in the world squatted on the pavement. It was a D Super, with turquoise metallic paint. The front had those Bugs Bunny headlamps, just like Papa Castaing's had had.

I drank strong coffee in a café called Madrague where I was befriended by a brown and white mongrel with no tail but enormous balls. The café had Baby Foot and dark red plastic seats. On the shelves behind the bar stood jars made of green and blue glass. Stuck to their sides were handwritten labels: coco, grenache, gingembre, ananas, vanille. I thought of ordering a pistachio ice cream for old time's sake but what then? Send out for ratatouille? Hunt down Joel and snog him?

Instead I paid up and headed once more for the lighthouse. I looked all round it one more time for luck, then turned my back and started to run. The sun shone and the road out of Cap Ferret stretched empty in front of me. After thirty-eight years and four months, it was time to see what was on the other side of the Bassin d'Arcachon.

THE GATHERING GLOOM

Runner's World Training Log.
Day: Monday. **Distance:** 4 m. **Weather:** Bipolar.
Course/notes: Cap Ferret to L'Herbe. First segment of
road round the Bassin. Have as my guide a booklet
produced by Arcachon Office du Tourisme – 'As a flight
over the bay, a genuine escapee in a world of white sand,
a little sea of blue–green color, in which, at low tick,
channels and oyster beds covered by their white shingles
are drawn.'

The road from the lighthouse took me past the lifeless
holiday homes of avenue Nord de Phare, left at a silent
rue des Mouettes and then on to avenue de Bordeaux
where I hurdled the wet, leafy rails that had been laid for
the *petit train*. I passed the deserted camp site and abruptly
Cap Ferret was gone; I was alongside the D106, pounding
a soggy carpet of sand, bark and moss with little star-
shaped leaves. I realized how closely I studied the ground
when out running. So this was what it was like to be a
hoover.

The road was hillier than I thought. Approaching the
graveyard, I slowed and took a drink. Brambles grew over
the graves as if someone had been trying to scribble them
out. I looked at the place for the last time; I knew I was
never going to have to go back. Then I plummeted
towards L'Herbe, rain suddenly bucketing over my head

and back. I veered right at the crossroads where a sign pointed the way to the Chapelle de L'Herbe.

I didn't normally go in for visiting old churches. They were too redolent of the gathering gloom. However, in that downpour anything with a roof made sense. The chapel looked out over the bay, had a dome like a bathing cap and was squat and Moorish in style. Tiles over the porch spelt out GLORIA DEO. They were white, gold and blue, like a numinous vanitory unit. The doors were barred and bolted. I had been half hoping that it would turn out to be the place at which I had worshipped with the Castaings; it wasn't, of course.

I sheltered under a pine tree. Its branches drooped to the ground as though bowing. When the rain eased off I followed the smell of wood smoke to a strangely circular building of twenties vintage which seemed to have grown a prefab on its side. Propped by the entrance was a blackboard on which was written in rain-stippled chalk:

> Retour de marche 110F
> Choucroute maison (cuisine au Riesling)
> Munster et sa petite salade verte

It was early in the afternoon and the sleepy restaurant was empty but for the middle-aged pair chewing companionably by a window. I sat with my back to the fire guzzling black olives and saucisson slices the size of cartwheels. I passed up the chance of Choucroute Maison. Life was too valuable to eat cabbage in French restaurants. Instead I plumped for oysters and a bottle of local white. The waitress asked if would like a *crepinette* – '*sa companion des huitres*' – to go with them.

I did not know what a *crepinette* was, but it sounded frivolously exciting, something you would, perhaps, wear on your stocking like a garter, and I signed up for one eagerly. It turned out to be a sausage patty. It arrived with the oysters on a bed of seaweed, out of which the feathers and old shoe had thankfully been sifted. My rucksack rustled at my feet. I wondered whether I should feed it morsels, like a dog.

A radio in the kitchen played softly: 'If You Don't Know Me By Now' by Harold Melvin and the Blue Notes. Always got to me, that one; came out when I first started bonking the Married Man. Years in abeyance, living in a leaky-roofed house with bare floors; I moved in and couldn't bring myself to unroll the rugs. I thought my prince would come to do it for me; he didn't turn up. I was rubbish at single parenthood, too; my oldest son never knew the feel of an ironed shirt or the taste of a proper cooked dinner. He grew up despite it, a testament to creases and crisps. I'm doing it again, making jokes, but it was the worst time in the world.

Suddenly another flood of remembered loneliness washed over me and dammit if I didn't start crying again, surreptitiously blotting my runny nose with a rather greasy napkin. Weird, isn't it? You can go on for years containing it all and then something sticks a knife into your shell and opens you up just like an oyster.

*

I went blind at Kikinette; at least, for all of five minutes I thought that was what had happened when I woke up in the night. Everywhere as black as black could be. I waited so my eyes could adjust but I still could not see. Groping around, stumbling out of my bed by the wall, blundering into the chest of drawers, tripping over *The Reader's Digest Book of Laughter*, I concluded I had lost my sight and began wailing for Benedicte. She switched on the light. She and Janie were sitting up in bed, mutually puzzled, like an old married couple disturbed by an intruder. I muttered my apologies and slunk back between the sheets.

In the morning, Madame Castaing felt my forehead and took my hot hand in hers. '*Pauvre* Julie,' she murmured. '*Malade.*' I was tucked up in bed where I embarked on my fourth reading in a week of *What Katy Did*. The other children went to the beach. They had smiled sympathetically enough but I wasn't fooled. My little outburst in the night had simply confirmed them in their opinion that I was crackers. Then again, they didn't know what blindness was to our family.

One day not so long after Dad died Mum and I were sorting out old photos. One in particular attracted my attention. It was of a woman in a long pre-war frock, posing in the back garden of my grandparents' house in Essex. She looked vaguely, jauntily, familiar. 'Who is that?' I asked Mum.

'Your grandfather,' said Mum shortly. 'He put on a dress for my wedding day.'

I've told you about Grandpa Fred already. He was the one who invented a hand grenade twenty-four hours after the Armistice was declared. Clearly he had been a bit of a card in his time. I'd seen photos of him in his youth, a wiry, perky, beaky-nosed lad, riding his unicycle, performing acrobatics, monkeying around collecting for charity with a notice round his neck saying BLIND. Isn't life such a bastard? Over the years he went blind himself, gradually robbed of tone, colour, definition, light itself: victim to our family's genetic curse of glaucoma. You can arrest it now, have a special eye test, drops, operations, but then there was no alternative to the gathering gloom. Poor old boy, he must have been bored out of his shiny skull by the end; couldn't even see to turn somersaults. All he could do was dictate articles to *Cycling* magazine about Great Uncle

King, begetter of the beaded rim of the pneumatic tyre. One of them was published. I have a copy. Pored over to death by the family, it's as yellow and sere as Grandpa Fred finished up.

Somewhere around the middle of the fifties he came to live with us. One Saturday morning he was just there, elbows on the kitchen table, hands together as if saying grace. His eyes were watering; he was staring ahead, not at nothing very much but at nothing at all. I don't know if he was having a quiet blub. His eyes were often watery because of his blindness. On the other hand his wife had just died, he was seventy-nine, it was pretty much the end of the road.

I haven't thought about Grandma Belle for years. She was the daughter of a Tottenham pork butcher, a tall, short-necked, high-shouldered woman, round eyes beady behind pebble glasses, with a judicious amount of frilly grey hair. Just thinking about her now I hear the click of needles, because Grandma Belle was always knitting. It always seemed to be the same jersey, lace-patterned, in shiny blue yarn. Years back she'd really put her shoulders into it; she took in knitting to fund Dad's school fees. He was educated courtesy of Aran, brick stitch, fisherman's rib and Fair Isle. By the time I knew her it was some decades since Dad had hung up his satchel but she couldn't kick the habit. I never saw anyone wear her jerseys, though, not even her.

Grandma Belle's house had four floors and was part of a terrace, built in very red bricks. It was Victorian outside and in: black and white tiles on the garden path, an aspidistra feeling its way along the dark hall. Grandma Belle spent most of her day in the front room, on a scarred chaise longue, knitting bag by her feet. She was as permanent as the grand piano which filled a good third of the room. It was a piano no one ever seemed to play. On the sideboard in the dining room where no one ate were bottles from which no one drank. The whole house was like that, a depository for furniture and people. One upstairs room was furnished entirely by stuffed birds. During duty visits I would slip upstairs to gaze upon them in their rigid immortality. They were mainly owls. Even then I could not but reflect how very like Grandma Belle they looked with their round, front-facing eyes, small hooked bills, lacy feathers, short necks. The only sign that they had once played a significant role was the existence of a family catchphrase much used by my dad, even in his declining years. 'Who stuffed that white owl?' he would bark, then chuckle mysteriously. But no one ever explained it to me and I didn't like to ask, come to that.

Grandma Belle was a Methodist. Her practising had fallen off a bit by the time I knew her and her only pew was the chaise longue, but when Dad was growing up she was an inspiration to them all. Mum said that's why Dad never went to church when he grew up, he'd been stuffed with church till the Methodism spilled out of his ears. Once you've had it, though, the religion never quits you completely. Most of the time Dad's Methodism-spewing ears stayed plugged but every so often, generally during *Songs of Praise*, the corks would fly out and there he'd be, singing along to something improving by John Wesley and surreptitiously mopping his eyes.

It was Dad's older brother who suffered the worst bout of Wesleyitis. 'Got religious mania when he was seventeen,' said Dad. Louis was tall like Grandma, and exceptionally myopic. As a boy Dad was whipped for hiding his specs. Later, after marriage had settled him, Louis became a keen amateur botanist.

As for Belle and Fred, you don't know whether to

laugh or weep. Let me say right now that this is Classified Information I'm divulging here; not a peep to be heard out of Dad when he was alive, and Mum needed a good few snorts of Chardonnay to oil the wheels of talk.

Poor Mum, she had it all on during the war. While Dad was away at OCTU, every relly she had took advantage of her kindness and expert domestic management and they arrived in multiples. Already crammed into the modest three-bedroom semi with her and the infant Big Sis were i) the equally infant son of her sick-listed sister-in-law, ii) her unmarried older sister, always on the look-out for diversion from her dreary life and iii) a Miss Moon, billeted on her by the War Office. Then, one afternoon, an ambulance drew up outside the garden gate and from it emerged Grandma Belle.

Grandma Belle had broken one of the more negligible bones in her ankle and had been escorted to this ambulance following treatment at the Jubilee Hospital. She leant forward and poked the driver's shoulder. 'Don't take me home,' she ordered. 'Take me to my daughter-in-law.'

She plonked herself down in the dining room and that was where she stayed. Mum had to install a temporary bed, plus a bucket as Grandma Belle declared herself unable to mount the stairs to the lav. Mum was in charge of emptying the bucket. In addition to this service, she had to provide Grandma Belle with a bowl of hot water in which to wash each day, and at two o'clock every afternoon wheel in the tea trolley so Grandma Belle could dispense hospitality to her best friend, a dwarf named Titch.

What a joy it must have been and a lasting joy at that; Grandma Belle stayed three months and Mum only got her dining room back when Dad came home on leave. He walked in expecting to see the table laid and staggered back because of the pong. 'You see what's happened to me,' Grandma Belle lamented. 'Would you mind emptying the bucket, dear boy?'

'I'll empty this one,' said Dad, 'and after that you use the bathroom. No wife of mine is going to perform such tasks.' He always spoke very formally when in his masterful mode.

'Dear boy, I can't climb the stairs.'

'Then I will lend you my arm and help you.'

Every day for a week, Dad helped her up the stairs, after which Grandma Belle underwent a speedy recovery and returned home to The Larches. But where, you may ask, was Grandpa Fred in all this? Oh, thereby hangs some tale. Grandpa Fred was eleven miles away in another part of Essex entirely (Ilford, to be exact) and had been for some time. This, he had told Grandma Belle, was because of the depredations inflicted on public transport by the war. Grandpa Fred worked in London and in order, he said, to ensure punctual and regular attendance at the office he had taken lodgings in Ilford, which boasted a direct bus route into town of which other parts of Essex could only dream.

Dad had never heard such nonsense in his life. He knew for a fact that when it came to bus routes, our part of Essex was without peer. Off he went to Ilford to prise Grandpa Fred from the arms of his lady friend and restore him to the bosom of his family. Belle got her husband back and Mum got her dining room back, though not for long, in that as the war dragged on and the bombing began, it was the only place Dad could fit the Anderson Table. This was to the Anderson Shelter what Wembley Arena is to Wembley Stadium; an indoor venue.

We move on to the air raids of '43, during which Belle and Fred's street was bombed. Back they came to stay with Mum, accompanied this time by Belle's other best friend Emmy who had not been bombed but wanted to be part of the action. They swelled a cast of characters which now included not only the infant son of the sick-listed sister-in-law and the dreary unmarried older sister but Mum's younger half-sister, Mum's stepmother Auntie Winnie and, of course, Miss Moon. Soon Dad arrived on a day's furlough, with, I dare say, his little stick at his side. At this very point, the warning sirens sounded. Out they all came into the hall, the unmarried older sister, the younger half-sister, Auntie Winnie, Belle, Fred, Emmy, and let's not forget Miss Moon. Mum stood there, clutching the infant Big Sis and her infant cousin. 'They were', said Mum, '*milling around.*'

When the air raid was over, Grandma Belle said, 'Fred and I are going to sleep in the lounge, Emmy, so you'll have to have the kitchen.'

'She can't have the kitchen,' said the dreary older sister. 'I'm in there.'

'I think you'll find,' said Auntie Winnie, 'that I'm in the kitchen.'

'We couldn't even have a little snog,' said Mum later. 'There was nowhere to have one.'

'Bugger this,' said Miss Moon. 'I'm going to sleep upstairs and I don't care if Hitler gets me,' and off she stomped. Meanwhile Emmy and Mum's younger half-sister dived simultaneously for the dining room, at which Dad became masterful again and took Mum by the arm. 'You can all bloody well sleep where you like,' he said, 'but I am going to sleep in here with my wife.' He took her into the dining room and locked the door.

In the morning Dad emerged to find a crowded hall. Grandpa Fred occupied one of the armchairs, bounced out of the lounge in a last-minute switch of tactics which saw Belle bestow the sofa on Emmy. In the other arm-chair, reluctantly facing Grandpa Fred, was Mum's step-mother Auntie Winnie. Their knees were touching; she'd probably made herself stay awake all night, her face was as long as a fiddle. Mum's younger half-sister had done what she could with the pouffe and the piano stool. Dad went to the kitchen, brewed up. As he passed by the lounge door with a laden tray, Grandma Belle called out, 'Are you making tea, dear boy?'

'No,' said my father, entered the dining room and locked the door again.

Eighteen more months and Hitler was beaten. Bus routes went back to normal and Grandpa Fred left for the office every day. Home came Dad in his demob suit and away went the Anderson Table, quickly followed by the rellies and, of course, Miss Moon. Big Sis would have got shot of Dad too if she'd had any say in the matter. Didn't recognize him at all after such prolonged absence defending Essex from the Hun. 'Go away,' she said. 'Mummy's my mummy, not yours.' A few more years and she was having to divvy up Mum between not just herself and Dad but me as well. I was born in the late summer of '48. I should have been a Leo but I missed the deadline by a month.

Grandpa Fred kept on leaving for the office every day but as it transpired he never arrived there. Instead he sat in the park with his briefcase and sandwiches until it was time to go home. 1946, it would have been. Retired from his job a good while back but had never had the heart to tell Grandma Belle. He kept bread on the table by borrowing on his expectations. These consisted of his slice of the fortune left by Great Uncle King, but the fortune had first to be filtered through Daisy-give-me-your-answer-do and she proved to be of a quite stunning and expensive longevity.

Came the day when the banks threatened to foreclose on Grandpa Fred. Out tumbled the whole sorry story over lunch with my dad, who did the only thing a dutiful son could do and got his father out of hock. Had to put off the purchase of the Morris 8 for another year. The Larches was sold and Belle and Fred installed in the red-bricked Victorian terrace, rent paid by Dad in perpetuity. The rest of the story you know: the knitting, the blindness. I've said it was a house of despair, and no wonder.

'Pretend you're ill,' whispered Big Sis one Friday afternoon in the middle of the fifties. 'Then we'll get out of visiting Grandma's tomorrow.' I crayoned red dots on my arm and gave my forehead twenty minutes under a hot water bottle. It did the trick but my efforts turned out to be superfluous. The next morning Belle went downstairs to make the tea and suffered a stroke. When she had not returned for some time, Fred felt his way to the kitchen. There he was met by an unwarmed pot and the body of his wife. Gone to knit for John Wesley.

The Christmas after she died, we went to the cemetery to put flowers out for her. A dank, pale day. Dad moving swiftly away from the grave because he was crying. 'I was just remembering her,' he said as Mum caught up with him. She tucked her hand in his arm. 'Never mind, dear. She wouldn't have liked this cold.'

Grandma Belle left me one of her Bibles. It was two and a half inches long by one and a half wide and half an inch deep. They were designed that way because Victorian churches were cold in winter. Baby Bibles that ladies could tuck in their, ahem, muffs along with their hands. The Bible was unreadable, of course, without a heavy duty magnifying glass. I tried to find alternative employment for it, handing it over to one of my dolls for a while, but Barbie Gets Religious Mania never quite caught on.

Emmy survived Belle for a goodly time though the years were not kind to her. In fact she went slowly bonkers and one day locked herself in the lav and wouldn't come out. The Fire Brigade were summoned to release her, followed by the people in white coats. I swear this is true, she'd grown to think she was an owl.

I never did hear what became of Titch but no doubt they're all together as I write, three old girls, jawing over the tea trolley in the Great Dining Room in the Sky.

And after that I can only remember sad things for a while. Dad's older brother Louis had just one child, a daughter called Margaret. A brown-eyed, smiling girl. She was eight years older than me, just old enough to have her first proper boyfriend when she caught polio. Mum said she'd picked up the virus in Islington, waiting for a bus to bring her home from college.

They put her in hospital, in an iron lung. In the winter, Grandpa Fred died and the very next summer Margaret died too. We were falling like England wickets against Australia. Ooh, another one gone! Margaret was seventeen. The whole idea was unbearable, the young girl in the city street, the illness tracking her as unseen and deadly as any rapist/strangler. How he would have plucked and dissembled if they'd brought him to trial. 'I remember thinking she looked extremely attractive. I wished her good evening and asked if she minded my walking with her. She said no. I didn't mean to kill her. I was sorry.'

I was judged too young to attend Margaret's funeral but afterwards Mum alluded to it briefly. She said Louis and his wife had been stoic at the graveside but my father had been broken up as they lowered the coffin of my lively, curly-haired cousin into that dark lonely place. I kept my grim knowledge to myself, that I was scheduled to be next on the list. But more of that, as they say, anon.

FREE WOMAN

Runner's World Training Log.
Day: Monday. **Distance:** 9 m. **Weather:** Pissing down. **Course/notes:** L'Herbe to Ares. 'Romanesque, gothic and moorish architecture stand in the heart of the villages. Paintings reveal one thousand and one colors inside churches and chapels, and on the local artists' canvas: a troubling ensemble, a rich patrimony.' – Arcachon Office du Tourisme, ibid. **Dogs:** 1. **Kerb crawlers:** 1.

L'Herbe was built into a small, steep hillside. From the top I could only see its reddish roofs; beyond them was a wedge of Bassin. Little boats floated on it, so immobile they might have been sellotaped into place. It was a peaceful, pure-aired spot. A series of important-looking signs offered the information that motor vehicles were banned in order not to disturb the oysters. Behind my back the Atlantic roared disobediently.

A mile beyond L'Herbe it rained again. At the top of a hill a black dog as square and big as a quad bike was waiting for me; I rummaged in the stinking roadside ditch and found a broken brick with which to defend myself. A couple of motorists slowed as they approached me, stared hard then sped away. For a moment I saw myself through their eyes – a sweating middle-aged woman in shapeless clothes, grimly combing verges. The dog, I then noticed, was chained to an iron fence. Dusk fell, and more rain. I was still half a mile or so short of Ares when the white van drew up alongside. I had junked my vow of not accepting lifts from strangers some half an hour earlier when I kept having to stop every 50 yards to empty water from my shoes, and by the time Ares hove into sight I would have got in a vehicle with anyone who wasn't Peter Sutcliffe. But the man in the white van only asked me the way. I told him curtly that I was an Englishman and paddled on into town.

The little place looked lovely. Give the French a December night and a few boxes of 25 watt pearl and they'll reward you with fairyland. Across main street in Ares, as they were across every high street in the Aquitaine that evening, pale stars shot from each tree. In the central square was a Romanesque church, huge, dun-coloured, still as a sleeping horse. It was closed, God bless it; I didn't have to Go Round it. Uptown was the hotel belt. Here I proposed to assess various Nautics, Petite Auberges, Corniches and Relais du Caps; however, they too were closed.

I thought of my dad. Our family began to take holidays in Europe in the early sixties. Normally Dad was rigid, organized and conscientious but, for reasons I couldn't quite fathom, the minute he crossed the Channel he underwent a complete personality restructure and was sadistically reluctant to book us into a hotel in advance. Our Austin Cambridge would sweep past sunset-washed chateaux, hotels de la postes overlooking serene town squares, modest but clean pensions and on and on past kilometres of pig farms and through one-granny villages till, with a put-upon sigh, in pitch blackness, he would bow to the pathetic moans of his dependants and pull up outside some appalling flophouse the external dilapidation of which would give way to an interior of sloping corridors and peed-in bidets. 'There! I told you to leave it to me,' he would beam.

I was beginning to assess alternative venues to lay my head – builders' skips, drinking troughs, open sewers, I was not a demanding guest – when I came upon a handmade plywood sign propped against an Ares tree. On it I could just make out a crudely painted arrow and, underneath, the legend HOTEL LE COLIBRI. OUVERT TOUTE L'ANNÉE.

Five hundred yards along was a small, modern building which the lashing rain had turned into a blur of adventurously applied white pebbledash. An iron staircase zigzagged up the front to a door set into the first floor wall. The structure seemed slightly lopsided, a bit crazy, the kind of place in which you would find a Hall of Mirrors. In front were some rutted hard standing and a drain from which poured a flux of brown swirling water, the cause of which I guessed by the smell to be 1) bovine, 2) dead. No lights were on in any part of the building.

I climbed the iron staircase and tried the door. It was locked but after slaloming back to the bubbling forecourt I noticed a sign which said '*Accueil*'. A telephone had been set into the wall next to another sign which invited me to *Téléphone ici*. So I did, and was delighted to discover that the Hôtel le Colibri was indeed *ouvert toute l'année*. Presently I heard the sound of a car approaching via the track behind the hotel. A silver Peugeot 205 drew up and Madame got out.

We zigzagged back to the first floor and I followed her, squelching, along a mesh of corridors. My room was number 13. I listened to her departing whence she came in her little runabout. I had the whole hotel to myself.

There. I told you to leave it to me.

I exchanged my wet, sweaty vestments for some wet,

clean ones and turned my thoughts to dinner. Before the start of my trip I had visited a shop which catered for the needs of the long distance walker and, in anticipation of finding myself stranded late at night in some underpopulated part of France, I had purchased a compact gas burner and a selection of boil in the bag meals. (I do of course realize that boil in the bag meals are for wimps and that what I should have picked up were a gun and hunting knife for the shooting and skinning of wild boar but I didn't think the gas burner was up to the demands of spit-roasting a whole mammal.) In any case, on the morning of my departure I heaved my rucksack onto my shoulders and quickly realized that no way would I manage to hike two hundred yards with what felt like a small armadillo on my back, so I jettisoned my modest kitchen and threw in a couple of Power Bars left over from the London Marathon.

It is not that I particularly dislike Power Bars – I would sooner eat them than sheep's eyeballs, for instance – but when it came to the choice between sitting on a bed in a deserted hotel chewing my way through a slab of banana-flavoured lino or getting wet all over again in the service of a *boudin noir* with *frites* and perhaps a little dish of *chanterelles* on the side, I put my X against the *boudin*'s name. Stopping only to apply my friend Alice's waterproof mascara, I headed back into Ares, where every restaurant was shut.

Cars sizzled past on the D3. I trudged in pursuit of their disappearing rear lights. I felt lonely and strange but also pleased; I was on my way from Cap Ferret, I had booked myself into a hotel, I was managing on my own. A couple of miles beyond Ares was Andernos-les-Bains, where I embarked on a damp saunter around the sea front, under the Christmas lights. What a buzzy, happening town Andernos must be in summer – a casino and landing-stage, little waterfront cafés, pretty shops, a couple of those marvellous family-run restaurants where Grand-mère works the till, Monsieur sips the profits and Madame slaves in the kitchen over your *tête de veau avec sauce gribiche et sa petite salade verte.* Alas, somewhere around the end of October round these parts the music stops, the lights go out and it's either the Bistrot Enzo or starve.

The Bistrot Enzo was on the corner of a square next to a bland but ugly modern apartment block and flew in the face of all empirical evidence about where and where not to have a meal in France. One should never eat anywhere where the chef is visibly at work, always avoid places with paper mats depicting Splendeurs d'Aquitaine, and walk quickly past any bistro with a T stuck on the end.

I was greeted by a Mademoiselle in Doc Martens and a black jersey which appeared to have a mullet sewn on the front. Now maybe I'm asking for the moon but when I'm going to spend 300F on a meal which I know before I even dirty my knife and fork is going to be a sad and leathery disappointment I do at least appreciate a smile of *accueil.* The best the Bistrot Enzo could do for me was a snapped, 'Non. Absolument pas,' when I asked if there was a non-smoking section. In no time at all I was sitting at the table next to the Toilettes with a large, shiny menu listing a number of confusingly embellished pizzas and taking my first sips of something which allegedly hailed from Bordeaux, possibly after a long and circuitous journey in a petrol tanker.

There's something so dispiriting about dining badly in France, I always think. You can do that in any football ground in the British Isles, plus there's a game going on to take your mind off it. But at least I was warm and dry and, in due course, pleasantly tipsy. I was also voraciously hungry and thus more disposed than I might normally have been to address a salad and steak which were both, intriguingly, buried under huge and numerous spoonfuls of *crème fraîche*. It was a bit like trying to eat your way through the roof of the Sydney Opera House and after a while, when I began to feel a distinct sensation in my intestines of a troubling ensemble, a rich patrimony, I gave it best.

On recovering my plate, Mademoiselle had the decency to raise her eyebrows. '*Tout était bien?*'

Had I been less wimpy, more fluent, I would have said, 'No, it was disgusting, like eating plimsolls with the Meltonian still left on and back in Britain, where we care about animals, we'd call in the RSPCA if someone fed that stuff to their dog.' Deterred by my makeshift French and the fact that my oratory would be accompanied by gusts of cod Bordeaux I cravenly settled the extortionate bill and marched out into the rain.

There's nothing like a two-mile walk in the white heat of a bad and costly dinner to garner your unruly senses and by the time I presented myself at the first floor door of the Colibri I was calm, sober and with a hand-to-eye coordination that was beyond reproach. I married the key with the keyhole straight off. It wouldn't budge. I must have spent a good half-hour scratching and fiddling at that door, but eventually it dawned on me that I could stand there all night, possibly all my life, and not get the key to turn in the lock.

I was aware things could have been a lot worse. I hadn't just been told I was suffering from a horrible illness. I wasn't abandoned with a broken leg on a one foot wide ledge above a canyon. I was trying to be jaunty about it but it was nearly one o'clock in the morning. I had run and walked the best part of twenty miles that day. I had spent the last of my savings on going out to France to end up tired, wet and helpless in some piddling outpost where they served crap food and booked you into your room by car, and I just wished, wished, wished I was home, standing over my kids' beds, watching them sleep, knowing they were safe and warm, and me too. More than that, I wished I didn't feel like an idiot, the way I felt in 1959, actually believing I could *do* it.

On the other hand, I wasn't at the breakfast table nervously opening the *Sunday Telegraph* to see if they'd used my piece. I wasn't on the phone, grovelling for a job to some prissy-voiced desk man who was going to say, 'I'm sorry, we're a bit short of space this week.' I wasn't at the morning conference, in the seat by the photocopier which was the editorial equivalent of the restaurant table by the lavs, discovering that whenever I piped up the blokes would fall silent, wait respectfully for me to finish, then carry on with whatever they had been discussing before I intervened. I was cold, bone-weary, panicky, homesick, forty-nine years old, broke, unemployable and bloated with *crème fraîche*, but I was free. And wasn't this why I had travelled here in the first place, to prove to myself that I was capable of my own delivery?

I retraced my steps to Accueil and telephoned Ici. On the twenty-fifth ring, Madame answered in a sleep-dredged voice and after another sopping wait I heard the silver Peugeot coming up the track. Madame got out and silently turned my key in the lock. The door opened immediately. I slunk to room 13 and caught sight of my reflection in the mirror. My face was red and dark lines ran down my cheeks; I looked griddled. And so I fell asleep on the first night of my journey towards psychological insight, the insights so far being 1) Waterproof mascara isn't, 2) Life is pissy.

RABBIT STEW

Runner's World Training Log.
Day: Tuesday. **Distance:** 13 m. **Weather:** Sunny and gusty. **Course/notes:** Ares to Le Teich, across the Eyre. ('Such as the mullet or the eel, a sensation of independence invades the one that lets himself drift aboard a canoe on the river where fresh water and salt water have mixed forever.') Salt marshes, oyster farms, pine plantations. **Lacerated toes:** 1.

In the morning I woke to silver-blue Atlantic skies and a breeze which sent the Christmas lights crepitating in treetops across the coast. The pavements were dry, apart from outside the Colibri where Madame was energetically unblocking the drain with a broom handle. In the glassed porch which doubled as Accueil and dining room, she had already laid out breakfast: bread, butter, jam, pot of coffee and a pink china bowl.

I'm reluctant to relate this because it makes me look a hick, but the bowl absolutely stumped me. I tried buttering my bread in it; the bowl lurched sideways. Madame must have been watching me discreetly from the sidewalk; she was no doubt curious about the dripping, smelly, middle-aged Englishwoman who had fetched up at her door on foot, two weeks early for Christmas. She hurried towards me with a plate for my bread, indicating that the bowl was a drinking vessel.

Suddenly I remembered my first ever breakfast in France. It had taken place before we set off for the coast, in the Castaings' town house in rue Traversière, Tours. There had been just such a bowl. Denis had told me it was for drinking from. Suspicious, I had insisted Paulette give me a cup and saucer. The other children got on with pouring tea into their bowls; Veronique floated rice krispies in hers and invited me to do likewise. I refused; they needn't think they could catch me out in cereal mismanagement, either. It was only a small incident, but enough, I fear, to mark me out as strange, no fun, a stuck-up bore. If I had unbent even just by scattering a couple of token grains of extruded rice over my cup, perhaps the entire holiday would have been different; I would have been befriended, comforted when I wept for home, and persuaded to have a wonderful time. And then, perhaps, I would not have been breakfasting in Ares thirty-eight years later, trying to work out where it all went wrong.

*

I set off through the town, pausing only in the square at the helpfully named Shopi to stock up on supplies of bread, cheese and pâté should the Power Bars still fail to tempt. I was heading for Arcachon via Biganos, a trek which required no map. All I had to do was follow the clouds of foul white smoke that its factory chimneys were pumping sulphurously into the atmosphere. I've no idea what they made there; certainly not *crème fraîche*.

Just beyond a cluster of houses called l'Agneau I rejoined the main road and crossed a narrow bridge above a brown snake of river, the Eyre. I walked beside a forest of beech and birch trees where small unseen creatures rustled and flitted and chewed each other to death, and I sat on a log to apply Germolene and a plaster to the second toe of my left foot; the adjacent toenail was shaped like a quill and often drew blood. After the London Marathon my sock was like something out of *Reservoir Dogs*. The sun shone. I felt very happy, like when I was a kid, taking the long way home from school. Half an hour or so in the day when not a single adult knew where you were.

I'd noticed this before, how when I was walking or running long distance a part of me seemed to turn into the child I once was. It wasn't only the feeling I got out there of the shackles being lifted for a bit, or the absolute joy I often experienced at finding myself alive in a world that could fill me with rapture and exhilaration as well as frustration and despair. It wasn't only the boredom, though running and running for miles on end could closely replicate the forgotten, barren dreariness of much of growing up. Quite a large part of it was the sheer pain, effort, fear and avoidance of humiliation involved; fighting to get by, to go faster than someone else, to not look too foolish, and above all to survive, the way I'd done as a child.

You'll remember I told you a while back about my childhood secret, which was that I occupied a prominent position on the Grim Reaper's hit list. I heard my death sentence over rabbit stew. I must have been around three at the time, squirming on Mum's lap during lunch at Auntie Winnie's.

Auntie Winnie lived in a bungalow in a hamlet on what is now the main road to Southend. I drove through it the other day, on the way to race in Canvey Island; didn't recognize the place. It's huge now, chock-a-block with signs saying Texas Homecare and McDonald's. The bungalow has, as you might say, gone the way of all flesh, as has Auntie Winnie. Got knocked over when they started to widen the road to Southend. Mum didn't say much but if she had a vale for her stepmother it would have been Good Riddance.

As I have already indicated, Mum's childhood was a bit testing. Maud, her mother, was one of four sisters. The others were Winnie, Lou and Bertie. Lou played the piano to just below concert standard; Bertie went to Germany as a governess and returned with child, without wedding band; Winnie I'll get to in due course. They were already old ladies when I met them, though energetic and verbal, marbles all present and correct, hair faded to flaxen rather than grey; I can see them now in Mum. But I've only ever seen one picture of Maud. I found it stashed away with a couple of pallid still lifes and some of Mum's unfinished embroidery while exploring the boxroom. She had marcelled hair and sapphire blue eyes; that's all I know about her. Mum inherited the eyes.

What was she like before marriage to Sydney? Was her piano playing as up to speed as Lou's, did she dance, sing, embroider, speak French? Was she ladylike, sporty, a bluestocking? How could I ever know when Mum barely knew Maud herself? The only thing she had to remember her by was rival siblings, because Maud was a cot-filler: seven babies she had in all, three singletons, two sets of twins, like pigeons fluttering from a conjuror's sleeve.

The winter came and took Maud away, some time around the First World War. Mum so young she can barely recall how young – eighteen months, three, five? It's your mother who tells you the age at which you achieved infant milestones and her mother was gone. But whatever age Mum was, it was far too early to be left jostling for love and attention in a full-to-bursting nursery expanded by the arrival of Bertie's fatherless mite.

Poor Sydney, drowning in children and sisters. Probably

thought he was doing his best by them all when he married Winnie – did he line up Maud's sisters and do Eeeny Meeny Miny Mo? But the way Mum tells it she had an absolutely monstrous childhood, fighting for her surviving parent's attention like a drowning child for air, dragged along corridors by her hair, served with bleak, poor food while her two young half-siblings larged it at the high table.

But I liked Auntie Winnie. A jollier prospect than Grandma Belle altogether – hunched, merry and spry with a frothy porridge of hair. Mind you, she didn't have to put up with Grandpa Fred and the House of Gloom. Shagging Sydney had breathed his last some time during the war. Nobody to bother her, kids all grown up. She was a free spirit.

I liked that bungalow, too. I used to go there on my own sometimes. In the back garden she kept hens and I used to spend some absorbing hours watching eggs emerge from feathered back ends. I won't say it was the equal of having a 64-bit Nintendo but in those days you had to take what was going. Her bedroom was at the front of the bungalow, by the door. She had a piano in there and the bed was covered by a green satin eiderdown. The rest of the room was taken up by a dressing table on which she kept a photo of Sydney. A giant one so there wasn't much room for the silver-backed hairbrush and trinket tray.

Old ladies. It's funny how you remember their bedrooms and their cuisine. It was Big Sis who reminded me about the piano. 'And the pickled sprats,' said Big Sis. 'That was what she did. Pickle sprats. They were very nice. You just got your little bits of small fish and put them in vinegar. Absolutely delicious.'

After we had eaten the rabbit stew, which was a stranger to seasoning but presented in a fetching green dish, Mum and Auntie Winnie embarked on a long and tedious conversation about which I have no recollection save that towards the close of it Mum revealed that she had once been to a fortune-teller. The session had clearly been a bit hit or miss and Mum was still looking out for the fair stranger with an M in his name who was going to introduce her to a life of fabulous wealth and luxury, though with dwindling hope. 'She was right about some things, mind you,' said Mum. 'She told me I'd have two and lose one.'

That was a bit of a shock, I don't mind telling you, because I knew immediately that if it was between me and Big Sis as to who was earmarked for imminent oblivion it would be no contest, because I was just the sort of unlucky person it would happen to, the way I knew when I was older that if I flew I'd be in an air crash.

I heard the news of my doom without external alarm and took myself off to the back garden where I could compose myself by staring up the backsides of hens. My impassivity wasn't really that extraordinary. Dying was not then something you talked about openly. It belonged to that class of subjects, such as diarrhoea or childbirth, which were alluded to with a lowered tone and euphemism: 'she's gone down with a bilious attack'; 'she had a very difficult time'. Grandpa Fred and Grandma Belle did not die; we 'lost' them. Even now if I hear this expression my mind conjures up images of mislaid geriatrics in their hospital clothes, waiting bewildered on street corners to be reunited with their families.

And that was it, really. I thought that while I was waiting to die I might as well go on living, and when I continued to live long after the fortune-teller's predictions might have been expected to be borne out I just assumed I'd imagined it or hadn't properly been listening to what

Mum was saying. It wouldn't have been the first time, nor the last.

I was a teenager before I put two and two together. Jane and I used to discuss my parents quite a lot. In certain moods, I think we saw them as interesting specimens. During one of our case conferences, Jane disclosed that my mother had suffered a miscarriage during the war.

'She says now that it was a stillborn boy,' said Jane, 'but I think it happened much earlier than that.'

Poor Mum, all those rellies milling around her house, and losing a baby as well. Like Jane, I thought it improbable that she had known its sex for sure. But longing can often harden into belief, and Mum craved a son so badly. God alone knew, I'd tried my hardest to make it up to her. But more of that anon, too.

THE LOST BOY

Runner's World Training Log.
Day: Tuesday. **Distance:** 4 m. **Weather:** Dry.
Course/notes: Le Teich to Arcachon. Had lunch on edge of some kind of bird sanctuary, found out later it was famous: Parc Ornithologique du Teich. Wondered whether I should Go Round it, then thought Fuck The Widgeon. Less than dutiful about Ports Ostreicoles and something called Maison de L'Huitre too. Felt tired in the last couple of miles. Road into Arcachon busy.
Dogs: 1. **Dead dogs:** 1.

I traipsed on round the lower rim of the Bassin, alongside a little railway behind a low, mossy wall. A train rushed by, under archways freshly painted in bright blue. I passed a toytown marina and roadside ads for *sapins de Noël*, executed in luminous green. A squat cream building announcing itself to be the Welcome Café Concert Pub told me I was on the outskirts of Arcachon. In front of me were the first high-rise buildings I had seen for forty-eight hours. There was a Seat garage, a Central Pneu Service and a showroom which boasted *Tout pour la piscine*. I felt vaguely surprised that Arcachon had such things; it could have been any medium-sized town in France. I had imagined it as romantic, lovely, embellished, with a preponderance of Disney-ish turrets and pistachio ice cream available in every shop. The lagoon would be blue. It was as though my mental picture of the place had been frozen in 1959, when I had longed to arrive in it as a means of escape from the hot loneliness of Cap Ferret. I believe a little train had a puff-on part.

The strange thing was that part of the town was quite magical. I don't want to get too guide-bookish, but there are actually two Arcachons: one for summer, one for winter. The summer town grew up around the borders of the lagoon when the railway lines were laid. But over a series of winters the residents crept up the long skirts of the hills behind: they built enormous, gaunt, fairy-story villas with clanging gates and stone trellises. Some have since been turned into hotels and at one of them, attracted by their advertisement which recommended its *tranquillité* and refined atmosphere, I presented myself. It was called the Semiramos and after the giant entrance door creaked shut behind me I realized it was very creepy indeed. Most hotels feature a bit of human activity, a suitcase or two in the foyer, the tinkle of spoon on coffee cup, the distant scherzo of adulterous bonking, but all I could hear were muffled voices from an adjacent lounge. When I peeked round the door, I swear, *nobody* was in there. All this, and the fact that at a minimum of 400F a night it was way above what I was prepared or indeed able to pay, convinced me I would spend an infinitely more tranquil, if less refined, night in some more modest hostelry downtown.

So I booked myself into the Hotel Aquamarina on the main road out of town. It was unable to match the Semiramos for oak doors and creeper-clad walls but my room at the back was more than adequate and an investment of 240F entitled me to an entertainingly complicated bathplug. It was adorned with levers and a dial; I idled away twenty minutes on the challenge of sealing the plughole.

Rested, dry and as dainty as two inches of receding bathwater (plug-in-plughole-wise I never did achieve perfect snugness) could render me, I wandered back towards town. No more than twenty-five yards along from the Aquamarina was one of those tiny French bars which manage to cram a coffee machine, two tables and twenty men in check shirts into a space barely larger than a pizza slice. I was tempted but even a cockroach would have found it a crush and I pressed on to the Café du Commerce.

Every French town has a Café du Commerce, I find, and externally they suggest consanguinity; red awnings, a lectern displaying the *tarif des consommations* under a brass picture light, the pavement filled with old-fashioned tables and chairs. Inside, the creativity of each proprietor is allowed to gallop free. This Café du Commerce exhibited a pleasing mismatch of themes: swirls of pearly neon on the ceiling, fly-blown fan, banquettes upholstered in beige leatherette, long troughs of plastic plants. These were threaded with tiny red Christmas lights. The effect was of illuminated herpes. In the glass-fronted cabinet by the bar were two crème brûlées, three slices of *tarte tatin*, a pair of *îles flotantes* and something unidentifiable but flamboyant in a ramekin. They looked like late night stragglers on a dance floor. The barman was listening to the radio. Still having a rough time of it in Niort, I noted.

I loved sitting on my own at that table, early in the evening, ordering my drink, knowing I had made it to the other side of the bay. Outside, a man walked past leading a ginger dog. He wore a flat cap, Fair Isle jersey and black trackpants. He looked very contented. So did the young lovers who strolled by soon after; she had dyed hair, he a pink sweater. A woman whose silver anorak matched her poodle scuttled across the street between passing cars. I thought Arcachon seemed a very nice place to live and started blubbing again, this time at the memory of waiting, waiting for Big Sis to arrive at Cap Ferret. Mum had said she was going to be in France with her university friends around the time of my trip to the Castaings, and would no doubt be dropping in to see me. She never did. I couldn't think why. It seemed perfectly reasonable to me that a twenty-year-old would break off from cruising the Champs-Elysées in an open top sports car driven by a French count in order to undertake a coastal detour of several hundred miles. I realized that for the second day running I had sat in floods of tears over a bottle of wine, so I paid for my drink and set off to look at the beach.

The summer town was still and grey. On the seafront stood a frozen carousel, fenced round and bolted; the *caisse* behind it was shuttered. But I walked around it anyway, in the childish wonderment that always came over me when I found a French carousel. They're always so beautifully *maquille*, aren't they? Visions in silvery pink, syrupy brown, sea green, mulberry, gold leaf, gingersnap, pea. This one was a cultural carousel, panelled with paintings (not wholly hideous) in the manner of the French masters. Corot, Lautrec, Manet, Cézanne, Pissarro, Sisley, Degas, the gang was all there. Rise and fall on your gilded charger underneath a Van Gogh.

By the jetty, the sea lapped gently. There were those flocks of little boats again, the sparrows of the maritime. White buoys bobbed, sand dusted the waterfront like eyeshadow. So this was it, the place I had been trying to see all those years ago as a lonely ten-year-old far from home. I looked across the bay. Smoke from Biganos scarred the sky. I could just make out an eyebrow of shoreline opposite. And I thought, That's where I was. A little girl, standing on a shore, on the edge of her known world. I could feel her presence. I knew she hadn't been able to see me but I could see her. I wanted her to know I was there and that I was looking out for her.

*

I remember the conversation long after I have forgotten why Jo and I were mooching down the road. I can still smell the fences and hedges we passed – warm creosote, tom-catted privet – and see the gardens decked with rigid dahlias, so I guess it was summer and school was out. I would have been nine, Jo ten, so we were probably heading for the high street where, in Woolworths, Jo was developing an interest in the displays of bras.

'Does your mother ever say, "Why can't you be more like Julia?"' I began.

'No.'

'Ah. Mum sometimes asks me why I can't be more like you.'

We mooched on a bit further, while I reflected on the gravitas, efficiency and social ease that had obviously made Jo such an appealing prospect to my mother. I then rather awkwardly began confiding that Mum had always wanted a son. I can't recall what Jo said in response. I suspect she'd decided that there was nothing *to* say. I only remember concluding brightly, 'I'm a girl who's as good as a boy, so it's all right.'

I suppose Mum's longing for a son began as normal admiration for her five brothers and was compounded by frustration that boys were allowed to do interesting things like go to university and fight wars while the girls of that pullulating household were sentenced to cross stitch.

Unlike her dreary older sister, Mum had been tomboyish, bouncing on beds till they broke, shinning up trees, hiding under the carriage horse to escape whipping. You wouldn't have thought it to look at her, the little blonde wisp. She used to sit for Jacob Epstein, who lived virtually next door. 'He called me his little bit of Dresden china,' she said later, more than once.

One of her favourite brothers was Ted, who before the war was apprenticed with Bob, his twin, to learn furniture making at Harrods. 'You'll never guess what I learnt today,' Ted had said to her.

'What?'

'How to put woodworm holes in antiques.'

Ted went off to fight Hitler by way of Sunderland. He dropped in at her house first to say goodbye. She was nursing Big Sis. 'I don't like to think of you going,' said Mum.

Ted heaved his kitbag over his shoulder and dropped a kiss on Big Sis's forehead. 'I don't have the responsibility of this,' he said and headed north-east to join his troop ship. He was climbing on board when it was dive-bombed. They rushed him to the infirmary but nothing could be done. Now all she had left of him was a gate leg table. Never bought antiques at Harrods after that, either, on account of knowing how they got the wormholes in.

I don't know exactly when it was that I became aware of not being quite what was wanted. Whenever I think of my early childhood I feel happy. It was a great time, that. My social life was fabulous. I had a choice of three little girls to play with, including the special one with whom I was allowed to share baths. I loved this little girl and after one of our joint baths fixed up that I would marry her when we grew up.

However, I found the girls too faint-hearted to mix with exclusively and allotted half my leisure time to the boys. With them I enjoyed pretending to shoot people, pretending to blow up people, cricket, roaming, moving cars along the carpet and riding bikes which we crashed into trees a lot, resulting in much barking of shins and bloodying of noses (as a child I must have smelt permanently of witch hazel). Among the boys I could be strong, rowdy and competitive and I liked being with them very much.

The summer I was four, I went through a sort of boy time myself, and asked if I could wear bathing trunks rather than a one-piece. And Mum instinctively did the right thing. Instead of reprimanding me for getting my genders mixed, she let me choose a pair of red trunks, explore my boyness, if you like, and to hell with what any of the other mums said behind her back. At Christmas, I was given the train set I asked for, and was made to feel enchantingly special rather than worryingly odd.

It was a boy toy that I constructed in a girl way: while my friends the boys built linear railways in accordance with the principle that males always follow a pointing dick, my railway was circular. I was, all the time, aware that I was a girl, and very pleased to be so. Poor boys, they had such colourless doll-deprived bedrooms: dull chests of drawers with dull brush and comb sets, dull underwear, grey clothes. I felt pityingly superior when they rolled around the grass fighting and also when one of them produced his penis for my inspection; it seemed frightfully inconvenient to have that thing dangling around all the time.

Nevertheless, to one of those boys I made my second proposal of marriage in two years. And that was how I lived then, with parents whose happiness was what had spurred me to want to set up home with my two friends. I had the boldness of a boy and the tenderness of a girl, and very carefree I was.

Well, we moved house one summer and I left my friends behind and, I guess, things changed. It's hard to say what happened to me or what turned me into that self-doubting nine-year-old trying to make the best of a bad gender. All I know is that in the September that followed that conversation with Jo, I returned to prep school for my eleven-plus year. The class headcount was swollen by a number of girls from Jo's form (she was a year above me). Unlike Jo they had not shone academically; indeed, so flickering was the candle of their academic attainment that they were required to repeat the examination. They included a ballet-obsessed girl with huge yellow teeth, the terrifying Murgatroyd twins (to whom I will return later) and the thick but good-natured Marie.

Marie was a big girl. It was whispered that her mother had to clean houses in order to pay the school fees so while everybody was very nice to her no one was ever her friend. She was, however, a good swimmer and her demeanour hardened up no end as the end of year swimming gala approached. She was clearly looking forward to kicking some ass.

I too looked forward to the gala. Jo and I were scheduled to close the show that year by diving off the top board. Jo had actually left the school by then, gone off to a posh boarding school, lacrosse stick under her arm, but their term ended before ours and she returned to the gala by special request.

That day I walked into the classroom with a quiet swagger but my entrance was ignored in favour of some far more interesting and pressing to-do: hushed voices, Marie weeping in a corridor. She was ushered away to see the headmistress from whose study she did not emerge to take part in the morning's lessons. In the playground, word went around quickly. She was ill. Well, not ill exactly, but laid low by something secret and embarrassing. 'It's something to do with blood coming out of your bottom,' the Chief Scout's daughter said importantly.

After lunch we went by coach to the Kingfisher, a country club which boasted an open air pool in its grounds. Pulled down now, of course, but in its day a natatory palace with marbled walkways, green lawns surrounding and, behind the shallow end, a handsome though erratically widdling fountain. When the gala was drawing to its close, Jo and I climbed the steps, past the low board, the semi-low board, even the middle one, while everybody below went Ooh and Aah. We stepped onto the top board, the smallest girls at the pool. Jo went first. Strode briskly to the edge and took the plunge. I had to do it then, because I had to live up to her. A bit clumsier than her, perhaps, but I landed with an efficient plop and surfaced to polite applause.

It was then I saw Marie. She had been allowed to attend the gala, but was still in her uniform while the rest of us were in our bathing costumes. She was smiling unhappily, separated from us by the chain link fence that divided the pool from the hotel grounds. She roamed up and down behind it, pressing her nose to it as Jo and I raced a couple of triumphant lengths. She looked like an alsatian chained behind a wall.

At Kikinette later that summer, I stood naked in the bathroom and saw to my horror that my breasts had started to grow. I tried to push them back in but they would not stay put, and I realized finally that the days of red trunks were over and I was soon to be stamped indelibly as female. I would join Marie behind the chain-link fence, a gulf of secrecy, embarrassment and misinformation separating me from my boys for ever.

Since I've grown up, I've never once wanted to be a male, though I've sometimes thought enviously of the ease with which men make their way in the world. But when I was nine, ten, eleven, the idea of womanhood seemed so depressingly complicated. No longer would I be befriended by boys, I would be judged by them, and in the qualities that they would judge me by – prettiness, quietness, bustiness – I was certain to be found wanting. I didn't want to be fettered by biology, I didn't want to become the Other, the enemy. I wanted to go on being me but as I stood in front of the mirror at Kikinette I knew that the me I wanted to go on being had died a long time back. Wherever I had travelled that year, whatever I had done, that realization would have come along and knocked me sprawling. My exile just hurried the crisis forward and the lighthouse symbolized it. It was nothing to do with France, I was already mourning a lost time. My boys, my old house, even all those rellies milling around. My first Gone Forever Place.

MOVING HOUSE

Runner's World Training Log.
Day: Wednesday. **Distance:** 15 m. **Weather:** Foul.
Course/notes: Arcachon to Blagon. Logging country.
Stubble, a smell of burning, the buzz of saws. Boggy
underfoot, fungus like mackintosh buttons.
Loony alsatians: 1. **Blisters:** 2.
Dead things on road: 7. **Kerb crawlers:** 2. (One
white van and a small bronze Citroën. Thanked them for
their interest and sent them on their way with a cheery
wave.)

I bade a reluctant goodbye to what the French Office du
Tourisme called 'A vast triangular shaped cut in the coast,
hemmed with pictoresque villages, ponctuated by never
ending come and go that makes the Arcachon Bay this
incomparable site that one discovers as it were for the first
time', and took the Bordeaux road, a spectacularly dull,
wet, dangerous one ponctuated by never ending come and
go of dripping pines, grey lakes, skeletal pylons and
Norbert Dentressangle lorries. It is said that when you
forsake your car for the pedestrian life you notice all the
things that you miss while whizzing by in several tonnes
of metal, and on the N250 what I would have missed had
I been awheel were close-ups of dead creatures.
 Depressed by hedgehogs as flat as sheets of filo pastry,
pigeons that had gone to meet their Maker and finally a

particularly deceased cat, I turned off onto the D5 to Marcheprime, after which my life expectancy improved immeasurably, if not its quality. I can't say I enjoyed running in the rain above all things, although it had the advantage over walking of getting me to my destination faster; not that I had anything as grandly definite as a destination. It was more a question of seeing how far I could plod on the D5's boggy verge before I was sucked in. That I would not be the first runner to achieve this fate was demonstrated to me by the protruding toe of a trainer under which, I had no doubt, lay its owner, who would be discovered in a millennium or so's time and put on public display as Marcheprime Man. (Evidence suggests that this late twentieth-century man wore shorts and met his end while foraging for his staple diet of Power Bars.)

It was a nothing road, winding between nothing villages. I passed the time redecorating our top floor bathroom. Then I pulled down the bay window extension in our living room and replaced it with a conservatory covering the whole of the back of the house. I bought the property at the bottom of our garden; it had been converted from what had originally been the stables when our house was built. I knocked down the dividing fence, added a garage and hard tennis court, then sold up and moved to Dulwich so the children could be nearer their school.

Sometimes when I was out running I got to work on the house where I grew up; that it had been demolished in 1985 was irrelevant. I haven't told you about that house. We'd been looking for somewhere since I was around three. I didn't want to move, ever. I bawled the place down in Porthcawl the year Dad saved the peardrops from meltdown because I thought we'd moved to Wales without them telling me and I would never see my home, bike, dolls, train set or fiancés again.

Gradually I got used to the idea. We entered a time of viewing Residences, as houses above a certain price were dignified. (If people asked about the house to which you were moving, you would say, 'It's *detached*,' so they would know that you were going up in the world.) We wandered in and out of empty Old Rectories, draughty Lodges, Halls throttled with creeper. We had two looks at The Pantiles. At £4000, it was somewhat less grand than the rest, but it was the one Mum really wanted, modern and manageable. However, there was a problem with damp.

One day, driving along a posh road on the edge of the forest, Dad braked the car suddenly and leapt out. He'd spotted a For Sale board. It was tacked to a tree that was half in a garden, half out on the pavement, bursting through the fence like a knee through torn trousers. Behind it a giant Victorian shoebox stood among huge lawns. There were fruit trees, pines, yew, holly hedges, flowerbeds the size of roundabouts, a pond big enough to justify a weeping willow.

Dad swung open a five-bar gate, strolled up the drive, pressed his nose up against grimed-up windows, tried doors.

'What are you doing?' Mum said faintly.

'Look around. It's empty.'

Mum obviously didn't much like the idea. It was trespassing and anyway she was still mourning the damp Pantiles. 'You can't do that,' she said. But he walked all around it and presently returned to the car.

That seemed to be that. A few weeks later, Big Sis popped her head round the kitchen door. Mum was dusting her hands on her pinny. 'Daddy and I are going shopping,' said Big Sis.

The pair of them returned some time later, Dad holding a set of keys which he placed with a characteristic gleeful solemnity on the kitchen table. 'A present for you, dear.'

'What is it?' said Mum. 'A car?'

But round and round the table Big Sis was already twirling. 'Daddy's bought you the house. Daddy's bought you the house.'

'*That* house?' Mum said with irritated desperation. 'I can't manage that.'

'Nonsense,' said Dad. 'We'll have a lovely time there.'

*

I was in 1B at prep school when we moved in, three or so years before Jo and I had the conversation I have already recorded. I also had chickenpox. The first neighbour we met was Jo, who walked down the drive from her house next door to introduce herself, her plimsolled feet crunching on the gravel.

We stood on the pavement, surrounded by firescreens, cushions, nests of tables, newspaper-wrapped figurines, all the flotsam of a modest three-bedroomed semi which even with the rest of the contents seemed barely enough to fill our new reception hall. I had seen Jo before, in the school playground, though we had never spoken as she was in the form above. She wore brown Start-Rite sandals, beige shorts and a pink aertex shirt. Her hair was also a kind of beige, though not dull; it was a sophisticated colour, and curled around her head like a little crown. For some reason she negotiated directly with my mother, asking if I would like to play while I swung on the five-barred gate. Mum sent her away on account of my chickenpox though Jo, already the GP in the making, assured her after checking dates that my infectious period was over.

The Avon Lady from our old road had sent us on our way with a gracious wave and, so that Mum would not have to worry about lunch, a cheese and bread pudding. An expression often used by people rhapsodizing over a memorable meal is, 'I can still taste the flavour now.' What was notable about the Avon Lady's gift of lunch was its entire absence of flavour and to this day I wonder at how she managed to generate such insipidity out of half a pound of strong Cheddar. In fact, insipidity implies too positive a quality. This sub-fondue was a kind of culinary black hole. She could have slapped one of her new lines in aftershave on it; at least that would have added sensual experience of a kind. The cat, a white long-haired neuter called Binky, had the better dining deal. Dad spread butter on its paws, the notion being that while licking it off the cat would come to associate its new home with butter and stick around for more.

We sat round the table in a home now indelibly associated with tasteless cheese and bread pudding and with a general feeling of, Where do we go from here? I'm not saying that roast beef and two veg would have kicked off our new life any better but that dreary meal adumbrated a feeling of disappointment. Materially we were up in the world but something mysterious and good had been lost.

I think it was that, through the entirely benevolent intentions of other people, Mum had had control wrested from her. Both the lunch and the house had been imposed on her, and while you can clear away an uneaten lunch an unsolicited house is not so easy to bin.

I never knew till after Dad had died that that was how we came to live there. Mum told me about it the other day, for the first time. She spoke in a tone of rueful indulgence, as though it was just a funny husbandly quirk, like keeping ferrets or ironing his own socks.

In the beginning I rolled my eyes and shrugged along

with her: '*Men!*' Later I reflected that though it was a bit of an odd way to go on it was simply all of a piece with the prankish side of Dad's nature, the one he inherited from Grandpa Fred, the slightly malicious cheerfulness with which, as a boy, he hid his older brother Louis's specs. Later still, after I'd pondered about it more, I said to myself, Hang on. What would I do if Ron bought a house over my head? Would I be like Mum and consent, whether reluctantly or with gratitude, to live in it? And then I thought, The fuck I would.

Because I knew, with a fierce and certain clarity, that if Ron were ever to bound whistling into my kitchen one morning, with my oldest child as co-conspirator to boot, and chuck a set of keys on my table with the news that come the date of completion our abode would be The White House or The Old Vicarage or Dunreportin I would reach for (in no particular order of merit):

i) his suitcase
ii) my lawyer
iii) a rusty breadknife for castration, purposes of

But as Mum said, he was a dear.

DOUBLE TROUBLE (1)

Runner's World Training Log.
Day: Thursday. **Distance:** 8 m. **Weather:**
Unremitting. **Course/notes:** Blagon to Martignac-sur-
Jalle. **Dead things on road:** 2. **Loony dogs:** 2.
New blisters: 2. **Holes in socks:** 1.
Kerb crawlers: 0 (obviously lost my glamorous allure in
the last twenty-four hours). But hurrah, a shining oasis in
a desert of vile thingummy: the Restaurant Loutrein.

I got to Martignac-sur-Jalle around lunchtime on Thursday. It was the kind of place that didn't have many streets
to choose from. I walked down the one in the middle
because that seemed the quickest way to get out again. It
was my fourth day on the road. I kept fantasizing about
hot showers, pedicures and taxis and I hadn't even
reached Bordeaux.

The street looked like a trailer park. HGVs and vans
discharged rumpled men in overalls and check shirts.
They streamed in line towards a dowdy old building above
the windows of which chipped lettering proclaimed: Restaurant Loutrein. Closer inspection showed a child's blackboard wedged against a window pane, displaying the
chalked legend: Menu 55F. With the possible exception of
'tax rebate', no other expression has such power to put a
spring in my step.

The Loutrein turned out to be one of the cheeriest

places I had ever seen. Every single table in its vast dining hall was filled by lorry drivers chomping, joking, quaffing and fumbling for cigarettes in the pockets of those special crap acrylic grey cardigans that only French lorry drivers know where to get. As I hovered by the door, a driver waved and pointed to an empty seat. His moustache was so big he looked as though he had stuck on two at once. I sat down. I was shivering and light-headed. My feet twitched, unable to believe they weren't walking. I drank a lot of water because Ron wasn't there to say, 'Don't drink the tap water.' Then I had soup. I can't swear on the Bible as to what was in it but I think I detected the odd nugget of carrot and tomato; some noodles swam to the surface for my inspection. I was the only woman there apart from the owner. She had middle-aged Frenchwoman's glasses and wore her hair up. Another driver poured red wine into my glass and I had a lot of that too. Then I had a lot of hors-d'oeuvre and a lot of steak and chips. The chips were particularly good. A trucker raised his wine bottle to me in a silent toast. I had a lot of cheese. The last course offered a choice of fruit or ice creams. All the drivers chose the ice creams. They were actually lollies. I didn't have room for one, but watched sixty French lorry drivers simul-taneously sucking child-sized lollipops with dainty con-centration. The coffee was great, too.

I visited the loo. It was clean and had a seat and soft paper. I put plasters on my new blisters. On the way out another trucker gave me a warm, appraising glance. I was sorry to leave; it wasn't often I found myself the toast of a small French town. Outside, the weather had settled into a fine, drizzling rain and things no longer seemed so dismal. I headed in the general direction of Bordeaux, mentally redecorating my new house in Dulwich.

*

I'd like to go back just once more to the first house I ever lived in, the three-bedroomed semi where Mum and Dad began married life.

The first time Mum ever saw him he was throwing stones into a pond. He had been ditched by someone called Ena; Mum said he looked lonely and miserable. She sat down beside him; she hadn't long turned twenty and was fair, small, with Maud's wonderful eyes. Dad wasn't too tall, either. His ears stuck out; his family name was Teeny-in-brackets.

She doesn't dwell much on the nuts and bolts of their courtship, which with all her siblings milling around in the front room was clearly something of a spectator sport. Perhaps that is why she speaks affectionately of visits to watch Queens Park Rangers at Loftus Road. You are never more alone than in a football crowd, as Denis Potter said, though he was alluding to Fulham.

They returned from their West Country honeymoon by taxi and as they stepped out, the front door – their front door – opened and there they stood. The dreary older sister and her equally dreary twin brother. 'Somehow they'd got hold of the key,' said Mum between clenched teeth, 'and moved in so they could welcome us home.'

The twins had Christian names – the dreary sister's was actually something quite flirty and unusual, like Marianne or Lucille – but they were universally known as Girlie and Boydie. Some people are simply destined to be a burden and an embarrassment to those of their kinfolk who are negotiating a more successful path through this vale of tears and in Girlie and Boydie Mum had double trouble.

Boydie was tall, gaunt and awkward. He'd been born with a cleft palate and never talked like other people, though when I was little I didn't find it strange or funny; it was just the way Boydie talked. I loved him. But he was shy and never married. He started to suffer from arthritis when he was still quite young and his long fingers inclined sideways at five degree angles. They were oddly neat and looked almost like furled wings.

I was never told what Boydie did for a living. He was just someone who came to our house, talked in his odd but melodious voice and remembered my birthday (it was the day before his) with book tokens, which I liked. I was all of sixteen when I found out his job. He was the janitor at our local public school. Some of the boys I was going around with at the time were pupils at this school. I was in love with one of them, a short, thin, witty boy called Richard whose ears were the most substantial thing about him. One day the boys were taking the mickey out of their janitor and then I heard Jug-Eared Richard speak in Boydie's voice. I pretended I had known all along, and how hilarious it was that my mother had for snobbish reasons kept it secret, and I betrayed Boydie by laughing along with them.

As for Girlie, maybe her life was filled with small joys and unexpected delights at which I could never guess, but I'd say she had a bloody awful deal. She was raped one day as quite a young lass, on the way home through the forest. She had no one to talk to; no one could ever bring themselves to mention it. I guess that's why she never married. Instead she tried to contribute to my mother's nuptial happiness in every way she could devise.

Thus it was that she was ready to step in when Mum went off to the nursing home to have Big Sis. My older sibling was born at seven o'clock in the morning, on Valentine's Day. Dad, having worn out his shoe leather and stubbed out the last of his cigarettes on the waiting room floor, put himself to work ringing round family and close friends with the birth announcement. Phone call after phone call brought forth the same answer: 'This is old news.' All Dad's thunder had been stolen because Girlie had already taken upon herself the happy task.

Nearly sixty years later, Mum can still be as cross as crabs about it. I suppose Girlie had annexed something of Dad's that Mum thought was all hers, and what S. Freud would have made of it all I leave you to speculate. But Girlie had her uses. The eve of the Coronation in '53, Mum and Dad went uptown to camp out overnight on the pavement and she was drafted in to take care of me. We slept in Mum and Dad's double bed and Girlie held me in her arms all night.

These days I put myself in Mum's shoes. It's hard enough when marriage makes the two of you step-parents, trying to knock the issue of two discrete families into a harmonious unit while trying to find time and space to do what nature intended with your new partner. Mum had to contend with a hydra of indigent in-laws, on-the-shelf siblings and a hated stepmother. She'd spent her childhood having to fight for everything, just one needy little person among many. Now here she was, a married woman in her own home, and instead of melting silently away into the dusk with a respectful adieu the rellies were squabbling over possession of her and Dad.

When we moved to the big house, I think Mum decided to take action. There was plenty of room in the new reception hall; the whole mob could have milled around and overnighted in armchairs, but those days were over. Slowly she dead-headed the hydra. They came, they were given the guided tour, but before they could get their feet under the table they were firmly shown the door.

There was a certain amount of stubborn regrowth. Auntie Winnie turned one afternoon tea into a week, all expenses paid. It was, as I recall, the year of the bat. I had found this bat on the floor of the forest, in what I failed to realize was a state of advanced moribundity. I housed it in a discarded Dinky toy box, placing it on a joist in the garage which Dad had just finished assembling at the top of our drive.

Dad was very proud of this garage and took Auntie Winnie to view it. Barely did she have time to expel her first gasp of admiration before a loud rumbling sounded and the edifice – brought down, perhaps, by the bat in its role as last straw – collapsed on them both. With a small dent in her brow caused by a hang-gliding rafter, Auntie Winnie departed soon after and Dad called the builders in to install a double garage with gardener's store and integral coalshed. The bat, of course, copped it, though I buried him with full military honours.

Apart from the garage when it fell on Auntie Winnie, the house was very quiet. Our old road was full of really interesting sights: lights in bedrooms going on and off, encyclopedia salesmen invited in, husbands' tipsy progress from station to front door illuminated by the fitful blink of lampposts every twenty-five yards. Here we overlooked the forest and every hint of vigour or any emotion warmer than tepid was repressed by arboreous soundproofing.

And it was lonely, too. Our former life had teemed not just with rellies but with neighbours, friendly women called Olive or Betty who wore headscarves over their curlers and could be nattered to in the street or visited for a drop of milk or, of course, in the case of the Avon Lady, aftershave. Here you'd perish of thirst rather than confess milk lack to any of the gorgons who set the social tone.

We weren't the only new people in the area. Our house was at the corner of two roads. One of these roads, that which was run by the gorgons, was absolutely, 24-carat, ruthlessly posh. The other was one of suburban Essex's bloodiest battlegrounds in the class war. At the bottom was a social oubliette comprising two pairs of artisan cottages and a block of maisonettes. A third of the way up, the road began to rise both topographically and economically, first with spec-built cul-de-sacs, then with Residences. These were of increasing size and pretension, as were their occupants. One entire family was as fat as it could get without actually needing to dismantle the door frames to enter the house. There were two fat girls, a fat boy, a fat baby and a Mummy and Daddy built like the Albert Memorial. The Mummy dressed like it, too. She never fitted in. Next door was a house where the foghorn-voiced Mummy lived; she lowered the tone, though not literally. Beyond that lived the wife who had an affair, and over the road was the woman whose husband gave her a Disease (you could find out no end of intriguing information by hiding under a card table at Conservative party whist drives).

The point of existence for these women was the obtaining of an invitation to one of the gorgons' Coffee Mornings. If you cut the mustard there, you could graduate to her Bring and Buy Sale and when you got the call to do Meals On Wheels with her you really knew you were cooking. My mum achieved it in time but it was a tough, cruel world. You could see them all along the street,

Mummies twisting slowly on the gibbet of social ambition, *pour encourager les autres*. The whole thing gave me the heebie-jeebies.

*

Some houses, you can just feel they're haunted. The one we live in now is a warm house. The central heating clicks and fusses on occasion and one top floor ceiling is particularly prone to collapse, but there is nothing remotely non-corporeal to vex and alarm you. But I never did like being alone in that Victorian house on the corner. Even as an adult I would sleep in it with a light on. As a child, I'd lie awake for hours not daring to pull the covers off my head.

Nothing much in it was ours at first. The previous owners had included in the purchase price a job lot of hideous furniture: a three-piece suite upholstered in bile green leather, a gas fridge whose effluvium filled the entire ground floor, a pianola. This sprawled across a good third of the living room, its body covered with an eczema of lacquered scenes from ancient China. My father was persuaded to buy it on the assurance that it was worth thousands of pounds, though a drawback was that part of an outside wall would have required taking down before it could have been removed to realize its value. The pedal case alone was big enough for me to hide behind though I never would because that was one of the places that was haunted. Others were the landing, the walk-in pantry and the far end of the attic above my bedroom, where there had once been a dovecote; the ghosts of these birds were very active at night. And yes, I do know that these frights and spooks were the projections of an insecure child. What I cannot reason away, though, is the woman whom I awoke to find sitting on the edge of my bed. She wore a green 1930s dress. Even in the fuzzy state between sleeping and full consciousness I realized that this was no Tory lady who had placed her gin and tonic on the drinks tray and tiptoed upstairs to hunt for her mink and gaze on me in tipsy sentimentality. I was house-sitting for my parents when it happened, being twenty-seven at the time.

The time came when Dad retired and sold his business. They stayed on for a while but the house was punitively expensive for two elderly people to maintain. Like I said, it was a barn of a place in which none of us had been as happy as we'd hoped, but it had Position. I didn't like to imagine it, the devastation of what I still regarded as my house, which for all its ghosts was very dear to me. I suppose they felled the weeping willow, filled in the pond, crushed the double garage with gardener's store, mowed down the beanstalks in the vegetable patch. Perhaps the woman in the green dress watched from the dovecote before flying around the rubble looking for a new billet. I would never know. I never went back there. But over many years I dreamt about it so many times; it was like an old film lot, some walls ruined, others unbreached, one or two crusted with gold. The front of the house remained undamaged, with its wide blue door and the magnolia blooming outside the living-room window. There would be holes in the roof which there was not the money to mend but in the kitchen, or the living room or the study I'd come upon Mum, Dad and Jane. They wouldn't notice I was there, being intent on their game of Scrabble.

The house to which my parents moved was a tad smaller but delightful. It too was sited on the edge of the forest and boasted a drawing room quite large enough to accommodate both the Scrabble trio and the pianola of which, by this time, they had grown fond, as one would of an old, farting dog. But Mum felt the loss of her

Position very keenly. She called this house her Little Cottage and developed a theory that had I been a son, to whom they could have handed over Dad's business empire, they would not have had to move.

I pointed out time and again that even a penis would not have prevented my talents and inclinations lying more in the direction of the printed word than light engineering, but this never stopped her. 'It would have been someone to carry on the Family Name,' she'd say, and you just can't deal with it, can you? At least, I couldn't. I'd bang the phone directory down in front of her and point out that one thing London, London *alone*, did not lack was people called Welch, when what I really wanted to do was scream, 'I'm me! Why can't I be good enough for you?' but I didn't because she was my mum and she was on her own and even though it was coming up to two years after Dad's death she couldn't seem to move on.

I'd murmur that Big Sis and I did our best and she'd say, 'Yes, but if I'd had a son I just feel he'd never have left my side.' There was so much loneliness in that statement your heart just went out to her, because you knew that eighty years hadn't been enough to heal the emotional neglect of childhood, and what she was saying was what she'd been saying since she was three: 'I wish someone would take care of me.'

And it seemed mean and indecent to whine on about it now when I was happy and healthy, so most of the time I laughed it off but every so often it got to me again, a big gnawing sadness. What usually happened was, we'd be chatting with some of my friends about our children. Someone would allude to their son, and because she wanted to be their contemporary, their equal, not a visiting granny, she'd nod at me and say, 'Of course, this one was meant to be a boy,' and I'd just stand there, dumb, caught between simpering and embarrassment – 'Silly me, I've gone and been a girl' – while inside I felt about two inches tall. I just wished she wouldn't do that.

KEEP ON RUNNING

Runner's World Training Log.
Day: Friday. **Distance:** 12 m. **Weather:** Pissy.
Course/notes: Aéroporte de Bordeaux-Merignac to
Bordeaux Centre. Military trucks on the road, smell of
aviation fuel, blinking lights and signs. Right instep
puffy. New, independent laceration on toe. All my
clothes stink. **Museums missed:** 5.
Historic districts not Gone Round: 2.
Old churches avoided: 3.

I was slithering round the western outskirts of Bordeaux
when another runner came towards me; I sped up
because that's what I always did when I saw other runners, and fell over, twisting my right foot. He looked
away; that's another thing you do when a runner falls
over, to save their embarrassment. 'No, no, I'm fine. I'll
just superglue these three parts of my tibia back together
and then I'll catch you up.' My foot didn't hurt too
much. I put some Voltaren on it, sitting on the wet grass.
I had a drink of water and a couple of cakes. The rain
made them a bit spongy.

I remember being very happy as I rested outside that
airport, breathing in aviation fuel, eating damp cakes and
waiting for the pain to ease off. I felt vindicated. It's hard
to explain tidily but I think I'd known intuitively that
going back to Cap Ferret would produce the catharsis of

grief and pain I needed to move on. What I had experienced there in 1959 had been a sudden, frightening awareness. I had realized I was unhappy and had been that way for some time. I didn't have anyone I could confide in and as the years passed I carried my unhappiness around like a stone suitcase. Now I'd taken it back to Cap Ferret and left it at the graveyard on the hill, next to all the other unhappy stone monuments. I'd run on without it.

At the time I was sitting there I hadn't worked all that out, of course; I'd just become aware that after four days of being pissed on, barked at and followed by leather-faced Frenchmen in rusting vehicles I was having a hard time keeping a deranged grin off my face. I watched a military convoy crawl past; I was glad I wasn't in a car, stuck behind it. The trucks were mottled, shiny, like bugs. I liked those moments on a long walk when I could stop and sit down. I always wanted to see as much as I could, while I could, in case the family curse stole up on me, the blurred words, furred edges, growing fog. I would sit anywhere, watch anything; the military convoy was a joy.

Another was that my knee didn't hurt. Damn, there I go again. I'd planned not to mention the K-word. One is not Shakespeare but one strives in one's small way to illuminate the human condition, the heroic struggle in the face of ultimate futility and oblivion, and what emerges instead is a load of loose talk about knees. I have learnt many things through running and one of them is that knees, like bunions, blisters, fallen arches and ingrowing toenails, are not heroic.

But now we're on the subject I shall go on. During the summer that preceded my trip to Cap Ferret, I embarked on a spell of demented physical activity. After running the London Marathon, I climbed the Three

Peaks and took part in the London-to-Brighton Bike Ride. I then attempted a sublime-sounding long distance walk called the Cloud Seven Circuit. It took place on the northern edge of the Peak District and coincided with the hottest day of the year, possibly of the century. The cold rice pudding they served at the third checkpoint was bubbling. It was one of the most ridiculously unenjoyable ways you could possibly imagine to spend a midsummer Saturday and when, halfway up Cloud Four, my knee made a kind of ker-chunk ker-chunk kerrr-*chunk* sound and refused to carry me any further, I was not far short of shedding tears of relief.

Two days after that I limped through the door of the nearest BUPA physiotherapy department where for the next six weeks a jolly Kiwi girl performed a series of excruciating experiments involving ice, fingers and thumbs on the offending gristle and sinew. At last she stood back, slapped my knee with a triumphant 'She'll do!' and sent me on my way. I skipped lightly home, got into my running shoes and came to a grinding halt two miles into the heath.

Essentially comic runners' injuries might indeed be but at the time it was hard to derive hilarity from mine and in fact I felt very angry that I could no longer run: a real, cursing fury at my body's betrayal. I tried telling myself that running was, after all, only an entertaining diversion, that other people of my age could turn themselves to a cornucopia of soul-nourishing pursuits – gardening, the theatre, joining a bridge club. I enumerated to myself all the things I hated about running. The first twenty minutes were always awful – being wracked with breathlessness, having my spine jolted by the pavement and my toes squeezed into shoes which never seemed big enough no matter what size I bought. The boredom, fear and paranoia (is that Great Dane scampering towards me looking for a friend or a snack? will that group of youths who have just acknowledged me with an encouraging wave follow it up with an elbow round my neck and a knife at my carotid artery?). The discomfort and weariness and longing for a pee. All those dreary five-mile slogs through Blackheath traffic. (In fact I very rarely took that route by then but the occasions on which I did coincided with the worst of my knee pain and the height of my failure to find work.)

I was going to say running wasn't a compulsion; I did have a choice. But that choice was to do with what I wanted to be like when I was sixty, seventy, eighty. I remembered Grandma Belle sitting all day in her chair; the most active thing she did towards the end was take to her bed and there, mostly, she stayed. I thought then that even if to run five miles took me half the day, I would want to do it for the rest of my life. If my sight had gone, I'd feel my way along the pavement. I would not go into that last dark decade falling over and spilling things and dribbling, and when the Grim Reaper called I would bloody well turn and run away as fast as I could, and if he was after me he'd have to catch me first.

It was in that frame of mind that I threw myself on the mercy of a nice podiatrist at the Lewisham Foot Centre. He got me standing on a chair while he walked all round me, staring at my legs from every angle. He made a video of my running on a treadmill, and plaster casts of my feet. We then struck one of the most important bargains I have ever made. I would give him £170 and he would give me back the pleasure of running pain-free. A few weeks later I took delivery of a cardboard box from the Benefoot TM Orthotic Laboratory, Edgewood, NY. Inside were two white insoles for my shoes and a little note which said, among other things, 'Sometimes your orthoses will squeak in the shoes. Be reassured that the device is dynamic and moves during walking.' I slipped them inside my shoes and they did indeed squeak, but what was that compared to having to learn the rules of bridge? And so I went on my way rejoicing, though having to rule out thoughts of any new career as a cat burglar.

DOUBLE TROUBLE (2)

Runner's World Training Log.
Day: Saturday. **Distance:** A very long way.
Weather: No different. **Course/notes:** Bordeaux to St
Andre-de-Cubzac. Houses, pylons, hideous pink
apartment blocks, factories, dark grey towns with names
like chewing iron filings: Carbon Blanc, D'Artigues,
Ambares et Lagrave. **Lacerated toes:** 3. (Quill-shaped
toenail seems to have turned into weapon of mass
destruction.)

I'd been fighting it for ages; in the end I justified it on
the grounds that my twisted foot needed a rest. After
running and walking for so long, I found the taxi went
almost insanely fast as we hurtled through the Bordeaux
traffic, sometimes at speeds of up to 15 kilometres an
hour. The taxi smelt of diesel and stale Gitanes. I
watched rain bounce off the windows instead of my head.
The driver had the radio on (keeping up with the latest
from disaster-torn Niort, I imagine). He had glasses hanging on a string round his neck and a severe case of BO.
The view from the nearside windows was partly blocked
by his blazer, which swung from a gilt coathook screwed
into the pillar and featured black plastic buttons the size
of old pennies. On the floor by the front passenger seat
was a wastepaper basket and on his lap a newspaper.

The bridge over the Garonne reared in front of us,

lights blinking. Under it, the river was pewter and brown. On the other side were austere town houses, half hidden behind ginger trees. I got out just north of Ambares at Lagrave and headed along the old road to St Andre de Cubzac. The bridge across the Dordogne was creaky, the road narrow and quiet. I felt I'd entered another country, one with valleys, chain link fencing and bright green grass. I'd left the Atlantic coast behind me, though I wasn't quite ready to say goodbye to the little girl of ten.

*

I learnt early on that you were punished for being clever. Teachers set traps for you, to prove to you that you don't know as much as you think. They celebrate your failures and shortcomings; Miss Jeffries (Transition Year, 1957–58) invited the entire class to applaud one girl because she had 'beaten Julie in exams'. I applauded along with everyone else, to show I was a good loser. I would publish the tomato-faced old bag's home address now except she's dead.

I'm always tempted when turning to the subject of my schooldays to wallow in the foaming bath of self-pity but compared to what some people had to endure I had it very easy. I was never the last person to be picked when you had to divide into teams for PE. Nobody held my head down while someone else flushed the toilet over it. My parents were no more embarrassing than anyone else's. Like I've said, there were concerted attempts from time to time to 'bring me down a peg or two', but teachers weren't mind-readers; they couldn't know how vulnerable I was underneath. And I'm sure I was pretty conceited, as it happened. That would explain how the Murgatroyd twins came as such a shock to my system; I just couldn't believe that anyone could possibly dislike me so much.

The Murgatroyd twins were repeating their eleven-plus year owing to general disarray and non-cooperation wrongly diagnosed, I think, as stupidity. They were fraternal twins but alike, with angry shoe-button eyes and a scribble of brown hair each. They were naughty (conduct mark) and I was good (effort point). These badges of vice and virtue would be recorded on a large chart on the 2B notice board.

An average tally of conduct marks for the term per pupil would be three. Five meant a visit to the headmistress, a large spinster who generated more excitement than she deserved because her father had been a fighter pilot. Seven conduct marks and you could be thinking of transportation. The Murgatroyd twins shared twenty-two, and I had one. Once. For a very short time. The teacher was so unaccustomed to my transgressing that she registered it in the adjacent effort point column. A week went by, after which I told her that she had incorrectly registered it and she promptly expunged this stain from my record. In fact, I am almost certain she let me keep the gratis effort point to go with the eleven I had already amassed. Whoever said creeps don't prosper?

Well, I didn't, actually. Unfortunately Mrs H. called the class's attention to my *beau geste*. I'm not saying that she had her own agenda but I always think in certain circumstances it's best to reward children by stealth. She was one of those women who put their arms round you and kind of suck you between the Scylla and Charybdis of bust and armpit. 'Julie has done a very honest thing this morning.' The tone she used was affectionate but the undertone was 'What a nauseating little ass'. Interestingly, Margaret Thatcher's manner was exactly the same twenty years later when required to present me with a sportswriting award.

The Murgatroyd twins left scrawled poison pen letters in my desk and marched around the playground arm in arm, crowing, 'Julia Welch got three for a mental arithmetic test.' I had no idea they'd even noticed me, let alone how much they hated me, and was taken aback by their passion. And – strictly in the interests of truth and accuracy, you understand – I would like to have it put on record that I never got three for a mental arithmetic test. Ten, always ten out of ten. Except for once when I got nine-and-a-half but that was when I had written two numbers the wrong way round by mistake and Mrs H. wouldn't let me alter them.

I was too much of a wimp to confront the Murgatroyd twins and not enough of a sneak to tell Mrs H., who by then would probably not have been inclined to take up my cause anyway on account of having gone off me suddenly. She had proposed we start a lunchtime handicrafts club – 'Why don't we call it the Busy Bees?' – and I had turned down membership in order to continue playing riding schools in the rhododendron bushes with my friend Sandra. We were the only two in the class to take a stand and Mrs H. took it personally. All they ever did was make papier-mâché plates. You couldn't get into the formroom for buckets of mulched *Daily Telegraphs*.

The end of term play approached. The title of the production now eludes me but not the part in which I was cast. I was The Showman, my elevation to this starring role driven no doubt by my possession not just of the necessary memory for large chunks of rhyming verse but also the strong bladder required to stand and recite them.

The character was an itinerant impresario. He tramped round the country, stopping off here and there to introduce his circus of weird and marvellous folk and creatures, which is rather my function in this book, perhaps. Even then the role seemed to harmonize with one aspect of my personality and I liked the idea of playing it very much. But as Grandma Belle would no doubt have told me, had she not by then set off to make that fatal pot of morning tea, Pride goeth before destruction, and a haughty spirit before a fall (Proverbs, somewhere or other). I was really, really *proud* of being The Showman and dammit if I didn't get jocked off. As we gathered for the first read-through, the Murgatroyd girls began complaining vociferously that my ownership of the role was unfair. They made no claims on their own behalf – a smart move, this – but were pleading for the girl with long, yellow teeth.

Mrs H. threw the vote to the floor. Who should be The Showman? The Murgatroyd twins came from a family of seven and were experienced in shouting. They led the opposition and quickly eclipsed the more modulated claque led by my friend Sandra.

'Well, that seems to be it,' said Mrs H. 'Do you mind, Julie?'

'No, not at all.'

That evening I confessed my humiliation to Mum. She was all for putting on her coat and going round to speak to Mrs Herrington *right this minute* but I dissuaded her. I thought it would only have made me more unpopular. And that was an end to it, really. The girl with yellow teeth turned out to be so crap in the part that I was reinstated for the final dress rehearsal, having learnt my lesson. I like to think I did the business, like Ian Rush coming on for Liverpool late on in the second half and scoring the winning goal with a minute to go.

In the Lent term I travelled by tube to sit the entrance examination for the London public school. As we gathered in a classroom beforehand I noticed the Murgatroyd twins had also been submitted for the once-over. We eyeballed each other across the desks but did not speak. They were not offered a place (conduct mark) and I was awarded a scholarship (effort point).

At the end of that school year I was also awarded a cup for academic achievement, presented to me by Mrs H. rather in the manner of Bingley's sisters to Elizabeth Bennett on the occasion of her engagement to Mr Darcy. I'm sure she would be strangely gratified to learn of my subsequent pratfalls, but she's with the mulched *Daily Telegraphs* now.

Meanwhile, you know the rest. I went to the London public school and turned into a dolt and yes, a big part of it was needing not to be disliked more than I wanted to be clever. But I was also *bored* witless. The lessons at my first school had been dreary but whatever needed doing had been achieved with a minimum of effort. Here was a higher, more demanding standard of tedium. Maybe if someone had explained why I needed to burden myself with this knapsack of dull facts, what they would lead to in terms of knowledge that it would be a pleasure to have and use, it would have been all right but as things stood I can't tell you how unexciting a prospect it all was. My output was poor, as were my notices: 'Julie is inclined to be self-centred at times, and can be a law unto herself.' I heard out Mum's entirely reasonable reproaches in silence, and went on exactly the same as before.

It sounds as though I underachieved through an act of will but in fact I just didn't seem to be able to do anything about anything, and my only comfort was that the Murgatroyd twins had not been there to enjoy my shameful failure. The headmistress said goodbye to me on the last day of the summer term, in July 1961. She was a tall woman of distant dignity, her white hair giving her a snow-capped appearance, like an unassailable mountain peak. The road in which the school stood was next to Fleet Street and the rattle of newspaper lorries accompanied her adieu. 'I will not say you have been a great success here. At your interview you were interesting to talk to.'

Years later I'd still catch myself thinking what I might have retorted: 'I will not say your Scripture lessons were the most interesting I have ever attended,' or, 'Go shit in your hat.' But I just disappeared from her sight. And as it turned out, I was wrong about the Murgatroyd twins. They would reappear in my life later and witness an even more dramatic downfall.

I used to spend a lot of time wondering why being clever was a mixed blessing, why not only peers but more importantly adults can feel so threatened by a very intelligent child. Now I'm a parent I understand more. It's so lowering, somehow, the realization that such a child is exasperated by your failure to grasp something so patently simple to him or her, especially if it is accompanied by swank. Perhaps it is also the independence of mind, a quality which requires courage and support to sustain into adult life. But I think the real trick, one which I never quite managed, was to do with tact and concealment, a kind of cerebral version of legeredemain. I couldn't keep my head down and succeed at the same time. I was too much The Showman. But I don't mind. I liked being The Showman. Still do.

MY LIFE WITH JONAH

Runner's World Training Log.
Day: Sunday. **Distance:** 28 m. **Weather:** Wet and chilly. **Course/notes:** St Andre de Cubzac to Blaye. Narrow verges, squelching feet, vines. A bridge called Pont du Moron. A pretty town called Bourg: narrow main street, a roofed market place, Listes de Mariage shops and a very old *mercerie. Joyeuses fêtes* on all the windows. A signpost to somewhere called Le Pain au Sucre. **Chateaux not Gone Round:** 4. **Fortifications not marvelled at:** 1. **Loopy dogs:** 2. **Loopy motorcyclists:** 3. **Leaps into ditches to avoid loopy motorcyclists:** 3. **Unscheduled comfort stops, one behind row of vines:** 3 (yesterday's pâté, I think).

I walked alongside the eastern banks of the Garonne. It looked choppy, wide and furious. Rain had begun falling again. Just before dusk, I reached Blaye. It was a citadel town, forlorn in the December half-light. Vauban's walls, banks and fortifications reared in front of me. They looked intimidating, like the sign reading THIS IS ANFIELD which terrifies visiting teams as they head out to the Liverpool pitch.

It was late in the afternoon. I sat on a bench in a car park under the ramparts, looking at the map. The car park was nearly empty, the ground was puddled and the two hotels I'd passed looked as though they'd have tilted corridors and the kind of bathrooms in which you burnt your arse on the hot water pipe every time you turned round. I seemed to have been walking for ever but had come such a small way. I felt gloomy. What I was doing seemed pointless, but impossible to get out of. I was going to have to go on walking. I'd have to wake up every morning, put on smelly clothes and shoes that hadn't dried overnight, hang a damp rucksack on my back and set off. I knew I wouldn't go off my head, start talking to myself or poking around in bins, I'd just do it. If I'd learnt anything at the school for country Sloanes it was that: to endure.

A flight of steps was set into the rampart wall. I trudged up them and crossed a little bridge with freshly painted green rails and dogshit-garnished cobbles. I was in what was left of Vauban's citadel: a grassy plateau traversed by neat narrow lanes, dotted with great old trees, and few lines of artisan cottages. I'd been told this citadel was Vauban's masterwork. I was too wet and tired to care. More exciting was the Hôtel de la Citadelle, serene, ivy-clad, carefully preserved and above all *ouvert*.

I surrendered myself to the usual end-of-the-day joys like hitting my head on the television set, drying out my money on the radiator, scrubbing blood off my left orthotic, opening a half-bottle of Chateau Perthus and reading the photocopied hotel brochure while stretched out on the bed with a glass in my hand. The brochure contained some good tips on getting washed. (Schower. A mixer top (the higher one), more you turn it, water is hoter. Bath=2 small tops.) Warmed and schowered, I felt more cheerful. I studied the view from the balcony, or, as the brochure put it, from its towers contemplated the setting sun over the most Europe important estuary. It was fogged over, like a steamed-up bathroom. All I could make out were two whiskery eyots in the foreground. Upstream, a dredger turned round sedately, blinking its bleary lights. The view was stimulating enough, but not for all of the four hours I had available between downing the last of the Chateau Perthus and going to sleep.

I went down to the hotel restaurant to gauge the possibilities of discovering own panoramix view over 'La Gironde', and tasting the products of the region according to the seasons and the day market, without forgetting the best greatwine from the area: 'Premières Côtes de Blaye, Côtes de Bourg and others Bordeaux.' A quick check of the menu indicated that the greatwine alone would have left me distinctly outpocket so, having been reassured by the hotel brochure that 'Our night auditor will welcome the lastest of you', I set off back to town to trough in others bar. This was a modest but friendly looking concern which I chose on the advice of its doorman, a large brown poodle.

Here I did what I always do in French bars, which is inadvertently catch the eye of the town drunk. This one had a beard, greasy trilby and white trainers and did to me what town drunks always do in French bars, which is to shake my hand, indulge in one-way conversation, shuffle away then return for a repeat performance. I set about the rapid emptying of two pitchers of Beaujolais and left before the arrival of the meal I had ordered, the combined effect of so much Beaujolais and so little *sandwich jambon* causing me to pursue a circumferential tour of Vauban's work before I found the hotel again. I don't know if I was the lastest back but I was quite definitely the pissedest.

*

I ran it the other week. Haven't been back to East Anglia for ages. Last time I set off there was to interview an ex-footballer who lived near by. I used to know the way like the inside of my Runner's Medicine Chest but I actually got lost seven miles out. I don't think I wanted to arrive, really. No disrespect to the ex-footballer, but the place just gave me the willies.

This race, the one I was running in, was a 20-miler. The Bury Chicago Rock Café 20, to give its full title. A notably well organized and marshalled event, perfectly timed for the build-up to the London Marathon, so one of Runner's World's Team In Training events with close to 1000 entries. There were medals for every finisher and hot tea and hamburgers in a warm hall afterwards. I recommend it, though it's a hard one to run. I did 3 hours 30, and was by no means the lastest. Was overtaking people, even. My small, slow triumph.

God, the landscape hasn't changed. That flat, bleak skyline – a dead tree is high incident – and wind syphoning in from the North Atlantic, and fields of frozen mangel-wurzels, and lanes caked with a psoriasis of dung. Worms, roosters, tractors. I would say the memories flooded back as though it all happened yesterday but firstly I'm not yet desperate enough to resort to cliché and, secondly, I've always tried to forget about that part of my life.

The school for country Sloanes was by the sea. It closed a handful of summers ago, victim of the trend away from boarding education. No idea what's happened to its buildings, the seven boarding houses, music school, classroom blocks, gymnasium, art room, chapel, tennis courts, swimming pool. Probably been taken over by some kind of sect now, though I don't know what they'd make of the lacrosse pitches. Mass suicide at cover point?

The library block where I was expelled had gone some years earlier. It burnt down.

The headmistress's nickname was Jonah, though she was built more on the lines of the whale. Her study was on the first floor, overlooking the ocean, and I sometimes wondered whether she had become beached one long ago day, but had managed to find her way over the boundary hedge and in through the French windows. Here someone handed her a tweed suit and a maths degree and showed her upstairs.

She was a forbidding sight, with fine grey hair which was rigidly disciplined by a slide, though a kiss-curl on the right-hand side gave levity. The school, as was typical of that kind of place at that kind of time, boasted a number of peculiar rituals and etiquettes, one of which had to do with meals. Each Monday, the more reliable and incorruptible sixth form girls would stand at the dining room entrance before lunch handing out alphabetically marked tickets. These would indicate your table and the randomly selected company in which you would square up to gristle-beaded rissoles, reconstituted scrambled egg and dreadful jugged hare (a complete set of leporine teeth was once uncovered beneath the gravy) for the next seven days. However unattractive a prospect this was – what is bread for, if not to be broken among friends? – the only alternative was more hideous still. Each Monday, too, a typed slip of green A4 would go up on the notice board. The girls listed thereupon would be on The Jonah Table.

Jonah's table was the most commodiously positioned in the dining room, in an alcove by those French windows through which, I fancied, she had first arrived. We would foregather in standing silence, broken only by the nervous tintinnabulum of dropped cutlery. Presently she would pound her way along the polished floorboards, kiss-curl bouncing, and pause behind her chair (it was made of oak, with throne-like features) to bark grace in a slurred but accelerating baritone. 'For what we budger receive maytheLordmakustrulythankfulmen. Sit down, hmph, mmph.' Shortly afterwards: 'Welch!'

What had I done? Some detour from the path of Dainty Eating, no doubt. Not that you could bring yourself to eat much on Jonah's table. Worse than waiting to have your teeth out. She called everyone by their surnames, not just me, though Welch-wise she could have qualified for a frequent-user discount.

We made fun of her behind her back, though not with any great heart. That woman could detect insurrection at 100 paces. Some antenna in the kiss-curl, perhaps. Another typed slip of green A4 would appear on the notice board:

Girls to see Miss Jones
Welch

You'd sit outside her study with the other detainees, the bench rocking and creaking under anxious bums. Into her chamber you would creep, feeling lilliputian; she was, as I've indicated, quite a considerable woman, and everything in her study was of a size and gravitas to match – the vast desk from behind which she interrogated you, the sea rolling and slopping a paper dart's throw from the windows, Her Majesty the Queen eyeing you above the fireplace (it was the Annigoni portrait).

'Good afternoon, Miss Jones.'

'People are saying you're conceited. Hmph, mmph?'

I think now that she was not without kindness or humour, despite her quelling solemnity. She certainly had her quirks. She drove an open top Jaguar in which on some evenings she would glide out through the school's narrow and pillared gateway, wearing an extra hide of tweed to withstand the sea breeze. It was believed that her destination was one of the better local hostelries or the golf club, from where, having sherry taken with retired colonels, she would later emerge, kiss-curl a mite less tamped, and once again negotiate the gateway, though not with such ease. Little dents and scratches were sometimes noted on the Jaguar's paintwork the next morning.

I don't want to give the impression I was completely miserable there. You learn to assimilate, don't you? Within days of my arrival I was calling hairdressing *wigging* and the lavatory *cab* (you said, 'Must go to cab' – it was vital not to use the definite article). For the first two years I was deemed to be 'refreshingly original' rather than crazy. I quite like good, clean, innocent fun and there was a lot of that to be had: midnight feasts, apple-pie beds, wrapping your chums' birthday presents in sanitary towel bags – what larks.

No chance of the other sort of fun, of course. All-female cast of staff, apart from subjects the teaching of which required a dick: science, the clarinet, tennis. For these Jonah hired the most ancient geldings she could find. The Head of Science was a bald, embarrassed man called Robertson. We nicknamed him Golly. Clarinet was with a sparse-moustached major, his pips possibly obtained in the Crimea.

Actually, he wasn't a bad guy, the old major. Wore a hacking jacket with gravy-strafed lapels and taught me how to play The Onions, with which Sidney Bechet had enjoyed success fifteen years earlier on one of those crackling 78s. We discovered a mutual interest in horse racing and used up a lot of the lessons bandying Newmarket gossip about. Sold me his saxophone at a very good price, too. Meanwhile Mr Cooper, the sun-dried tennis coach, introduced me to the Western-grip fore-hand and men's capacity for lying to get what they want. 'I'll give you sixpence if you hit that,' he said, placing his floppy hat on the service line. I hit it first time, but sixpence came there none.

And then it started going wrong again. I was top of the form, and then I wasn't. Nothing happened out-wardly, nobody impugned my mental arithmetic, I wasn't struck down like the two sisters whose father died (heart attack) mid-term. We watched their uncle's car draw up in the gravel drive. Dreadful sobbing from the dormitory, we weren't allowed in; they were hurried into the back of the car with coats over their heads as though under arrest; we never saw them again.

I just seemed to get lost. Some people should be let off adolescence on compassionate grounds and I was one of them. Everyone else was blossoming into Womanhood and I was stuffing my face with food and bursting out of my tunic. My body wouldn't do anything I wanted it to do. Hair like a hedge, eyes squinting (it was either that or the shame of specs), cheeks permanently blushed, spare tyres, chins, apology for a bust.

Things weren't very happy back home, either. Dad working his socks off to build up the business empire and cut a dash at the council, Mum (as she put it) 'slaving like a skivvy over a hot stove'. Big Sis was grown up and all but gone. No more holidays in France for the four of us. There'd been an empty space in the Austin Cam-bridge for some time. Dad really missed her when she was away on her student travels. They had terrible rows, immigration, boyfriends, all that jazz, but the same as with Jane, he'd light up like a bulb when she was around.

My sister was a linguist, spending a lot of time abroad. We'd be sitting around the garden waiting for something to happen when a taxi would draw up behind the fence. Dad would go to look, then he'd leap around, his voice vaulting to a joyful bellow as he called her name. From abroad she brought home sophisticated talk, wit, a kind of fellowship with Dad which I never seemed to match. She was cool, zany, blonde.

Then she got married (me the pinkest, burstingest bridesmaid you ever did see) and went to live in Australia. Waving goodbye at Heathrow Airport, we stood on the observation roof and watched her and her new husband walk from the departure gate across the tarmac and climb the steps into the big jet. Mum hugging herself though it was a warm day. 'It's such a long way away,' she said. I offered Mum the contents of my post office savings account to help expedite her first visit but it didn't seem to make her feel any better. Nor me, either. Poor thing. One daughter in New South Wales, the other a stupid, clumsy, disappointing lump.

Mum went out to Australia the next summer. Trip of a lifetime, she sent home loads of lively letters, it was a time to have shares in Basildon Bond all right. 'This morning I woke up to the sound of footsteps. A postman was on the roof.' (Later it transpired that I had misread her eager writing and it was in fact a possum thus aloft.) Mum came back to be met at Heathrow Airport by Dad and Jane and that was when the fur started flying, owing to The Hotel Bill For Two. On an April day some thirty-five years later Mum and I agreed that Dad was indisputably innocent of all charges but at the time – I don't care what she says now – they had not just one cross word but a multitude. The atmosphere terrible, Mum trying to pull me one way – 'Never mind, Julie, you stick up for your mum' – and Dad the other. Bleating irritably behind the steering wheel of the Austin Cambridge as he chauffeured me to my riding lesson. 'I wish your mother would be reasonable. We could have such a happy home.'

Can't look at a hard hat now without thinking of that horrible time.

I sleepwalked through my O level year, getting nine with largely mediocre grades, growing simultaneously more uppity and hopeless. Mum and I had so many fights we could have been Frazier and Ali. No use asking Dad to referee, he was just a man, completely out of his depth in that big wild sea of female emotion. Back at school I acted the goat.

> *Girls to see Miss Jones*
> Welch

'Good afternoon, Miss Jones.'

'You could be a likeable child if you weren't so desperate to attract attention. Mmph, hmph?'

I suppose what I needed to know was that living is like running marathons. Sometimes you just have to grit your teeth and run through all the pain and tiredness and cold. Presently you'll get to a place that says Finish and someone will step forward and hand you a cup of hot tea. But no one was in a position to tell me that then. Women were barred from running more than a few miles, the prevailing medical opinion being that to travel further would cause our fannies to fall out. Even had that not been so, Jonah could not have enlightened me. Her distance was the 100-metre dash from the dining-room doorway to her table. Any longer than that and she took the Jag.

She was right about one thing, though. I was desperate for attention. A boyfriend would have done nicely.

All the successful, pretty girls in my year were embarking on postal romances with boarding school boys met at Christmas dances. Names like Charles and Chris, schools like Eton and Charterhouse, wrote mainly about house rugby results, but caused the occasional flutter by signing off 'Luv by the gallon'.

The winter of 1963, Jo had a Ball. Her house was bigger than mine, with rose garden, tennis court, hint of a maze, bespoke Wendy house and a ballroom that opened off the dining room. Billiards table at one end, and a parquet floor around which we'd spent many happy hours roller skating on long past afternoons. I wore the bridesmaid's dress let out and converted and at midnight found myself marooned during the Fireman's Waltz with an underdeveloped boy called Nigel.

I don't suppose anyone does the Fireman's Waltz nowadays. You stumbled round and round, the lights went out, the music stopped and you kissed your partner for as long as it took. Lights on again, music, and off you waltzed again.

It was meant to be fun.

'I think we'd better sit the rest of this out,' said Nigel nervously after the lights went out for the third time. I chose a book from Jo's library and read in the loo for the remaining two hours. Later, Mum tried to buy me a roll-on. 'You're not fat, dear. You just need a little control.'

Off she went to Australia again. While she was away I'd go with my dad to functions, in the role of Council Chairman's Lady, bulging out of my black Mary Quant skinny rib and beige halter neck skirt (impossible to describe; it was the sixties, you had to be there). With me glowering at his side, Dad would fall casually into conversation with Young Conservatives, about whom he would afterwards sound me out. 'What did you think of him?'

'Dunno.'

'That's the sort of young man I'd like to see you with.'

My darling dad. Kind, good, tactful, if at times rather bemused. All he was doing was his fatherly duty, which was to make sure that his daughter chose the right man. I thought he'd gone mad, or blind. Couldn't he see that I was ugly, scowling, unlovable, never in a million years to be the object of interest of one of those fresh-faced, curly-haired young men? (Just like he must have looked at their age, they were.)

I can't have been a complete write-off. I caught the eye of a Haileybury at ballroom dancing class and could in consequence hold my own with any girl in the matter of Edmonstone House rugby for the Lent term of 1964. In the Easter holidays I exchanged kisses and letters with a Dulwich College encountered over the lemon barley jugs at a tennis club dance. Bishop's son, lived off Belgrave Square. He was American. I loved the wide, confident sound of his voice. We held hands in the college chapel during Stabat Mater and he gave me his signet ring, despite being irritated by my hat. The ring was a heavy, clunking thing of pewter, with a dull brown stone. Two weeks later he told me he was returning to New York with his family and asked for it back.

Henrys, Jeremys, Iains, Alistairs. Fruit cups, MG Midgets, YC barbecues. I did my best but it wasn't really my thing. Just didn't find public schoolboys sexy, to be honest. 'I say, would you mind awfully if I kissed you?' Talking as though they had doylies stuffed down the back of their throats.

God alone knows where Jean-Pierre was being educated. I met him on a school trip to Menton, he was there with the rest of his orphanage, on a holiday at the Paris taxpayers' expense. April 1965. Enticed by my Vidal Sassoon geometric cut and green denim trouser suit (another of those garments which you had to have been there at the time fully to understand) Jean-Pierre took my bra off by the light of the Riviera moon and wondered aloud about *peut-être se marier, qui sait?* Who knows indeed? One false Oui and I could have been writing this as the wife of a Bercy garage mechanic.

I said I'd keep in touch and I did but by then I'd met him. Jug-Eared Richard, though the remarkable wing-span of his organs of hearing was a matter of supreme indifference to me, shielded anyway under the delicious silk of his black-brown hair. Why him, I don't know. I suppose I'd been running through all the pain and the cold and he was the one who stepped out at the Finish line. Handed me not a cup of hot tea but a beaker of youth club orangeade.

He was the first boy I'd met who made me laugh.

It was a time of A level set books, pirate radio (the good ship Caroline, remember it?), that wasp-striped vest dress from Biba – from the first shop she owned, a long march down the Abingdon Road from Kensington High Street tube. Mary Wells sang 'My Guy', the Byrds did a cover version of 'Mr Tambourine Man', the Beach Boys charted with 'Help Me Rhonda'. Hemlines went up and heels were beginning to clunk.

Jug-Eared Richard didn't ask permission to kiss me, just got on with it as we sat entwined in the back of his friend Dave's Ford Cortina. (They put twin halogens on the front and rallied it. Made the results table of *Motor Sport News* once. He sent me the cutting. I stuck it inside the front cover of *Le Malade Imaginaire*, having underlined the name. Jug-Eared Richard's, that is, not Molière's.)

And back at school we wrote to each other. Dear Rick, Dear Julie. Then Darling, then the apogee, Dearest darling. I lay awake after lights out, intoxicated by the sound of falling rain. That's love.

*

He was a public schoolboy, his place there owed to some kind of scholarship. Beyond that, his credentials as the suitor of my parents' daughter fell away sharply. I made the mistake of telling Mum where he lived. 'It's a council house,' she pleaded with me. 'Have a little pride, dear.'

I went on seeing him in secret. I'm told by more sophisticated friends that undercover relationships are a vital part of adolescence. Perhaps I was frightfully pious at heart, but I felt damaged and seedy. I went around all butter-wouldn't-melt, but something inside me was like a peach that had been run over by a car. Mum wasn't taken in for a moment. 'Where have you been?'

(On his bed, wearing nothing but a pair of flowered pants from Netawear.)

'I *told* you. I had to go to the library.'

'We looked for you in the library. You weren't there. Where were you?'

'Yes I was. You must have missed me. I was researching in the alcove.'

'Ho! In the gardening section?'

Two implacable wills.

*

Back at school was the first girl in our year to announce she'd lost her virginity, on a reproduction chaise longue after a carefully plotted assault on an amazed but grateful Felsted. She'd been letting us in for months on the slow postal build-up, like Sky Sports whipping up consumer interest in a pay-per-view fight. We were awestruck, we never thought she'd really do it. A spotty girl, very good at chemistry, and always one of the keenest at Confirmation class. Then again, if your surname's Smellie I suppose you've got to pull out all the stops to give people something else to remember you by.

> Dearest, darling Rick,
> If the world's about to be destroyed by nuclear war, will you make love to me before it starts?

> Dearest, darling Julie,
> It won't take imminent nuclear war for me to make love to you, just you and me alone somewhere warm and quiet.

In the outside world, Jean Shrimpton went to Melbourne races with Terence Stamp. She wore calf-length white boots and a simple lawn shift adorned at the neck by a single brooch, though it was the size of a saucer. Goodness me, what a stir to be caused by three yards of flimsy blue cotton. Made all the front pages except *The Times*, which still led with its classified ads. I was handy with a sewing machine and equipped several friends in my class. Sixth formers were allowed to wear their own clothes at weekends. I led the white-booted charge into the dining room for Friday night supper, to audible gasps from impressionable Upper Fourths.

> *Girls to see Miss Jones*
> Welch

'Good afternoon, Miss Jones.'
'White boots. We don't wear things like that.'
'No, Miss Jones.'

She reached out for her in-tray and handed me two sealed envelopes. They were addressed to me. University of Bristol was printed on top of one. The other had a Cambridge postmark.

I *felt* them, looked and looked. Her Majesty the Queen regarding me with steady gaze from above the fireplace. My heart going boing-boing-boing. 'Shall I open them now, Miss Jones?'

'Up to you. Let me know later, if you want.'

I opened them in front of her. She probably knew what was in them anyway, the old poker-face.

'I've, um, got interviews at both.'

'Well done.'

'Thank you, Miss Jones.' Fingers round the door handle now.

'Welch!'

'Yes, Miss Jones?'

'Bound to get into Cambridge. They'll like you there because you're mad. Mmph, hmph.' There was a low rumbling sound which I realized was Jonah chortling at her own joke.

*

Exhilarated, I went home for half term and got Dad on his own, behind the steering wheel of his car. It was a new one, a turquoise Austin 2000. They had funny-shaped boots, the design never really caught on. Me, I was terrified, stuttering.

'Dad, I've got to talk to you.'

'What's that?' he exclaimed jovially, as if in a desperate attempt to inject a carnival mood into proceedings. He knew what was coming. Poor man. Like I said, just couldn't cope with all the *emotion*.

'I can't stand it any more.'

'I knew you liked someone,' he said gently.

'More than like.' I started blubbing. That set him off, of course. Mopping his eyes with a crumpled check handkerchief. 'Your mother and I are very proud people . . . I suppose I imagined you meeting a lord or someone like that . . .'

Snivel, sniff.

'I'll have a word with your mother.'

That weekend we went to a Function and I was allowed to take Jug-Eared Richard as my boyfriend. Round and round we waltzed. I've still got them, the Paco Rabanne earrings I wore. White and black plastic, like bull's-eyes. The dress, I think, was a Dollyrocker. Dad managed to claim me for a foxtrot. 'You look lovely, dear.'

'Thank you.'

He glanced at Mum then out of the side of his mouth he said, 'Dance with some other boys too. Don't push your luck.'

*

A week later, Jonah hurtled up to me in the library block and drew me aside. She was wearing a new suit, I noticed, Winalot-coloured, with long, narrow lapels. 'Letter from your mother,' she said. 'Wants to come to your Bristol interview.'

Bloody hell. I'd told Mum I was going up there on my own. Can't say why, it was just how I wanted it. Can say why, actually. Didn't want to be told what to say, what not to wear. Because that's what parents do if you let them. Hijack your things because they've no faith in your getting it right for yourself. I'm a parent myself. Trust me, I know. 'She probably thinks I'm going to meet my boyfriend,' I told Jonah.

'Are you?'

'No,' I said. The absolute truth. 'She doesn't approve of him because he lives in a council house,' I went on. 'But he's got an interview at Oxford.'

'Not the road-sweeper's son, then, hmph, mmph? No? All right. I'll write to your mother and tell her I think you should be allowed to go on your own.'

*

I went by train from Paddington to Bristol Temple Meads, overnight case at my feet. Mum's admonitions ringing in my ears. 'If they offer you a place, don't accept it. Tell them you've got an interview at Cambridge AND FOR GOODNESS SAKE PULL YOUR SKIRT DOWN.' I read letters from Richard and Jean-Pierre, and thumbed through the sports pages of the *Daily Telegraph*. The boy in the opposite seat started chatting to me (I'd whipped off my specs when he sat down). He was going for an interview at Bath, having been turned down by Bristol at UCCA form stage. He wanted to write to me so I gave him the address of an irritating girl in my class.

After he got off at Bath, I couldn't help it, I looked at my reflection in the window.

Eyes.

Fringe.

No plurality chin-wise.

Cheekbones, even.

In fact, overlook the specs and it wasn't such a night-mare vision, really.

Could have been yesterday, stepping onto the plat-form in the November darkness. Not quite a foreign city, but wooded, hilly, exciting. Past the station went the teeming road to Bath. Little streets threaded off it like capillaries, rising steeply, lined with terraced houses.

Totterdown, the area was called. A domino effect waiting to happen.

I caught my first-ever-by-myself taxi and went crawling up Park Street to Clifton in rush hour, noting cafés and shops. A cold evening, but dry. I liked the look of Bristol. Big Sis had done her French degree there: Upper Second with, as Mum liked to emphasize, distinction in the Oral. She was very proud of Big Sis's academic achievements, though it had taken her a while to come to terms with Bristol. Most put out when Big Sis firmly headed west after refusing to stay on the extra year at school to retake Oxford entrance. She'd hit the bell first time around, but they'd only offered her a place to do German. Given the choice between fluency in the land of *wurst* and potatoes or the language of Papa Jean Castaing it was, of course, no contest.

She told me: 'He explained to me everything about Sartre and Camus. He was the only man I could ever have taken as a lover.'

What had really got Mum's goat was that the daughter of a particularly pushy neighbour had won a scholarship to Cambridge to read Maths. The girl had not been well in the days leading up to the entrance exam.

'You know what *she* [the neighbour] did, don't you? Wrote them a sicknote and they let her in. Well, we could all write sicknotes if we were prepared to stoop that low.' A happy ending was that the girl dropped out midway through her second year, after a nervous breakdown.

What a pressure cooker it all was for mothers in those days.

I'd been booked for the night into a place near the Students Union building. It turned out to be one of those strange hybrid places like Dolphin Square, half hotel, half apartments, with a restaurant on the ground floor. I commanded a table for one and dined off liver and bacon, with a book propped up against the condiment set. *Giles Goat-Boy* by John Barth. I didn't crave Richard at all. He didn't belong in this place. This was about me. And I can feel it now, the way I felt then. I felt clever and mysterious and quiet and powerful. I felt absolutely great.

My interview clothes:
Black wool Foale and Tuffin skirt
Black and green check work shirt (Millett's)
Emerald green needlecord bomber jacket (Netawear)
Black knee length boots (Ravel)
Apple green tights (you had to be there)

Ten past ten the next morning, I presented myself at the door of Professor Korner's study in the Faculty of Philosophy. A boy waited on a bench outside, knees knocking. 'They interview you then send you outside while they talk about you. Then they call you back to say whether you're in or not.' The door opened. He was called back in. He emerged and hurried away.

Stephan Korner was one of the world's leading experts on Kant. A small, close-coupled man with tight grey curls and interested eyes. My other interrogator was a man with a beard. (There were a lot of them in the philosophy department. One had to search for distinguishing subtleties, like their preferred shade of duffel coat.) The interview went well. I dismantled existentialism in three crisp sentences and was sent to wait outside, but the man with the beard had reopened the door before my bum hit the seat.

*

Looking back on how I felt on that journey to Bristol, it dawns on me how much it resembles the way I feel in the middle of a race, in the one-hour place between fighting and coughing and wrestling for breath and, at the other end, the dying of my legs beneath me. I felt so *in charge*. It wasn't just the confidence a plain girl finds from being the object of male attention, though having two boys vying for me was nice. I think it was to do with the way Jonah had talked to me. She and I had enjoyed rational, adult conversation. She had listened to me and treated me with respect. She'd told me I was mad, but implied it was a condition to be revered and applauded. She'd teased me as an equal and for a very short time, no more than a week but what a week it was, I knew what it felt like to be a normal clever girl with a normal and enticing future.

PAPER CROWN

Runner's World Training Log.
Day: Monday. **Distance:** 17 m. **Weather:** Hurrah,
dry. **Course/notes:** Blaye to St Ciers à Gironde. Fallen
leaves, empty roads, farm buildings. Villages with saints'
names. **Dead rats:** 2. **Dead birds:** 1 (brown and
yellow: very pretty). **Dead person:** 1. (Must have
happened within the last forty-eight hours. Road sign
with fresh bunches of flowers propped against it.)

By dint of holding the remote upside down and position-
ing myself on the far side of the wardrobe, I was able to
operate the television in my room before breakfast. A
weather girl in a maroon velvet jacket gave forth a
message which roughly translated as rain, everywhere, all
over France, all of the time (and as for Niort, they really
had it coming to them). I abandoned my plan to linger
over coffee and croissants beside Europe's most important
estuary and set off at a lively wade in the vague direction
of England.

Just outside Blaye the D255 veered away from the
forested banks of the Garonne and started a mercifully
level wind through the fields and villages. It was just past
nine in the morning and with stunning abruptness the
rain stopped and all over France – or, at least, the part in
which I was walking; I cannot vouch for Niort – the
countryside began shimmering under pale, tenacious

sunlight. A woman buzzed past on a moped; her small dog rode pillion in a basket behind. Horses grazed; two bays with white blazes jerked up their heads to watch me pass. Blue-black pansies grew in stone troughs bolted to walls of rusty brick. I walked alongside what looked almost like a toy farm, with motionless sheep and stationary tractor, a yellow yard of still hens and rooster, silent despite his splendid red cravat. Perhaps when I'd gone from view someone would come along and put them back in their box.

At lunchtime I stopped to buy food in a St Village, from a shop at the top of a hill. The front room was a bar; the shop part was at the back and had shelves stacked with jam-making equipment, fishing tackle, disposable nappies and suspenders, none of which seemed quite to address my dietary requirements, but I tracked down some bread and cheese and ate it there, at a mottled formica table, with lukewarm coffee in midget cup. I felt glum again, and lonely, imagining what I would be doing at home. Just talking to someone, in English so I wouldn't have to think hard before I spoke about gender and tenses. I started to think about the early morning conversations I had with Ron over the tea tray: the private, marital archive of jokes and references. But that wasn't going to do me any good at all, so I paid up and set off to count dead things on the road again.

*

I hate talking about this. It's the period of my life I'm really ashamed of, the one which I can't seem to make excuses for or joke about. I feel strange and embarrassed coming to it now but it is, I know, an important part of the story.

I'd been allowed to do Bristol solo, but Cambridge was another matter. We drove there on a November morning, Dad, Mum and me, a glum, tense undertone to our carefully bright conversation, like people waiting in hospital while a relative is undergoing exploratory surgery. We arrived at last in the city of Mum's dreams and pitched our tent right outside New Hall where posses of dead leaves chased along the pavement and Dad assessed the neighbourhood with a firm set to his jaw. Perhaps he was thinking of moving us all up to Cambridge once I got in.

New Hall was a modern building; its pale walls hadn't had time to be discoloured by exhaust fumes and rain. There were paved steps, corridors, big windows, something metallic and restrained in the statuary slot. And everywhere, so many girls, shiny girls, hair tumbling over their shoulders just so; tall, kempt and sparkling girls in their interview suits. One girl wore an orange two-piece; she was hoping for a place to study Mandarin. As tall, shiny girls have always done and will always do till I'm old and grey, they made me feel dwarfed, scruffy and tarnished.

I was interviewed by the Dean in her long, commodious study. I wanted to do Moral Sciences, which was Cambridge's way of saying Philosophy with a modicum of Psychology thrown in. On being called up for interview, candidates were given the names of three books which might prove helpful. Mum bought them for me; they're still in the family bookcase for all I know, in mint condition because I hardly looked at them. Consequently, the Dean and I didn't have much to discuss, despite my attempts to swing the talk round to existentialism.

'Don't you think you're a bit young?' said the Dean after a while (this is now known as counselling out. It is meant to be better if the applicant herself makes the decision to withdraw rather than be turned down). 'Wouldn't it be better if you applied next year?'

I never could take a hint. 'No. I want to come this year.' We ended up talking about the importance of going to the dentist regularly. When I returned to meet my parents, they asked how I had got on.

'I did my best.'

'Well,' said Dad heartily, 'that's all you can ever do, your best.' Phut. Phrrrrip. You could hear his dream balloon deflating. He knew, bless him.

So that was how I failed to get into Cambridge. Not because I couldn't get on with my mum, or because Dad was too wrapped up in his work to take enough notice of me, or because I was in the throes of star-crossed love or had been forced to dress for the occasion in a porridge-coloured suit which made me look like Don Estelle in *It Ain't Half Hot Mum*, but because out of conceit, laziness and a kind of stupidity, the most obvious symptom of which was deafness (had I really not heard what every teacher of mine had been saying from Year One?), I hadn't done the work. It seems absurdly simple now. 'Here's three books. Read them. Then let's talk about them.'

Took me thirty years to figure that one out.

Then Jug-Eared Richard gave me the elbow. Can't say I blamed him, a young man has his pride. Won't bore you with the details, but it all blew up at a party one night, at my place: Mum glimpsed us on the early Victorian love-seat. A muttered but furious row ensued between me and her in the reception hall which left me grimly glowering at my feet as she glided away (how much scorn and dignity mothers can invest into the simple sentence, 'And now I'm going upstairs to have a bath').

I returned from the fray to find Richard awaiting enlightenment by the Dansette.

I told him: 'Mummy doesn't like you because you live in a council house.'

Richard reeling. He had no idea I'd been seeing him in secret. I'd been living a double life on two counts, see. We'd been due to go to the cinema the next day, I believe, but when I phoned him about arrangements it was, as the clarineting major would have said, off at all meetings.

'It isn't me,' said Jug-Eared Richard, 'all this cloak and dagger stuff.'

I think he'd become a bit tired of me anyway by then; the Dearest had been lopped off his last two letters but, like I said, I never could take a hint. I replaced the receiver on the hook and staggered away to find Mum pretending to deadhead the floral display in the hall. 'Will you be going out tonight, dear?'

'No.' No cinema, no Cambridge, no Richard. My crown, my foolish crown, my paper crown.

Mum took me in her arms. 'What is it? I can't tell – are you laughing or crying?'

Suppose it was a bit of both, really. Crying, obvious. Laughing because I was being comforted by my persecutor.

'I know you're glad it's all over,' I said, 'but I can't help being upset.'

'Glad? Whatever kind of parents would we be to feel glad you're so upset?'

This is called ambiguity.

Richard's rejection hit me hard. We'd been together nearly a year. A long time when you're that age. Kept thinking of all the if-onlys and might-have-beens. Never cooked for him or tidied his room, never spent the night with him (God, it was innocent; I never even got to see *son sexe avec son fourrure . . .*). The first day after he'd gone, I couldn't eat a thing. Perked me up briefly, that did, a bit of wasting would have done me no harm, I could have experienced the novel joy of wearing size 10 flares without splitting the seams. But the day after that I was back to stuffing my face – I couldn't even die for love, for heaven's sake – and the day after that and every subsequent one for quite a while I just went haywire.

I was very angry. It was a horrible feeling so I turned it into self-pity in order to be able to attack from the moral high ground. No, I can't precisely follow the logic in that either, but we are in the steaming, hissing realm of Emotion where Reason is stranger. Curiously, I did not lose my sense of fun and adventure, but they were now in service to my Shadow Side.

I'm sorry about all these capital letters. That's autobiography for you: encourages megalomania.

Let me see now: back at school I took a screwdriver to the public phone box down by the golf club. Two like-minded girls at my shoulder, a cold March night, pinhead stars. I indulged in several other acts of petty vandalism around that time but this one I remember most clearly, as you always remember first times: the noisy shower of coins when I finally achieved access, the hailstorm of threepenny bits bouncing off my sensible school shoes, the divvying up of the spoils which none of us spent but kept in our top right-hand drawers like love letters and other objects of sentimental value. I bunked off lessons and helped myself from W.H. Smith's and Woolworths but my *coup de théâtre* was to organize a night on the town for myself and the two like-minded girls. The boys were friends of ours from the Christmas holidays.

Oh what a night. You've got to bear in mind that I was, for all my acts of hooliganism and truancy, a carefully brought-up girl, one who had no idea that if you invite three adolescent males to party with you in a seafront flophouse at midnight they will expect more return for their journey than shandy, potato crisps and light petting.

Might have made a difference if I'd fancied the blind date earmarked for me but he sparked nothing in my wounded breast but a mild feeling of déjà vu – he was a public school scholarship boy who lived in a council house. I made my excuses and left. One of the other girls lingered long enough to foster a dalliance but prudence got the better of her and she caught me up as I was climbing in through the dormitory window; she'd run all the way from the seafront at a five-minute-mile pace. Well, she was Vice-Captain of Games.

The other one, who had a *tendresse* for the boy involved, stayed to hand over her virginity but got back at ten minutes to six so she could change into her surplice; she was on the rota to be a server at Communion.

Lord knows how we thought we'd get away with it, our plan had been all round the school for days. At Sixth Form assembly just before Sunday lunch, Jonah hurtled from common room door to centre stage and uttered the terrible words:

'Three girls were seen out last night. Would they please stand up.'

Gasps, murmurs, scraping of chairs.

'Thought you'd have something to do with it, Welch.'

She marched the three of us off to the library block where she grilled us in the entrance hall while I stared at the floor. Red tiles and a large cardboard box printed with the exhortation SELL YOUR EGGS IN ROTATION. The shadow side of March outside: yellow-grey sky, wind rattling the panes. Long-sighted eyes enlarged formidably by her spectacle lenses, Jonah quickly extracted our sorry tale, pausing only when it came to the identity of our swains.

'Is he', Jonah asked me of mine, 'the one who lives in a council house?'

'No,' I said. But couldn't help adding, 'Though oddly enough this one lives in a council house too.' Perhaps I thought she'd exclaim at the coincidence.

'You'll all be expelled, of course.'

Our parents were summoned. I was, I remember, halfway through a tennis coaching session when an Upper Fifth rushed up to tell me they were there, trembling with self-importance at the task allotted to her. I aimed one last ball at Mr Cooper's hat, missed, and ascended to Jonah's study, still clad in my Fred Perry whites.

It was awful. Dad mopping his eyes, Mum a wounded icicle in yellow Jean Patou. She and I fell to immediate contumely. 'If you'd let me go on seeing Richard—'

'Ho! If I hadn't been so free with you—'

'Shush!' bellowed Jonah. We both shut up. Sat there with our mouths hanging open like unruly children; even Dad, in fact, gave an impression of bated breath at Jonah's intervention in our dysfunctional family. And I do suspect that all along that's what Mum and I had been waiting for Dad to do; tell us to put a sock in it, enlighten me on exactly what was and wasn't allowed, then take Mum away somewhere and make her happy. And then I wouldn't have had to try and take over his job, and then I could have treated her like my mother again and she could have treated me like her daughter.

But that's all by the by.

In the end, Jonah didn't expel us; we were three of her best A Level candidates and even though it was well before the days of league tables, she had to have something to flaunt on the school prospectus. And looking back, it seems pretty tame stuff really. No drugs, not even strong drink taken, just a bit of pinging of suspender belts and heavy breathing. I mean, hardly Trainspotting.

I was put in solitary confinement, in a room with just a bed, desk and wardrobe. But it wasn't so bad: conveniently situated above the shrubbery so I could hang out of the windows at midnight, smoking Gitanes and throwing the butts into the disguising rhododendrons. No one wanted to talk to me, of course, but I suppose that was good training for my life ahead with Ronan Goldblatt. I didn't go to school meals, mainly dining off Birds Eye custard which I made in the boarding house kitchen. I found its golden colour cheering, though I still felt the same. Anger, anger in my heart.

One of the worst things was that Mum and Dad had recently struck up a warm friendship with the parents of one of the girls I'd led into perdition, the five-minute seafront miler. The bridge evenings, the visits to the West End theatre, all had been balm to my mother's social insecurities, and now I'd gone and smashed all that to pieces for her. The Communion server and the five-minute miler both apologized to Jonah in due course, and I wouldn't, not even when Mum begged me. I couldn't see the point. I wasn't sorry. It was all I had to hang on to. I might have been a thief, a liar, a bad influence and a monster of teenage depravity but I wasn't going to be a hypocrite as well.

Life went on. 'Hear you've been in a spot of trouble,' said the Major, knocking his clarinet on the floor to divest the mouthpiece of accumulated spittle.

'Yes. But I'm NOT GOING TO APOLOGIZE.'

The Major nodded and adjusted our music on the stand. 'Want a tip?' he said.

I'd thought he was going to utter a few wise words

about the necessity for humility in these troubled times but he said, 'Sandown, 3.30 Friday. Joe Mercer on Nil Illegitimum.'

'As in Carborandum?'

'The very same. Now where were we? Ah yes, Jesu Joy Of Man's Desiring. One – two—'

He was all right, the Major.

OUR SON IN WHOM WE ARE WELL PLEASED

Runner's World Training Log.
Day: Monday. **Distance:** 11 m. **Weather:** Thumbs down. **Course/notes:** St Ciers à Gironde to Mirambeau. Narrow road with 200 yards of chained dogs either side; an avenue of slobbering maws. Coming into St Ciers, a giant zit in a field: a swimming pool just like the one at Lesparre, except white. Looked to see if a German and his woman were in there, but it was closed. Thought I heard the sound of metronomic splashing, though.

On the far side of St Ciers the road ran between a wood yard and a cemetery. A funeral was about to take place; either that or the French put on sober suits in order to buy kindling. Don't know who they were seeing off, but his friends had paid particular attention to their shaves that morning and were standing close to each other, patting backs, pumping hands. I loved getting little glimpses of other people's lives, and deaths. Once in Brittany we were enjoying an open air drink when the auberge doors opened and out danced a bride and her six young bridesmaids to the wheezing music of the best man's concertina. They had frocks of inky blue and primped hair and looked very happy. They linked arms, polkaed round and between the tables and danced back in again. The doors closed behind them, the music faded to nothing.

They'd been dancing to the sort of tune that's called 'Traditional Air'. Makes your heart sink when you see it on a school concert programme, but it was lovely. A beautiful, quick minute that you wanted to go on for ever.

From St Ciers to Mirambeau I walked through a horror movie, on a two-foot-wide verge (grass a stranger to the mower) between the devil (a road which the vineyard lorries had appropriated as a racetrack) and the deep blue sea, or, more accurately, the deep stagnant dyke. From the direction of this dyke every so often would come a *Ploop!* which is what a plunging rat sounds like.

Still, who can blame the rats of the Gironde for enjoying a bath while they can? Eat, drink and pass on the plague, for tomorrow we die. All over the verges and the tarmac were victims of the vinicultural Damon Hills, once living, breathing kings of the vermin world, now strewn around the D255's murine scrapyard in a collage of exploded guts like burst balloons, coiled thick black tails, whitened skeletons, bloodied bristles, curled paws, squashed snouts. I had a lot of tiptoeing to do, but the alternative was worse. Any foolhardy attempt to walk on the road and I would have been charcuterie myself. It would not, I felt, be a dignified end.

Then the rain started tipping down again, six miles short of Mirambeau. It was here that I also picked up an alsatian, a vivacious one who gambolled around me in and out of two villages; I ignored it, I threw stones, it wouldn't go. I remembered shuffling along Lower Thames Street, drained and hurting in the last few miles of the London Marathon; that was where the kid had jumped out of the crowd and started to run alongside me. He'd had a big grin on his face, he was joining in, he was happy, and I wanted to wipe him out. I wanted that dog to be toast, too, and anyone else who looked as if they were having too good a time. I realized that somewhere in the rubbish dump of my unconscious was a load of vicious, deadly, jealous rage which under normal circumstances I never had to own up to but which in extremes of tiredness, abandonment and deprivation began to smell and smoulder. I feared it, I was ashamed when I expressed it, but in some grim way I was proud of it; it was what had made me a survivor where other, nicer people had fallen.

So I did what I did in the London Marathon, which was to stop, drink a lot of water and eat something sweet. I didn't know precisely how or why water or sugar worked on my neurological processes, but presently the ancient, primitive part of my brain retired, muttering, and I was able to think straight. It was an OK dog. I wasn't going to take it home with me but at least its teeth weren't in my carotid artery. I walked along with it to the junction where I threw it a Power Bar so it would have something to remember me by and hopped aboard a bus. I didn't know it then, but I'd just about reached the end of the road.

*

I saw him last September for the first time in ages and I didn't even recognize him. Said to Dilys with whom I was conversing, 'Who is that thin guy who's rather good-looking?' and Dilys rolled her eyes. 'You used to be married to him.'

I don't usually go to these university reunions. Time's depredations are so lowering. The beauty of our year, an olive-skinned girl of Italian extraction, was one of the first in the temporal firing line, hardly having collected her Upper Second in Art History before the rot set in. Shook the hand of the Chancellor and her hair had turned white before her family had stopped clapping.

Only joking. Considering it's only another fifteen years odd before we get the bus passes we've none of us, the class of '69, worn too badly. The boys have done their best in the face of male pattern baldness and the girls are swilling with HRT. A few teeth gone by the board, a divorce or two, a couple of eighties bankruptcies. One suicide, poor little lad. The life and soul of every party, he'd been. Always is.

There was the girl who'd been a dead ringer for Goldie Hawn. She'd filled out a bit after marrying well but it suited her; she'd been born to look rich and well-dressed and acquire the services of a good colorist. She'd had the flat above mine. 'I shan't forget,' she said, 'your mother arriving for graduation day after you'd done a bunk. I had to take her upstairs and give her tea.'

I'd forgotten about that.

'We all admired you so,' she claimed. 'You were so eccentric.'

'I was a basket case.'

The reason I went to the reunion was because Fred wanted me to. His dad was going to be there and I think he warmed to the idea of having both his parents gazing on him at once. A double share of doting.

When he was a baby we called him Freddy but somewhere around his teens he threw out one D and the Y. Didn't relish a lifetime of entering stage left through the French windows and asking, 'Anyone for tennis?', I assume. He wasn't consciously named after Grandpa Fred and he isn't like that old devil at all. He doesn't ride a unicycle and has never invented a hand grenade though when in his wild teens he briefly sported a highly coloured coat-dress of unisex nature, according to the then fashions of his teenage sect. What he does now is whatever it is a solicitor does – solicits? A tall, curly-haired guy with a big laugh, ferocious frown and pinstriped suit. A sub-three-marathon man to boot.

Well, best begin at the beginning, three years almost to the day before he was born.

*

Fade up soundtrack: 'Good Vibrations' (The Beach Boys)

> Dear Miss Jones, (you had to write to her after you'd left)
>   I have just completed my first week here and am starting to get to know the ropes. I have lost my virginity to a vicar's son (from Cambridge, incidentally!) and have quickly found out which pubs you can buy dope in. This morning Professor Korner gave us a most fascinating lecture on syllogisms.

Some of the above is not verbatim.

> Dear Julia,
>   Thank you for your letter. I am glad to hear you have settled down at Bristol and if only you could get a First, I feel your parents would be very much happier.

A First! What insane optimism was contained in that one sentence. I was one of those people targeted in the newspaper advertisements of the day which appeared downpage in a 6 x 3 box:

> **TAKE UP PELMANISM**
> for Courage and Clear-Thinking
> You know the people with 'Grasshopper Minds'
> as well as you know yourself. These minds nibble
> at everything and master nothing.

I and my grasshopper mind nibbled at three lectures in Term One and after that none, scraping into second year thanks to the kind heart of a dowdy girl whose notes I copied on examination eve. Only had to retake Philosophical Logic. I can remember her large, life-saving handwriting to this day. Went into the civil service. I wish her well, and a sumptuous pension.

University life. The heartbreaks, the hangovers. The usual things happened to us: keeping ourselves awake all night on bennies to revise, going to parties in flats which had fungus growing on the carpets, taking acid with the third-year architects. What a seat of learning Bristol was in the late sixties: two drama schools (the Young Vic and The Other One), an art school, a polytechnic and a theological college down in Fishponds though we never swam in their aquarium. One of the drama school girls – she had legs like pipe cleaners – got a summer vac job in an uptown boutique and that was the last we saw of her; she was whisked away to London by a smooth Mancunian in jeans who'd spotted her among the thigh-length boots and Foale and Tuffins; she got her name in one of the national papers, next to the knitwear advert.

At the end of the first year we all moved into flats in a shabby Georgian area of Bristol called Clifton, where we could wave at each other from our rusting balconies like babies in adjacent cots; university life has its harshnesses and griefs and it was very comforting. We occupied three sides of a terraced square: The Mall, West Mall and Caledonia Place. I don't remember what the fourth side was called but nobody lived there anyway. One boy was killed riding his motorbike back to base late at night, dramatically throwing a pall over June 1967. His girlfriend spent three weeks languishing on the forerunner of a bean bag in her West Mall living room, wearing nothing but a shortie nightdress and repeatedly playing one track from the same LP, of which I remember only the gruffly lilting refrain:

In the night time,
In the night time.

We grouped in the sitting room of someone's flat, among the stinking sofas and mould-decked coffee mugs, to watch the Beatles play on the roof of Aeolian House. What was it called? The Summer of Love, that's it. We girls wore sunglasses with yellow plastic rims and feather boas from Biba, and carried bright green handbags. Things had gone pear-shaped with the vicar's son and I spent the summer feeling a bit on the low side, not that that was anything new. Listened to a lot of Bob Dylan ('Sad-Eyed Lady of the Lowlands' still gets me right here) and got rid of a lot of money at Bus Stop in Kensington Church Street (bright pink bomber jacket and matching culottes; you had to be there).

In the autumn I took a room in The Mall above an antique shop. Our place had been converted out of a vast and elegant drawing room into four hen hutches with walls as thin as pamphlets; you could hear everything that everyone was doing to everyone else but when you're that age you don't turn a hair. 'Den of vice!' exclaimed Mum on visiting it, though had she but known it my life was one of quite depressing virtue. That winter of '67 was the coldest I'd ever known. Look out of those big windows and all you'd see was snow on car roofs. Everyone seemed to get sad around that time, first-year relationships breaking up all around us, one of my flatmates bursting into tears at the sight of a Pyrex dish because it reminded her of her mother. 'It all seemed so simple then.'

I wrote a lot of embarrassing poetry and set it to music,

sang in the university revue and got hauled up before one of the men with beards because I hadn't been attending any lectures.

'We have to ask,' he said, 'if your place wouldn't be better going to someone else.'

'Don't throw me out,' I said. 'My parents will kill me.'

I made a reasonable fist of lectures for a while but found them no less dull, and in March 1968 I met my first husband.

He's not someone I talk about often because Ron doesn't like me to, but I remember the first sighting of him to this day; on a black leatherette banquette in the Students Union Long Bar, later rechristened the Nelson Mandela after the trend of the time. My first husband in a giant overcoat and a Russian hat. A sweet, gawky young thing of great height and skinniness with a buck-toothed smile and soft, brown hair. He was a second-year architect. He was a legend.

He was a legend because of his ceiling. On rolls of white lining paper he had painted the heads of the four Beatles in black, blue and red and sellotaped them into an 18 x 12 rectangle which he then tacked to his West Mall cornices so that girls to whom he was making love in the missionary position would open their eyes and find a crudely executed Paul McCartney looking down on them sideways. One of the cornices suffered damp, resulting in Ringo Starr peeling off at the waist.

His name was Jack. Did I tell you that?

I was wearing a smocked mini frock when I met him, ashy-blue background with pink and brown flowers. I'd run it up on my machine out of some flannelette I'd found reduced in price at John Lewis, its primary purpose I'd imagine being for pyjamas. We went to bed and stayed there. I didn't know very much about sex; the vicar's son hadn't been very adept in that department, though he had lovely dress sense. But I always was a quick learner and after a week Dilys brought round my effects from The Mall and instructed me on how to get the Pill. A good Catholic girl, always ready to help others.

'There's a lady doctor opposite the Students Union who'll give it to you if you say you're engaged.'

She had a ring at the ready, it had served her and several others in good stead, though lately the lady doctor had started to question her more minutely about wedding plans after she'd reported in with a case of crabs.

Went on the pill, put on a lot of weight, somehow got through my second-year exams. Jack and I bought a blind white rabbit whom we called Grapefruit and regarded in the light of a first child, unsuccessfully trying to housetrain him; he dispensed rabbit pellets all over the floor and bed with the efficiency of a blunderbuss.

Had an argument on West Mall's cracked pavement, having snogged beside the Georgian iron railings and come up for air. September '68, a chilly night. 'I love you,' he said, 'and I'm going to love you for a very long time.'

What on earth did *that* mean?

'Just what I said.'

'But I want you to love me for ever and ever,' I wailed.

'For ever and ever is a very long time,' he said. Comforting in his funny old overcoat.

Funny how in times of high emotion you lose your composure, your temper, your underwear, but never your pedantry. I said, 'In the sense you meant it, *a very long time* is finite.' I added that we might as well pack up that minute if he was not going to love me for ever and ever.

'There, there,' he said. 'I'll love you for ever and ever if that makes you feel better.'

He was just wiser than me, I guess.

That month we heard of a flat going over the road in Caledonia Place. The rent was a bit steep at 3 guineas a week but it was on the ground floor and fetched onto a walled garden, where we installed Grapefruit and bought a buddy to share his hutch, a black rabbit at whom Grapefruit took one look and leapt on in an ecstasy of homosexual fervour; you couldn't have prised them apart with a crowbar, we had to wait till he fell back exhausted. Then we rescued the black rabbit and set him down in the garden. He shook himself and bolted through a hole in the wall, never to be seen again. Grapefruit passed away shortly after, but at least he'd had a bite of the apple.

There were giant windows in the front of the flat and French doors at the back. It could be divided into two rooms by the original folding partition through which Jack once, in the only fit of temper I ever saw him throw (he was the gentlest man I ever knew), kicked a hole.

My first married home, it would eventually turn out to be.

He was a Taurus, like my dad who was also kind, and sweet, and stubborn. Jug-Eared Richard was a Scorpio. Ron too. Brown bullets for eyes, the pair of them. There's a lesson in that somewhere, if only I could work out what it is.

Every wall in the front half of our flat was coral pink and every wall in the back was stained white. It was like finding yourself in a set of dentures. Beyond was a kitchen big enough to dine in, and a bathroom of rare squalor. We moved in and set to work.

Everything I know about design, colour and furniture is due to my first husband, who repainted three of the front walls cream and the other one bicycle-saddle brown, built a platform on which he mounted his desk and sewing machine and carpeted the floor in coir matting, which sandpapered the soles of my early morning feet and was soon stained with spilt tea. I've never thought there was anything wrong with shag pile, myself. At first we slept on a mattress underneath the giant front windows; the back room was filled with timber out of which Jack gradually fashioned a mezzanine floor reached by a spiral staircase. We tugged the mattress up there and used the space below to hang our clothes which swung emptily in the copious draughts that whistled from front to back and from the street gave the impression of a party constantly attended by anorexic guests.

The front room became our living area, for which he made a sofa bed with £50 given me by my parents to purchase same. They'd visited me for the weekend and we'd had to pretend Dilys was my flatmate. We set her up in state on the mezzanine, coached her in where the conveniences lay, and adorned the front room with a makeshift bed of borrowed mattresses for me.

It went OK till Mum asked Dilys to show her the bathroom. 'It's a bit dark in here,' said Mum. 'Where are the lights? Dilys, dear? Lights?' Onward Dilys blundered, we hadn't thought to tell her where the lights were, she thought all was lost. I reached the bathroom just in time. 'It's because she's got her back to you,' I said in a whisper. 'She's actually quite deaf and has to get by on lip reading.'

'You don't have to whisper, then,' giggled Mum. But later, as we made our farewells: 'Your flatmate is a very nice little girl. How wonderful that she's done so well despite her deafness. Now, you can't sleep on a mattress on the floor.' She then wrote out a cheque for £50.

I still blush.

On his sewing machine Jack made the curtains, as well

as trousers for himself and friends, and on the old tomato-splattered cooker in the kitchen he fashioned adventurous meals such as *boeuf à l'orange*. (Not a triumph.) But therein, I think, lay a central problem in our relationship: this wonderful man was domestically hermaphroditic. Not only did he perform the man's duties, the decorating and the carpentry, but he did the woman things too: he chose the colour schemes and the furnishings, he sewed, he cooked. There was nothing left for me to do.

Went to no lectures, got terribly depressed and even more fat, stopped taking the Pill because I was going home for Christmas. God, what a sadster I was. However, going off the Pill both cheered and deflated me. On the eve of returning to Bristol for the Lent term I spotted an item in a back number of Mum and Dad's *Daily Telegraph Magazine*; it announced a competition, The Young Writer of the Year Award. You had to write an essay on Britain Today. I cut the item out and packed it with my books and clothes. This was something I could do.

I composed my entry in the university library. Foreign territory always did inspire me. I wrote about us, all the boys and the girls, our summer of love, the autumn and winter too. Posted it off to the *Daily Telegraph* twenty-four hours before the closing date and I won't say I forgot about it exactly, but there were other things on my mind. Won't go into that yet. Instead I'll fast forward to spring and the telephone call, The Telephone Call Of All Telephone Calls, the one you get maybe once or twice in your life. Or every time there's an England international pending, I suppose, if you're useful at football.

To say you've won, or you've got the job, or you're required to spearhead the attack, or whatever.

I'd won £200, a portable typewriter, a piece of sculpture by Eduardo Paolozzi (sold later at Sotheby's to pay the deposit on my first house: cheers, Eduardo), a trip to Canada and one or two other baubles the nature of which now escapes me. I was interviewed by Sir Kingsley Amis (I am aware that this was long before he received his K but even in those days he was terrifyingly Sir-ish). A photographer accompanied us to lunch at the French Horn, Sonning, where while we addressed our steaks Sir Kingsley winced at my eating habits. 'One does not eat the side salad, of course,' he chuckled in an aside to the photographer as I nosebagged the iceberg and tomatoes. Sir Kingsley's interview was duly published in the *Daily Telegraph Magazine*. He described me as bantamweight and my winning article as unoriginal.

Mum and Dad over the moon. Always knew I could do it, etc. Numero uno, the golden girl. I went to the Ascot races with them and Jane, in a loose Ossie Clark dress and a roll-on out of which my waist kept bursting. Sat next to Jane at lunch. We discussed my winning entry, which with its focus on shagging, drinking and drug-taking had caused some raised eyebrows in local Tory circles. One of the characters in the article had had an abortion.

'I think everyone thought you'd been harry preggers,' said Jane.

'Well, I wasn't,' I said. Me being pedantic again. I hadn't *been* pregnant, past tense, done away with. I *was* pregnant.

Didn't tell her that, of course. Didn't tell anyone till the time limit for abortions was safely past, then I told Jack, who wasn't at all surprised. Went to the Student Health Practice, saw a very kind doctor with ginger hair, freckles and a rugby-player's torso who reassured me that wearing a roll-on wouldn't have harmed the baby and started campaigning for Jack and me to get married. Had five kids of his own, kept giving us good cast-offs. 'Any news about the jolly old wedding yet?' he'd say, handing over another boiled-clean, neatly ironed bagful.

The kindness of near-strangers. Professor Korner, whose lectures on Kant I had been giving a miss since Year One, wrote the warmest of letters. I have heard of your trouble, please let us know what we can do to help.

I completely messed up my Finals, of course, but they gave me a degree anyway.

I hadn't communicated with Mum and Dad since the day at Ascot. Mum rang up the university to find out if I'd passed. She sent a telegram: CONGRATULATIONS ON YOUR DEGREE. COMING TO TAKE YOU TO LUNCH ON GRADUATION DAY. The telegram arrived twenty-four hours before the ceremony. 'I haven't received it,' I said to the Goldie Hawn lookalike in the flat upstairs. 'I have gone away for the week, to stay with friends in Wales.'

They arrived, they had tea with Goldie Hawn, they left.

It was as bad as that.

Jack wrote to them in the end to break the news. Mum wrote, asking me to come home, but I wouldn't. I went to ground completely. In the end, Dad rang up the local police. A WPC drew up outside the flat in a panda car. I watched her from the window, a casserole dish in my hand. (Odd, the detail you remember at times like these.) I ducked behind the sofa but she banged on our front door. 'Come on out, I know you're in there.'

It was her duty to check that I was alive. My father had requested this, in case my alleged absence was down to Jack having murdered me. I've wondered since if this was what my father, subconsciously, fantasized had happened. I confirmed that I was indeed alive and saw her out of the flat. The casserole dish was still in my hand. Mind you, I suppose she saw that kind of thing every day.

And that was about it, really. The summer wore on. Man walked on the moon. I grew vast, ate peculiar meals at odd times, wrote nothing, renounced the world. In the early hours of the first of October I went into labour, squeezing down the spiral staircase from the mezzanine floor to be driven to the Bristol Maternity Hospital where a day and a half later our son was born. He was handsome and creamy-skinned. I stood by a window with him in my arms, looking out over the hospital grounds. Beautiful October sunlight. I was so happy to have him. I always have been, ever since.

*

It was pretty awful, though. Electricity cut off because we hadn't any money, infant wailing non-stop, me with no idea how to look after him, and oh my, the squalor. In November we set about the jolly old wedding. It was at a Registry Office in the city centre. We had three guests, one of them our baby. Most of the boys and girls had left Bristol by then; they'd gone down to London to rent West End flats, pair off in different permutations and look for exciting jobs.

My wedding clothes:
  Last year's pale green crêpe skirt and blouse (Ossie
    Clark)
  Fair Isle sleeveless jersey (jumble sale)
  The last of my supplies of Coty's Emeraude
  Can't remember my shoes but then again my feet
    hadn't been on the ground for a long time

Mum turned up at our flat one afternoon, out of the blue, getting out of a taxi in her best hat and insisting upon entry. I told you she was a brave old bird. Took one look at the baby and gathered him into her arms. 'Poor little mite.'

'He's *not* a poor little mite.'

'No, darling, I suppose he isn't.'

Jack took the baby up to his mum's for Christmas and I went home. A strange old time. They hadn't told anybody about my baby, not even Jane. The poor dear things, trying to do their best in the worst possible situation they could imagine. They'd explained my absence by saying I'd gone to Canada as part of my prize for winning the writing award. Mum had obtained a pile of brochures from the Canadian Government Tourist Office in order that I could answer confidently if anyone asked about my trip. So for a week I answered enquiries from local Tory dignitaries about Canada and acknowledged congratulations upon my award while, invisibly, my young husband and infant son hung about like ghosts at the feast. As I left to return to Bristol, Dad hugged me. 'You and the baby are always welcome here, any time. You know that.' The inference was that his new son-in-law wasn't, that by doing the unspeakable to his daughter Jack would never be allowed across the family threshold. I might have argued the point but I just didn't have the spirit.

Maybe it's wishful thinking, but I can't help feeling my shame-making plight brought them close. Dad had wanted to tell Jane but Mum wouldn't let him. So if I'd done nothing else, I'd given her a place where she could be alone with Dad at last.

*

We stayed in Bristol another year or so. I didn't get out much at first. I had post-natal depression, not that anyone diagnosed it as such; nobody warned young mothers about that kind of thing then. I spent most days in a formula-encrusted dressing gown, cackhandedly boiling bottles. Our baby stopped wailing when he discovered communication, babbling jovially and conducting an unseen orchestra, despite the fact that he hardly ever wore clean clothes, was a martyr to nappy rash and slept in a crib colonized by cats.

Jack bought a pram in a junk shop. A vestige of grandeur still clung to it: it had springs, a careful line of gold leaf around the chipped navy paintwork, chrome mudguards. Terrible roadholding, of course; take a bend too sharply and it would flop over at right angles, tipping my infant solicitor onto the pavement. I was out with the pram one summer day, negotiating it over the lights at the top of Park Street, when two young women stopped and said, 'Excuse me, aren't you Julie Welch?'

I had forgotten the existence of the Murgatroyd twins. Now they stood before me with shiny, neat hairdos and smart suits, boggling into the pram while I boggled at them. *The Murgatroyd twins. At my university.*

They were in their final year. I suppose if I'd gone to the library rather more often I might have bumped into them.

Their eyes were like RAF roundels, but I couldn't blame them. I would have been thrilled if I'd been them. 'We had no idea you were married,' one said, while the other visually frisked my third finger left hand. 'It isn't widely known,' I said, and wheeled the pram away. It seemed a bit late in the day to confront them about their calumnious behaviour regarding my mental arithmetic test and, anyway, they'd be wanting to get on the phone home as soon as possible.

*

We moved to London. Mum paid for me to take a secretarial course. I got a job on the sports desk of the *Observer* and in time became Fleet Street's first female football reporter. Heady days. The marriage would have ended anyway, we were just too young. The next time around we made adult choices. He's got two more kids and so have I. But only Fred is ours, ours alone.

When Fred was still very young Big Sis came back from Australia and tried to put together the shattered pieces as best she could. When she moved to Scotland, she would invite Fred up there with Mum and Dad for Christmas and New Year. She had two boys of her own, one either side of him in age. They were blond and tall like him, they could have been brothers. She said: If you want me to look after him for a while, I will, or for ever if that's what you like.

I'd never really been regarded as married, so I couldn't really think of myself as being divorced either; I was a sort of half mother (my son's existence was still not alluded to in the company my mum and dad kept); I didn't know what I was, actually. I envied Big Sis, imagining her staggering to the dinner table in Scotland with the oven mitts clamped round the trencher of turkey, slurping champagne, slipping on dropped Brussels sprouts, ear-rings dangling, fringe askew, kids fighting, parents agreeing to differ, husband snoring on the sofa, while back in London I'd go to whichever married friends would have me. I'd arrive armed with much-too-expensive presents for them and their children (I was rich, I was successful), fend off the husband (I was thin, I was glamorous) and go home to wait for the Married Man's phone call; the new jogging craze was quite a boon, he took it up so he could get out of the house and to the phone box. Pip-pip-pip and then plop-plop-plop, the sweat dripping onto the receiver.

Big Sis was always inviting me up there for Christmas but I wouldn't go. I would have felt like Girlie.

I'm talking about my childhood again. After we moved to our new big house and Mum cast the embarrassing rellies out of her temple (we'd still see them, but it was by fixed appointment and there was to be *no milling around*) Girlie suddenly seemed to be a bit of a nuisance. She'd phone up on Sunday afternoons; Mum would make Dad answer the phone: 'If it's Girlie, tell her we're on our way out.' I found her wretched and insipid, a silly creature, jerky of movement and trivial of discourse and, oh, that excruciating miasma of inner turmoil. If she came to stay I'd barely speak to her, though she always made an effort to communicate.

She went to live in Devon where she joined the medical constituency of the unwanted, having a nervous break-down and being hospitalized for some months; when she started coming round she wrote to tell us she'd seen the Pearly Gates. Throughout all the years left to her, how-ever, she thought of me every September and December, giving me birthday and Christmas presents to her dying day. Her last gift was a glass ornament, a somewhat shapeless cat with innards of red and green.

Her dying day? In the summer of 1981 Mum and Dad were summoned to the general hospital in Exeter where she had been taken following a stroke. I drove there independently; I just wanted to see her. She was on an intensive care bed, strangely in the middle of the room. All Mum's brothers and sisters turned up; what a crowd they formed; even the dead ones seemed to be there, milling around. I'm like my dad, a bull in the china shop of grief; I burst into tears on seeing Girlie laid out on that island of a bed, hair as ever in its neat blonde French pleat. 'She's had such a horrible life. Everyone was horrible to her.'

One of my aunties, clearly regarding this as some sort of rebuke, assured me that her husband, Girlie's oldest surviving brother, had rivalled my transports, but invisibly: 'He's always controlled his feelings.' Mum was rather embarrassed by my jeremiad and when it was time to leave insisted on giving all her siblings a guided tour of my new Renault 18, resplendent in the hospital car park: 'She paid for it all herself.'

A few days after I drove myself home, I rang the Samaritans. I know I've said before that the last shove in the shoulders towards the psychiatrist's chair was delivered by Ronan Goldblatt; that was certainly part of it, but the person who really sent me there was Girlie, the embarrassing relly, the gawky unmarried daughter, hovering around the edge of the family for scraps, the omega animal, the lowest member of the pack.

Big Sis and I were talking about her only the other day. 'Did you know she drove ambulances in the war?' she said.

That I wasn't aware of.

'In Paris. She always used to bring me perfume.'

A life not so relentlessly horrible, then. Not without excitement or perfume or travel.

Adrienne. That was her name. Not Girlie, or Marianne or Lucille. Adrienne – I thought that was beautiful.

I still have the glass cat.

SOUP WITH PEGGY

Runner's World Training Log.
Day: Monday. **Distance:** 2 m. **Weather:** Rain.
Course/notes: Beyond Mirambeau and back. Mistake.
Life quality: Shit. Want to wear my Monsoon fur coat again, want to smell nice, want to throw away my running shoes, want someone to talk to, want it to be summer: riding my bike across the heath early in the morning to fetch bread, sunlight bouncing off the front mudguard.

During my years in Fleet Street, in a career which brought me into contact with some of the most dedicated drunks the world has ever known, men and women (but largely men) who fell into ditches, wrecked fashionable eateries, threw up in ice buckets and brought home ladies of the night to meet the wife then coolly strolled into Wembley to ad lib a thousand award-winning words on the Cup Final, the drunkest of them all, King Sot of Sotsville, was my friend Edinburgh Al.

Edinburgh Al worked for the Press Association but had a sideline in antiques. In an early attempt at niche marketing, he spent his entire savings trying to corner the market in lap desks. (Since you ask, a helpful item of furniture for ladies too idle to get up out of their chaise longues and hike to the writing room to pen filthy letters to their lovers. They were, well, miniature desks. Without legs. You placed them on your lap. Or, if you were tired, I expect the butler did it for you.) At first Al stored the lap desks in his Putney flat but after his girlfriend became a bit shirty about disappearing under a mahogany and walnut avalanche every time she wanted to get a frock out of the wardrobe he took out a lease on a Tooting warehouse. It burnt to the ground, the lap desks cremated along with it.

Since Al was permanently down to his last bean and his cheques bounced more than a Barnes Wallis bomb, it was widely assumed that his was the match that had lit the petrol, but the sad fact was that he'd been too broke to stump up the premium for the insurance which would have been his to claim, and with every antiques dealer in the British Isles after him (those ricocheting cheques) he decided to relocate to Argentina.

Al found himself a flat in Hurlingham, not the posh-part-of-Fulham Hurlingham but a suburb of Buenos Aires. Well, you know how it happens. You've been in the bar all night, making lively conversation, getting through the entire session still able to pronounce anomaly and Chislehurst without fucking up. Come closing time, you walk outside with the intention of returning to the bosom of your family and realize that, unknown to you, someone has given you a lobotomy. Some time later you wake up on a stationary train. You are in a siding in Eastbourne.

One night in Buenos Aires Al, though even more comprehensively rat-arsed than usual, managed to get himself to the station. On asking, in Spanish, 'Does this train stop at Hurlingham?' – no easy linguistic/elocutionary test in the circumstances – and on receiving the assurance that yes, indeed, this train stopped at Hurlingham, Al lurched aboard.

He woke up in Chile. It was the Trans-Continental

Express. Made one stop, in Hurlingham, then rumbled on through night and day. Still, he'd always wanted to see Santiago.

I've mentioned Edinburgh Al because when I settled down on that bus I spread my legs out and leant my cheek against the glass. Oh, the joy of being out of the rain, away from that bloody dog. I drifted off, probably not for very long, but when the bus came to a jumpy halt and I woke up I had no idea where I was, or, more importantly, where I would end up. Marseilles? Austria? I reached the driver just before he pulled away from a tin-roofed shelter by a line of trees which might have been anywhere. 'Mirambeau. *Où est?*'

With a jerk of his head, he gave me to understand that Mirambeau was a thing past.

I got off. I could vaguely make out a distant huddle of roofs and spires on the horizon. By keeping my eyes firmly fixed on them (when I looked at trees they started to move) I found my way back to Mirambeau.

Incidentally, if you've been wondering why it is you can't get a lap desk for love or money these days, now you know.

*

Mirambeau looked big enough to qualify as a town. It featured a pleasant square which had been paved in large, pastel-coloured flagstones then pied with oil from all the cars which people parked over them. I ducked inside the first doorway I could see which bore a sign saying BAR. My teeth were chattering like an old Telex machine. I stood in the doorway for ages; I didn't seem to have the will left to walk further in. The floor was bare and brown. Facing the street was a big picture of John Wayne. Above it was a high shelf on which stood a line of toy horses.

Beyond the bar was another room with a pool table, and behind that a cavernous diner with a glassed roof and deeply ineffectual stove. The diner featured cactus plants, check tablecloths and a sign above the door: Peggy's Grill. Behind the bar stood a Frenchman in chaps, ten gallon hat, check shirt and holster. He watched my shivering inspection of the diner then smiled pleasantly. 'It must be very cold in there.'

'It isn't cold in there, in fact it's humid,' snapped the cowgirl squeezing between the pool table and bar stools. Clearly the stove was a source of contention between them. She had a blonde ponytail, striped T-shirt and specs and was, at a guess, in her early 50s. She spoke French in a strong deep voice and an accent that I struggled to place before realizing that Peggy was as Gallic as me, in fact somewhat less by a few thousand miles, being a native New Yorker. I suppose what had happened was that one day the French barman in chaps had walked into Peggy's Bronx grill, realized that here was not just the woman but the diner of his dreams, thrown them both over his saddle and galloped back with them to Mirambeau. Here they lived happily ever after, apart from occasional wrangles about the stove.

The cowgirl turned to welcome me. 'I'm terribly sorry,' I said in English, 'but I think I've got hypothermia.'

'I think this calls for chicken noodle soup,' she rasped. 'In New York we call it medicine.'

In the diner I ate chicken noodle soup, crudités and three slices of pork, each with a tiara of crackling, while trying to pour water into my glass with the cap on to the sound of Frank Sinatra. After that I went out to the pay phone by the square to call Ron. I asked him to come and fetch me.

I didn't feel angry with myself for jacking it in; I'd

spent the last seven days proving I was hardy, fit and capable of finding my way. Thirty-eight years back I'd had to spend three miserable weeks in Cap Ferret because I was powerless to do anything else. Now it was different. I had gone back to Cap Ferret and re-edited the script. Not only could I cope alone, but I didn't have to. I felt gifted, loved, worthy. I had someone who would come and get me. I *had* someone. I kept turning it over and over in my mind, like a beautiful jewel.

All the time I was walking and getting wet and moaning about my feet, something was going on inside my head. I was making new decisions about myself. Maybe I wasn't crazy or flawed or warped or a failure. Maybe I wasn't fated to make the same mistakes over and over till I died. Some things happened when I was growing up that weren't very good, but they were just that: things that had happened. Some of them I could have dealt with better, others might not have come about if I'd done them differently, but that was irrelevant; I couldn't change them. And now I knew that even if I had been able to change them, I would not have wanted to. They were my life.

And just because they'd happened it didn't have to mean that anything nice that had come my way was sheer luck. You have to work for luck, and I had worked; I'd put myself in positions where I could get lucky, and when the luck had come my way I'd made the best use of it. I'd worked with all the power of which I was capable and I knew now that power was something I had.

I'd never admitted this to myself before, because my power was on the same emotional axis as my rage, the rage which had leaked into my consciousness on the road to Mirambeau, which burned in me when I was tired and sore and nearly done for, which made me wish death and destruction on those who obstructed me, and which I had once turned on my parents. But it was this power which made me a survivor. I could not repudiate it; it was as much part of me as my slow, dogged spirit and my capacity to love.

NEW WAYS WITH TURKEY

Runner's World Training Log.
Day: Wednesday. **Distance:** 7 m. **Time:** 1 h. 10 including interruption to give directions to man in Escort looking for Corelli Road. **Weather:** Sharp, snow in the offing. **Course/notes:** Lewisham Hill, Lee High Road, back through Blackheath Park via Morden Road. Abandoned hubcaps and slushy litter on the pavements, except in Blackheath Park where there were laurel leaves and confetti. A better class of winter there. Felt emotional. Home, home.

I spent a night at Chinon with my driver, in a place called the Diderot to which we found our way after that brisk salvo of expletives always exchanged by married couples trying to find a berth in the dark in a foreign one-way system. The Diderot was withdrawn from the road behind high white gates. These opened on to a big gravel drive surrounded by walls, in the shelter of one of which grew three banana trees lagged against the winter chill by copies of the *Voix du Midi*.

What a pleasure it was to draw up at one of the Touraine's wackiest and most lovely hotels in a large, expensive car, to know that beyond the subtly lit porch was a proprietor who would not wrinkle his nose as I advanced towards the reception desk while the rain from my anorak formed puddles on the carpet, to remind myself that the next day I would be reunited with my children, my underarm deodorant and my books. It would be a demanding but ultimately gratifying task to adjust to the notion of turning pages again after a week spent reading nothing but the instructions for blister plasters and the odd signpost.

And so I travelled home for Christmas, stopping only in Calais to buy ten white *boudins*, the use to which I was intending to put these I shall lose no time in explaining. When I was a bride at the start of the eighties one particular aspect of wedded life came as a great shock to me. This was that I had married into a family which didn't want turkey at Christmas. *Boeuf bourguignonne* had served them more than adequately for two decades and *boeuf bourguignonne* was how they intended to go on. They were not completely inflexible. They were more than happy to have it cooked with diced *pancetta*, or with venison in the place of Mr Dring the butcher's best braising steak, but beyond that they would not go. They wanted something with gravy, in cubes, and without drumsticks.

So every Christmas, while other families were pulling wishbones and squabbling about whose turn it was to put up with the brown meat, we sat slurping and mopping up something in red wine sauce. It was very good but all along I yearned for turkey, because when I was a kid we always had turkey. My dad cooked it. He had two acts in his culinary repertoire, basically. The first was brawn. Never more at one with himself, I sometimes think, than when he had a pig's head bubbling on the cooker. I won't tell you how it was made; no one actually ever attempts the recipes in cookery books, do they? They buy them for the pictures. I'd put one in here, but brawn doesn't photograph well.

Dad's star turn was the turkey. He cooked that Christmas bird with real love, basted it with dripping on a regular basis, swaddled it in streaky, watched over it like a baby; if it had woken in the night, he would have rushed to it. Did the sprouts and potatoes too. Mum had no peer as a good plain cook but every December 25th she was marginalized into bread sauce.

In the sixth year of my married life I served two Christmas lunches simultaneously: bird and *bourguignonne*. The bird was as delicious as the beef, so much so that our dining room soon resembled that scene from *Aliens*, the one in which Kane's stomach bursts and bits of viscera finish up hanging like paper chains around the walls. We agreed that this truly was excess gone mad and set to hammering out a peace agreement which was that next Yuletide and every subsequent one till divorce or death intervened we would serve bird and beef in alternate years. We would also move the dinner forward to be consumed on 24 December, leaving us free the day after to concentrate on the more important Christmas issues, like sleeping through *Chitty Chitty Bang Bang* and having terrible, bitter arguments about who lost the remote control.

P.S. If you're wondering about the *boudins*, this is what you do. Split them open and discard the skin. Stuff the turkey with them. Anoint the bird with dripping, cloak its breast in foil and place in oven at 180 degrees. Take phone call from your mother who prior to flying to Scotland for the festive season chez Big Sis has given you £40 to purchase a black velvet hat.

Mum: Have you bought the hat yet?

Self: Yes, yes! It's wonderful! Thank you so much.

Mum: You haven't bought it, have you?

Self: Yes I have. The only thing is, it's green. I couldn't find a black one I liked.

Mum: It's still in the shop, isn't it? That £40 has been swallowed up in your overdraft. I can tell by the look on your face.

Go off and start getting pie-eyed but remember to visit the oven about an hour before dinner. Remove foil and ornament bird with streaky bacon.

Open another jeroboam of champagne. Revel anew in your good fortune in having a stepson who is the wine correspondent of the *Observer* and always arrives with a lot of excitingly clinking and gratifyingly free cases of the glugging stuff. Move on to the retailing-at-£25-a-bottle red and in due course sit down, having first rounded up any members of the family too intoxicated to remember where the dining room is. Ask head of household how he is enjoying the turkey.

'It's fine. I don't know what's wrong with a nice *boeuf bourguignonne*, myself.'

Later, at Midnight Mass, reflect on the Christmas mystery, which is, of course, how your mother, by phone and at a distance of 700 miles, can tell you are lying.

WHAT WILL SURVIVE OF US

Runner's World Training Log.
Day: Boxing Day. **Distance:** 40 m. by bike.
Weather: Cold but dry till late on. **Course/notes:** Essex
and back, via Rotherhithe Tunnel. The tunnel empty,
fast and scary. Echoes made by the noise of the bike
wheels. Had promised Mum I'd check on her house
while she was away. No burst water tanks, break-ins, etc.
She'd left a box of chocolates for me in the garage,
with a note: 'So you'll have something to open on the
day, dear.'

Among the many delightful attributes of long distance
walkers is a tendency to be utterly cavalier about trifles
such as time, cost and prior commitments ranging from
an audience with the Pope to imminent open heart
surgery when it comes to the chance to go walking. Invite
any ordinary member of your acquaintance to devote the
best part of a week treading the highways and byways of
a foreign country for nothing but the dubious reward of
your company and without exception they will exclaim
about your cheek or question your sanity. Ask the same of
any walker and their response will be to ring round their
friends to see if they too would care to tag along. 'Any
time, any place, anywhere' is the walker's motto. They are

the Martinis of the pedestrian world. This is how, a few days after Christmas, I found myself re-entering Chinon with Janet, Reg, Avril, Elaine and two men called Peter. For the sake of clarity I'll call them Walking Peter and Driving Peter, as those are the actions they respectively performed.

Not only had Elaine, Avril and the Messrs Peter never set eyes on me but I hadn't had the pleasure of meeting Janet and Reg since the Three Forests Walk in November 1996. It was, in short, quite wonderful when, in response to my stammered invitation to walk with me from Chinon to Tours, I heard Janet almost purr to the inquisitive Reg at her shoulder by the phone, 'Wait till you hear what she's got in mind for us now.'

What I had in mind for them turned out to be a 450-mile drive on HGV-cluttered roads in unimaginably awful weather to a town whose historic delights were quite invisible in the wintry dark. It was close to midnight, we were starving and every café except one was shut.

I have to say that until you have sat in a crap French café sipping tepid coffee and eating sugar lumps you have not known the true cruelty of life, and stopping only to appropriate the long-abandoned half of a Pastry of the Day from the waste trolley we retreated to our beds at the Diderot. And if you still retain doubts about the tolerance, the good humour and sheer decency of long distance walkers let me tell you that throughout all this not one of them offered me a single word of reproach. Though I'm glad the walls of the Diderot were old-fashioned and thick because Lord knows what they were muttering about me in private.

The next morning we fell with exuberant relish on the Diderot's baguettes, croissants and home-made jam and set off at a determined clop into the old town, whose every corner gave forth to a new treasure by way of cobbled pathways, intricately built turrets and oriole windows. But soul-nurturing though it is to traverse 17 kilometres of major wine-growing region with four of the liveliest people it is my pleasure to know, the sad fact remains that after a while even the renowned Forêt de Chinon becomes a blur of dirt tracks, D roads, one-alsatian hamlets and wintry vines. So while we get on with staring at our maps in a gale, comparing our blisters and nipping behind bushes for windswept calls of nature I propose to say a few words on the subject of Hundreds.

The Hundred is the sternest test in the LDWA calendar. It is at once its Premiership – a long, solid slog – and its F.A. Cup, a knock-out contest in which luck and steady nerve play an equal part in deciding who will survive to the next stage. A Hundred is what it says, a walk of 100 miles, and it must be accomplished in one go. No, I can't quite get my head around that either, but once every year if you happen to be in the vicinity of the Yorkshire Dales, the South Downs or other areas of lonely rural beauty you may notice a handful of people behaving strangely in a field. Some will be hallucinating, some will be walking in circles or, if female, asking, 'Where's my handbag?' This might be a reasonable enough query at turning-out time at the Locarno but it is altogether more mysterious and plangent when aired repeatedly at nine in the evening by a moving bundle of thermals and Goretex in a line of bushes west of civilization.

These are all people at the closing end of a Hundred. They have been walking without pause for nearly forty-eight hours, have seen the sun come up twice and have feet like minced beef, so it is hardly surprising that their internal narratives have become a bit garbled and that, though chilled to the marrow, they have the overwhelming urge to lie in a ditch to cool down. Possibly in order to keep the mortality rate at a manageable level, the organizers at the last few checkpoints dispatch marshals to keep an eye on them. Walkers are not often moved to poetic metaphor but if it's going to happen it's usually when asked to elaborate on the last, desperate, be-fogged hours of a Hundred, when all that may lie between themselves and untimely demise are a couple of friendly faces with torches. 'We are', said Janet, 'like big ships with the little ships guiding us into harbour.'

As I've indicated, the walking personality is not wholly at home with introspection, and if you invite one of these stout-hearted, energetic but unassuming people to explain what psychotherapists would call their motivation they will say, 'Goodness me. What questions you do ask. Um – bloody-mindedness. Now for God's sake pass the rice pudding.'

*

Just after one o'clock we stepped footsore, bedraggled and enormously hungry into the nondescript Touraine village of Riverannes and there, in a sturdy and capacious bus shelter in the rue du Commerce, next to a Christmas tree decorated with windblown bows of red foil, were Reg and Driving Peter. They had been shopping in a St Village. Then they had spread a plastic cloth the width and length of the bus shelter's floor and strewn it with baguettes, Brie, various intriguing and flavoursome salads, quiches, tartes, rillettes and pink, grapey Chinon. We fell on them (the food, not Reg and Driving Peter, I hasten to add) with little cries of, 'Look! Bottles! Ooh, pâté!'

I doubt that it could have been achieved in Britain where these days you're lucky to get one bus in Hampshire per week and where those bus shelters which have not been decommissioned are vandalized and splattered with graffiti. Which is a real shame because when you're sitting on an iron seat with a plastic cup of rosé in your hand, chewing baguettes while the Brie runs down your chin and watching a gale blow the tiles off the roofs opposite it is possible to know the purest happiness.

Afterwards we tramped on past apple orchards, white-fenced farms and tiny hilltop settlements to Azay-le-Rideau where, in the town square, Reg and Driving Peter awaited us with the news that they had booked us into a hotel called the Trois Lys. This, besides being commodious, elegant, inexpensive and otherwise perfect in every way, was also the only one open. My companions went off to inspect their rooms with little cries of 'Ooh! Showers! Look, central heating!' and I slipped across the road to the Maison de la Presse to buy a road map of Tours.

Azay's hilly streets were pleasantly busy in the Saturday twilight and with my map stashed somewhere in my anorak (one of the more disturbing features of the anorak is its pocket mountain; one is forever chancing upon a long forgotten zip which, undone, reveals a stiffened Kleenex and a cheese sandwich which has been there since 1996) I strolled round the shops. In the window of the *boulangerie* was a tray of meringues. How white and sacred they looked in their frilled cases, like girls in their First Communion dresses. The New Year cakes were already getting into party mood with paper hats. Loaves the size of HGV tyres rested on wooden slats at the back. Across the street, a young couple with a baby in a pushchair pressed their noses to the window of Jean Charles Daugeron (Sport Camping Chasse Pêche) and in low voices discussed the merits of a lorry driver's grey cardigan. A van drew up outside. On its sides were painted 'Le Dansant, Le Sloopy's (La Formule 1 de la

Discothèque)' and 'Le Marilyn Dancing'. Its driver jumped out and, folding his leather bomber jacket around him, went into the Bar le Commerce.

I wandered back up the street to the gift shop where I searched briefly for a memento for my dear children but could find nothing that would have distracted them from their diet of televised violence. They were slightly too old for the lopsided toy cat and not quite of an age for the underpants which featured three pockets embroidered 'Matin Midi Soir' and each containing a condom. Finally I entered a small bar across the road from our hotel, which I had been planning to do for twenty minutes past so I could order a big glass of red wine.

On the counter was a little plastic Christmas tree, lights flashing. Madame, the owner, sat at one of her own tables, sorting out lottery tickets and conversing in a Gitanes-deepened voice with a man in the room beyond. He never showed his face; perhaps he was in his Matin Midi Soir underpants as a preliminary to joining the youth of Azay in the Marilyn. A poodle, grizzled and arthritic, made its way across the floor, ears trailing on the tiles, too tired and old to lift them clear.

I sat with my back to the radiator and felt warm and comforted. My lipstick left a mark on the glass. On my table was a tall vase filled with stiff plastic roses. A poster on the wall extolled Les Douceurs de Villandry and a flyer from the Club Kalimba thanked me for my visit and hoped it would see me again soon. Through the window I could see couples drift home with their Saturday evening shopping, and a mother and daughter with armfuls of baguettes.

I spread my road map of Tours over the table and moved my upper torso back and forward and my head right and left till I'd found the angle. This is how I read small print in dimly lit bars these days. I was looking for rue Paul-Louis Courier, the street where Madame Castaing now lived. I was hoping, if I didn't get all knotted up in shyness and embarrassment, to meet her again.

I'd imagined this meeting several times. My fantasy was that nothing much would have changed. There she would be, preserved in her serene, unfazed, bosomy mid-thirties in her navy slacks and white blazer. Maybe she would be behind the wheel of the very same Citroën 2CV in which before breakfast on the morning of our departure to Kikinette she had careened through old Tours to the *boulangerie*. I remembered this vehicle so well; nothing like any car I had ever seen, hardly a car at all, but something bolted together out of the detritus of a pile-up on a pleasure beach, all dented metal, smashed lights and canvas seats like deckchairs. It had the smooth, cushioned ride of a kangaroo. You didn't so much open the doors as kind of hang them from the roof and hope they stayed straight.

I hadn't told anyone that I was going to Tours to find Madame Castaing. Maybe it was something to do with this fantasy of mine, that every mirror I looked in was making a mistake and I was not the battle-weary middle-aged woman who was proposing to stand before her the very next day but the plump, self-important child she had collected from Paris Orly in August 1959. It was probably just as well that at that moment the door of the bar swung open and Avril trilled, 'Oh, there you are. We've been hunting for you everywhere,' because otherwise I'd have started blubbing. I followed her back to the Trois Lys, where we ate and drank lots and had a good time, and I realized that wanting to be ten again was a pretty drippy ambition.

They made me Go Round the chateau at Azay in the

morning; it was probably their revenge for the deprivations of Chinon. Corniches, façades and prospects duly
admired, we drove into Tours, travelling the last half mile
in a sudden sleetstorm. It's hard to convey how violent
and alarming it was but imagine having frozen West
Highland White terriers hurled at your car.

I knew from Big Sis, who had assiduously exchanged
Christmas cards annually with the family, that none of the
Castaings now lived in rue Traversière. The children were
grown up and gone; Papa Jean was dead. From my street
plan it looked as if rue Paul-Louis Courier was in a
pedestrian precinct just a short stroll from the Loire,
between two bridges. We parked on the edge of the
pedestrianized zone, in a square between Rouget Isle and
Voltaire, where, in an I-expect-you've-all-been-wonder-
ing-why-I-brought-you-here voice I explained my project
and my friends, with every appearance of enthusiasm,
agreed to spend two hours in a car park in a squall of
hail, snacking off yesterday's leftover picnic.

I girded myself in waterproofs and with Janet riding
shotgun set out into the unknown. The narrow streets
were high-walled and Sunday-peaceful. As we crossed
Rouget de Lisle the hailstorm stopped as abruptly as it
had begun and we walked the last two hundred yards in
watery sunshine, peering at street names and exclaiming
at the elegance and nobility of every second building. The
words rue Paul-Louis Courier were carved high into an
old wall. We inched up the road, peering through venerable iron gates that gave way to stupendously classy old
dwellings beyond courtyards. Me not really knowing
whether I wanted to find it. Now I had come this far,
couldn't we give up and go back to the sanctum of Reg's
Audi? But a short way along, I happened on it: a high
wooden gate set into a stone wall, on which was a row of

bellpushes. Beside one was printed the name of Jean Castaing.

Forever on my bellpush, dear.

I could see through the bars of the gate to a sumptuous ground floor apartment, with a big front door of plate glass set into the old walls around it.

My hand hovered.

'Well, go on,' said Janet. 'Go for it.'

'I don't like to.'

Janet looked at me, incredulous. I said, 'She hasn't seen me for thirty-nine years, and that was for just three weeks, during which I cried most of the time, and if she's infirm or maybe a bit gaga isn't it going to give her quite a turn having two strange women in anoraks banging on her door for admittance?'

'Strange? Speak for yourself,' said Janet firmly, 'and if you don't ring that bell I will because I'm dying for a pee.'

I think Madame C. must have been watching me minnying around by the gate all along because at the first ding of the bell the plate glass door swung open and there she was, gliding across the courtyard towards us. And whatever the French is for a million dollars, she looked it: honey-coloured hair caught back by a gold-patterned Alice band, camel cashmere cardigan, silver grey sweater (angora), dark taupe slacks with a check so subtle you had to look at it twice for confirmation. Her lace-ups were chocolate leather. Glasses, very nice ones. Not so bosomy now, of course. And smaller than I remembered her, only a couple of inches between our respective heights. I don't think she'd shrunk; I'd just overlooked the fact that when you're ten all adults seem like Gargantua.

I identified myself in loud and execrable French and after I had quite possibly informed her that I had been walking in France for ten years she dragged the gate open and beckoned us into a big high-ceilinged flagstone-floored living room where in no time at all we were drinking black, perfect coffee from white, perfect cups. Throughout all of this Madame C. was so serene and unfazed she really did make me believe she could think of nothing more charming than to have her Sunday afternoon disrupted by two Englishwomen in rustling water-proofs, dripping rain like wet dogs over her rugs.

She said the apartment had been converted out of an old chapel which several centuries ago had belonged to a great house. The porch was almost a room in itself, with a round table on which sat a small box of choco-lates, white and perfect like the coffee cups. The dining area had a long table of dark old wood, subtly tapestried cushions, shelves of Papa Jean's books. Light entered from the high-up stained glass window and a small shel-tered patio that Madame C. revealed proudly, sliding back a plate glass sliver: her *court*. Every bit of antique wood gleamed, every rug was straight and the whole place was tidy and beautiful yet indisputably *lived in*, right down to the discreetly placed cardboard box which contained a few presents, wrapped in gay paper, not yet given. Who were they for? Had some of her grand-children not yet been to see her, though it was now well beyond Christmas? I decided, rather, that they were for maintaining the unfazed state, to have something to exchange with visitors who brought unexpected presents for her.

Over more perfect coffee she told me what had become of her children. Benedicte had been married for many years to a Swiss vineyard owner, gratifyingly rich and double-barrelled of name; she had grown-up children and had moved back recently to the land of her ancestors, being stationed in Rochecorbon just a short trot from where we sat. Denis, like Papa Jean, was a medical consultant, though his field of expertise was *foie* whereas Papa Jean was a bones man; at least, this is what I understood Madame C. to have meant. I have always got my *os* and my *oie* confused and if her late husband was in fact in geese I can only apologize for the misunderstanding. There was something else I wanted to apologize to Denis for, but my French didn't quite run to, 'Tell him I'm sorry I doubted his word about the bowl. He'll understand what I mean.'

Veronique lived in Paris in the rue de Grenelle, worked in *arts et métiers*, ran marathons and had three children: two medical students and a ten-year-old. Sophie, who also lived in Paris, had not married. She was working for L'Oréal though Madame C. thought she might be about to leave that job. Sophie loved to come to London, where she had many friends. Finally, Laurent – Laurent? Here was something I didn't know. Papa Jean and Josephe had one more child, a second son, Laurent, born the year after I went to Kikinette. He was a *médecin* too.

I told her that I had been back to Cap Ferret and that Kikinette was gone. 'Ah, Kikinette!' she said. Her eyes danced and she clasped her hands and led me to a tall chest of drawers by the writing desk. A wooden box with a dark screen framed by oyster shells; looked like a primitive TV set till she flicked a switch and there it was, a beach scene with real sand stuck on the plywood, a seagull perching on a bank in the middle above a glossy shell, and nothing between the painted sea and the sky. Le Bassin d'Arcachon. Kikinette wasn't gone after all.

Papa Jean made it. Well, a bones man, good with a hacksaw. Madame C. twiddled another switch. *Voilà!*

Lights, action. Two razor shells rose above the waterline, then two more, to form eyebrows and closed eyes. The shell eyelids opened to reveal shell eyeballs. The seagull twitched to the right: a nose. The conch on which it had been perching turned upwards and pouted in a red-lipped smile.

What will survive of us is Kikinette, I suppose.

And that was it, really. We embraced, me babbling '*Merveilleux, merveilleux*,' and Janet and I walked off up rue Paul-Louis Courier, mulling over the visit the way you do. Janet expressed surprise that I had been so iffy about ringing the doorbell. 'I mean, you have to go out and meet strangers in your job all the time.'

But Madame C. wasn't a stranger and that, I suppose, was what had made the prospect of our encounter so loaded. In my head she'd been with me for more than thirty-eight years, reclining on her deckchair in a shiny blue bathing dress, one of the least weird and most wonderful acts in the Showman's circus. A beautiful Frenchwoman in her mid-thirties with the mysterious serenity of wedded bliss. Whenever I stepped on to French soil and felt that much more chic, that bit more bosomy, it was not just because I loved France, or because Frenchmen were any more bowled over than Englishmen by small female sportswriters who spent their declining years running marathons, but because in my head Madame C. had just smiled at me, got up off her deckchair and beckoned me into her house.

When we reached the car park we found our friends had saved us some of the picnic leftovers, bless them, and so I passed what was left of a very happy afternoon munching on a giant baguette filled with Salade Paysanne and feeling as chic and bosomy as I possibly could in a rain-stippled waterproof and with a blob of mayonnaise on my nose.

*

The rain held off, so we walked out of Tours, north-east past walls of carefully piled grey stone, alongside the silvery Loire. Rochecorbon nestled in the side of a near-vertical bluff of cold bronze rock. We clambered towards the little town up a narrow road, no more than a paved slit banked by modest cottages prettied up with flower troughs under windows the size of men's handkerchiefs. The road widened and levelled off, and we looked down into a sweeping valley of fine trees, green banks and graceful old buildings. On our left was the Mairie, an unremarkable pile in itself but notable for its public address system. This adorned the roof and featured a dozen or more horns arranged in a circle like flowers in a vase.

Benedicte's house backed on to the hillside. The lower storey was obscured behind white railings and an immense garden wall lined the road as far as the eye could see. Access seemed to be achieved by a pair of vast blue-painted gates pierced six feet up by a beady spyhole.

'Go on, then,' said Janet, just a bit wearily. 'Ring the bell.'

Brrrrri-ing!

A dog barked but no one came.

'Perhaps Madame Castaing rang ahead to say you were coming,' said Janet.

I walked a little way along the road and hung on the wall, staring in through the windows. I could see honey-coloured drapes in the shadowy dining room, a polished wood vase on a landing sill, flashes of soft cream and gilt.

But of Benedicte and her husband and children there was no sign. Madame C. had said she was out '*souvent*' and so it proved. But Benedicte's house, like her mother's, looked *lived* in, I was glad to see. So we wandered back to Reg's car and left the dog to its barking at shadows in an empty house, which were, of course, not shadows at all but Veronique eating cold flageolets from a glass dish, and Benedicte and Janie sitting up like an old married couple, and Denis flicking rice krispies at Sophie over the breakfast table while Papa Jean taught them the rudiments of existentialism.

PART THREE

FRIENDLY YOURS

Runner's World Training Log.
Day: Saturday. **Distance:** 11.5 m. **Time:** 1 h. 45 min.
Weather: Mild for end December.
Course/notes: Dulwich and back via the College, taking in vile hill that goes up from Honor Oak Park station. Bum muscle hurt. Ran through it and had a sore right leg afterwards. Don't think I'll run that route again: the South Circular, lorries, grime, noise, not much for the soul.

Good afternoon Julie,

I think I forgot to send you a fax about the New Year Corrida on 31 December at Frevent, near Arras. 9.2 kilometres, departure for women 15.30 pm. Dial and aske for Mme Devillers. I think you already recieve the inscription form. Entrance is 25F. Noo reward and no appearance fee.

If you need some help further, just send a fax.
I kiss you everywhere.
Friendly yours,
Jacques.

*

'Hello, is that Karen? I don't suppose you remember me but we met on the Three Forests Walk last year. I was the one who fell over the sleeping cow. I know this sounds crazy but do you think any East End Road Runners

would come to a race with me? On New Year's Eve? In
France?'

Phew.

*

Let's begin at the beginning. If you want to run in a race
in France, it's simple. All you have to do is get hold of the
Nouvelle Année issue of *Jogging* magazine which, despite
its title, is as French as garlic breath and in the January of
each year publishes a calendar of every challenge of track,
road and fell taking place in every corner of Gaul from
the most teeming metropolis to the obscurest boar-infested
backwater.

I know this now, but did not when I was casting about
for a road race with which to round off my journey from
Cap Ferret and after several frustrating attempts to locate
something suitable in terms of standard (undemanding)
and Frenchness (I'm not quite sure what I had in mind –
fun runners dressed as the Eiffel Tower?) I gratefully
handed over the baton to a Paris-based old friend, the
charming and debonair sportswriter Monsieur Jacques
Brunot. For noo reward whatsoever M. Brunot devoted
the best part of his Christmas to finding me a race and
were I not a respectably married woman I would kiss him
everywhere right back.

I had indeed already received the inscription form,
which told me that the 21e Corrida de la Saint-Sylvestre
was being organized by the Frevent Olympic-Club with
the assistance of the Town Council and Tradespeople of
Frevent and its surrounds. I dialled and asked for Mme
Devillers and after inflicting upon her a barrage of no
doubt incomprehensible questions to all of which she
replied, '*Oui! Tout est possible!*' we established that the 21e
Corrida de la Saint-Sylvestre was the one for me.

There were races over 5k and 9.2k, *nombreuses récompensées* and *coupes*, prizes for the best fancy dress, and, at 12.30 at the Piscine, something called the Remise des Dossards which I fantasized on first reading to be some arcane local ceremony similar to Demonstration of Medieval Ducking School but transpired to be Handing Out of Competitors' Numbers. Frevent itself was a negligible blob at the confluence of two D roads on page 7 of the French road atlas. It was, like Martignac sur Jalle, the sort of place you would never normally spare a thought for if you were travelling through France and apart from that slight disappointment over the ducking stool it promised to be perfect.

Perfect, but for one thing. Race-wise, it was bad enough going it alone in England; at least it was when, like me, you were one of the Trabants of the running world. The starting gun went boom, you surged forward in a crowd of jostling elbows, snorting nostrils and flapping shorts and for half a minute all manner of exhilarating thought bubbles exploded in your head: 'Wow! Yesss! I can run at this pace!' What was really happening was that you had become the object of a kind of collective peristalsis, and 50 yards up the course the squeezing, pumping pack would leave you steaming on the road. For the next 13 miles or whatever it was just you and the steady squeaking of your orthotics. You'd get triumphantly to the Finish to find everyone had gone home apart from one last marshal looking rather pointedly at his watch. Call me a wimp, but the prospect of enduring one of these solipsistic trundles along foreign pavements to nothing but the sound of muffled Gallic laughter was not an enticing one.

I must tell you that almost a year ago to the day, while training for my first London Marathon, I had toyed with the idea of joining a running club. It would, I reasoned, be both a spur and a reassurance to step out on training nights along heath and pavement with friendly like-minded women of my age. I pictured us in our club vests, pacing each other through those early miles, talking each other through the wall zone round Canary Wharf, beguiling the harsh later stages of the race with sisterly encouragement.

I applied to join a club near where I lived. I can best describe it as 'august'. Wood panelling on the clubhouse walls, framed photographs of ancient leading lights. On my first training night there I set out with two friendly like-minded women of my age. We began by running up a sizeable gradient in the well-known Himalayan district of Bromley, Kent. I toiled, I puffed, I cursed. 'You'll soon feel better,' they said kindly. I nodded, then toiled and puffed and cursed some more. And so it went on, for ages and ages till eventually we reached a signpost that told us there was only one more mile to go. 'Nearly there,' said my companions, who by now were quite aglow themselves. I nodded again. 'We can make it,' I said. 'Yes,' they said. 'As you're so close to home now, would you mind if we stretched our legs a bit?' And off they floated to do another circuit of the Himalayas.

'You'll soon improve,' they said kindly when we met up again in the clubhouse afterwards. I nodded some more. And I knew. I knew that never in a million years would I ever be able to keep up with them. I had to face it: running-wise, I was unclubbable. The sad conclusion was that the sport I most loved would have to be a solitary vice.

All this is a roundabout way of saying that while I was desperate for company in Frevent I was also embarrassed to seek it out. God, how I wavered over that phone, trying to work up the courage to ring Karen's number. I had, it is true, lured the long distance walkers out to Chinon but at least in the intervening year since the Three Forests we had enjoyed contact by way of Christmas cards and occasional letters. The East End Road Runners, on the other hand, had last clapped eyes on me in extremis in a Sawbridgeworth scout hut, waiting to be towed away like an old broken-down car. I wasn't a sleek, sub 7-minute miler, I was a forty-nine-year-old with wonky knees and no pace; I had nothing to offer apart from a day trip to France.

Oh, I don't know, it just seemed such a bizarre thing to ask of anyone.

I'd like to claim I had begun to realize that this attitude was particularly stupid; the worst outcome would be that Karen would say no, and whatever the psychological reasons behind my bashfulness it was high time that I put a stop to it. I'd also prefer to say that when I called Karen it was an act of prescience; I'd known that meeting the East End Road Runners again would be the next stage of my journey towards self-healing. But the truth was far less admirable. I made that call because the alternative – being on my own in a foreign country, in a race in which I would indubitably finish last – was worse.

There they were, on my doorstep, four of them, at half past seven on the last morning of 1997. Karen, Joan, John and Mick. I'll flesh them out for you. Karen not much bigger than me, gamine haircut and oh, the energy; imagine a pretty jumping bean. Joan – and I couldn't quite believe this – older than me. An elite athlete once, before there was any money in it, and still a good match for a deer. John a young boxer, nose intact but his knee no sight for the faint-hearted after a motorbike accident. We were soon showing each other our orthotics. And then there was the club chairman, a very tall man with iron grey spikes for a haircut, used to work on the docks. Possibly as a crane. 'I'm Mick,' he said. 'I never stop talking and I always finish last.'

Music to my ears.

We rode on the Shuttle, we drank tea the colour of manilla envelopes, ate Mars bar after Mars bar, told each other our sun signs and got lost south of Boulogne. A mild day with silver clouds and a fuzzy, flickering sun. I fretted. What if this was a women-only race? What if there was a men's race, but separate and due to start before our time of arrival? They told me to shut up and gave me an East End Road Runners vest. It was shiny and purple like the end of W.C. Fields' nose. Handed it over with a kind of ceremony. I hadn't felt so proud since that day at Brownies when Brown Owl made me Sixer of the Gnomes.

When I am an old woman I shall wear purple.

Between Montreuil and Hesdin it began to rain in stair rods but by the time we reached Frevent the sky had rained itself dry and not another drop was to fall on us all afternoon. It was a nice little place, Frevent. A typically French arrangement of cafés and a Place du Marche and streets lined with typically French shop window displays: toilet seats, cardigans, joke underpants, meringues. We parked outside a small roofed alleyway beneath the grey stone arch of which, under Mick's command, we performed ten minutes of physical jerks then jogged in a purple line to the Piscine for the Remise des Dossards.

The entry fee for the 9.2k was 25F.

'Go on, you ask.'

'No, you.'

'No, you.'

Karen stepped up to the registration table with a

confident clearance of the throat. She said, '*Est-ce-qu'il est le même temps pour les hommes?*'

The women behind the table exchanged quizzical looks. One glanced out of the window. '*Oui,*' she said uncertainly.

Fixing numbers to fronts in the turquoise-tiled vestibule. The usual trawl through fluff-bottomed kitbags for safety pins. Always one too few. Joan murmuring to Karen, 'You asked if it was the same weather for the men.' Back in the Place du Marche we were interviewed by the local press. *La Voix du Nord* was ruddy-faced and plump and *L'Abeille de la Ternoise* was small with straggling grey hair. Each had a camera before which we arrayed ourselves, arms linked. John, Karen, me and Joan, with Mick behind us like God the Father. Couldn't stop smiling. Couldn't believe I'd organized this. It was my Showman's smile.

The Cyrano café had a yellow sun blind for a nose and its name picked out in grey on the white-walled side. Inside was a two-foot counter for sweets and *tabac* next to half a horseshoe of bar. Frenchmen's bottoms on cherry-red leatherette. We bought Mars bar after Mars bar, spread ourselves at a round table by the window and drank coffee from doll-sized cups. A large number of runners thundered past. We downed cups, abandoned personal effects and set off in the slipstream. Fifty yards up the road we established that we had joined the 5k race. We resumed our places at the Cyrano. After half an hour we lined up for the 9.2 start. Joan, John and Karen sleek and anticipatory at the front of the pack. Mick and I forming the rump.

'Remember,' said Mick, 'I always finish last.'

'You wouldn't say that', I said, 'if you knew me better.'

Gun went bang, everyone belted off. Wow, Yesss! etc. Fifty yards up the road, I was duly deposited. 'I thought for a minute you was having me on,' said Mick, catching me up. 'I thought you was really a fast runner.' We plodded along companionably, past rusting metal shutters, low white railings, PNEU SERVICE signs. One short loop of Frevent, one slightly longer loop, two very long loops. The marshals signalled our way with red and green lollipops. Not club runners but locals, feeling very important. On the second loop we were lapped by the first of our fellow competitors. Zoom, another and another. Karen, John and Joan glided by. Mick thought I looked stronger than him. You go ahead if you want to, he said.

'But you'll be on your own.'

'Then I'll just have to talk to myself, won't I?'

Away I ran. Round and round Frevent. The sun shone milkily, the pavements were clean and dry. I had one more loop to go when the marshal outside the Place du Marche stuck out a red lollipop and signalled me left.

Perhaps he was under the impression I was completing my last loop, I thought. Or perhaps everyone had got fed up waiting for Mick and me and had decided to call time on us. A sour-sweet moment. It had been embarrassing being so much slower than everyone else. On the other hand, I was knackered. I joined the line at the finish. At that point in thundered Karen and John. Karen's face dropped. She said, 'You've got another lap to do, haven't you?'

I said, 'I thought they'd decided to pull the plug on me.'

'I've just seen Mick set off on the final loop,' said Karen. 'You might be able to catch him.'

I ran and caught Mick. I passed him to finish second from last. Someone handed me a small square of cardboard on which was written '89me' in spidery blue. Someone else gave me a T-shirt. On it was a picture of a man and a cow putting on a display of bravery and agility. A few feet further along, a woman at a trestle table roofed with tarpaulins was waiting to present a lidded saucepan, jade green in colour and decorated with a still life involving vegetables, a giant strawberry and a pineapple. I thanked her, adding how nice it would look in my cooking.

Karen, John, Joan and Mick received cardboard squares, T-shirts and a paraffin lamp each. Karen was well pleased, she'd come second in the Femmes, there was a trophy waiting for her at the post-race reception in the Salle Polyvalente. This was a small hall made memorable by being painted in marzipan colours. It was like entering a giant petit four. Inside, Christmas decorations were still garlanding the ceiling and trestle tables bearing wine ran the full length of the room from Christmas tree to stage. I must tell you that the reception was magnificent. You just don't get them like that in England's running circles: a cup of tea, a queue for the loo and that's it, goodnight, sweetheart. But here people lined the walls five deep. The stage groaned with cups, bowls, salvers and statuettes, not to mention the mayor and a whole raft of slightly lower-ranking dignitaries. We had speeches: *'Mes chers amis sportifs ... mesdames et messieurs.'* We had a formal prizegiving. Karen went up to collect; she'd changed into a pair of kingfisher velvet trousers and looked gorgeous, the mayor was smitten. Shook her hand and kissed her, then slipped to the other end of the line of slightly lower-ranking dignitaries to do it all again.

After this, the East End Road Runners were called to the stage to receive porcelain plates depicting the Place du Marche. Stirred by the pomp and circumstance of the moment, I took the liberty of inviting all of Frevent to the East End Road Runners half-marathon in April. The mayor kissed Karen again and invited us to drink champagne with him. He looked quite crestfallen when we said we had to go.

We drove back through the Pas de Calais in early evening darkness. In five more hours it would be 1998 but all the houses in the small towns we passed through were shuttered and silent. St. Pol de Ternoise, Hesdin, Brimeux, Montreuil, Samer. At Boulogne we stopped off at the Buffalo Grill, perched high on a hill above the roadworks where we had got lost earlier in the day. We had *bavettes* with Roquefort sauce preceded by Salade d'Accueil.

Felt as though I'd known these people for years.

Riding back on the Shuttle we were tired, elated, amazed by the hospitality and formal kindness of the French. Over Kent the night sky was the colour of charcoal. A pinkish glow rose above London and red dots glowed on high-rise towers. Canary Wharf, floodlit, looked like a melting ice cube. It was not much short of midnight when we got home. The new year followed us in through the front door. We kissed goodbye, my new friends and I, and then after sharing a modest bottle or two of Uva di Troia with my husband I went to my desk and I wrote, I honestly wrote, 'Say goodbye to stone cold tombs! Choose life over death! I belong! I belong!' After which someone called the Exclamation Mark Police and I was led away burbling to my bed.

BREAKING AWAY

Runner's World Training Log.
Day: Saturday. **Distance:** 14 m. **Time:** 2 h. 10 min.
Weather: January squalls. **Course/notes:** Blackheath–
Chislehurst and back. Ran with Fred. His first long
training run for the London Marathon. He towed me the
first 6 miles in 54 minutes. Wearing his red Liverpool
hat. My legs going like Catherine wheels while he was
barely out of a canter. So cold on the way back. A
monsoon in Mottingham, had to shelter from it in a
phone box. Wanted to give up, just sit in the phone box
and die, but Fred wouldn't let me. Gave me his hat and
plodded home with me, not leaving my side. Oh, what
Mum would have given for a son like him.

The letter said that now the paper's budgetary problems
of the last few months were past, both he and the editor
would like me to be in the paper as much as possible. A
football feature on a bottom-of-the-Premiership Northern
club was proposed to launch this new career of mine: a
double-page spread with colour photos and interviews
with the manager, players and fans.

I set to work with enthusiasm and for a few weeks in
the new year I was a football reporter again, driving up
and down motorways, eating cod, chips and peas in Little
Chefs with Mike King, bellowing at copytakers on my
mobile in press boxes, dashing into Monsoon in my lunch

hour to pick up a little suit (shade anthracite) for Saturday night appearances on *Hold the Back Page*. I went to Highbury and The Valley and Stamford Bridge, sauntering into the press room half an hour before kick-off to be greeted by friends who had known me for years, with whom I had shared two decades' worth of terrible meat pies at The Dell and Portman Road and long beery journeys back from Anfield and Goodison and when we were all much younger, after midweek fixtures, had snogged in badly lit Fleet Street pubs. I was even snarled at by Ronan Goldblatt. It was as comfortable and familiar as a lasting marriage. Why had I been so reluctant to go back into football? This was where I belonged, what I did.

It ended as it always did these days, with my finely crafted double-page-spread-length article held over for two weeks, condensed by a third and wedged between 'Women's Golf' and 'Sport in Brief' at the bottom of a live page. Some other, more important feature material had had to fill the space originally allocated. I hacked and shaved it into shape myself, then forgot about it.

By then I had lost all desire to be a football reporter again. Nothing was ever as easy as to slip back into my old performance and nothing now was less what I wanted. The day before it was due to be published I went out for my Saturday afternoon run. I'd planned it as an undemanding 6-mile canter but when I rounded the corner by Lee Green Sainsbury's I felt that rush of energy that on good days took me up the long hill past the station and over the choked South Circular. A mild fresh breeze would sweep me through Sundridge Park and I'd pick up pace; I wasn't Liz McColgan or anyone else good but what I was was *me* and what I was doing had turned into what *Runner's World* called the Long Steady Run. Before I knew it I was bounding along Chislehurst Common with the worst hill in the South-East behind me and only another two big hills and 5.7 miles to go (I knew this because I was once sad enough to measure out the precise distance on the car tripmeter). I staggered back covered in dribble, snot and small flying insects to find Ron hastily rewriting my copy on his laptop because the bottom-of-the-Premiership team featured in my article had half an hour previously defeated Liverpool which changed the picture entirely.

Like I said, nothing was ever as easy as slipping back into football reporting again. Most of the time it was a pretty good world to be in; I had a place there of sorts, I could make a living there of sorts. I'd probably pick up another of those short-term contracts which was all you could ever get these days and in due course it'd come to an end, leaving me with a huge lump of fury, sorrow and resentment and an enormous sum owing on my Monsoon credit account, so I'd have to pick up another short-term contract to pay it off. And so it would perpetuate itself.

But the longer I thought about it the more I realized how much it was like a relationship ending, a relationship out of which you hadn't been getting what you wanted for a good while but had hung on to because the alternatives – insecurity, isolation, not belonging anywhere – seemed worse. The other person involved had tried to end it a few times too but kept coming back, and neither of you could quite make the terminal break, and each time he came back you kidded yourself that this time it was going to be different. And it never was any different, of course.

All of the above thoughts occurred to me in the few seconds or so that I stood watching Ron urgently rewriting my copy while he left the phone to ring and ring; it would only be the sports desk shouting at me to file because the first edition was about to go to press. It crossed my mind briefly that I should take over from him but I knew he was doing a far better job of it than I ever could, and it was at that moment, handing over the burden to my dear, good, talented husband, that I stopped being a football writer. Granted, I'd stopped being a football writer on numerous previous occasions but this time I knew I would make the decision stick.

I won't claim that, at forty-nine, my future didn't suddenly look blank and frightening. It did, but in a crazy way it also looked interesting and bright. In the weeks to come I would enjoy poking around in it to see what I might find. And with that last bracing thought, I wiped my nose on my sleeve again and hauled myself off to the shower.

REASONS TO BE CHEERFUL

Runner's World Training Log.
Day: Thursday. **Distance:** 6 m. **Time:** 1 h.
Weather: Life-threatening. **Course/notes:** My first
club night at the East End Road Runners. Ran with
Mick and two beginners past the old docks to Woolwich.
Rickety walkways, haunted pubs, black choppy water.
Planes taking off from City Airport, so close you can
almost see faces at the windows.

Three weeks into the new year, on a wet and gale-lashed
Thursday night, I paid my first visit to what was called on
the club letterhead The Terence McMillan Stadium,
Home of the East End Road Runners. I had been told
that the clubhouse was at the end of a driveway and as I
approached I made out through my flooding windscreen
and with astonished pleasure a commodious multi-
storeyed palace with gymnasium, café and bar. This,
however, turned out to be the Newham Leisure Centre.
The clubhouse was a rather more modest affair round
the back, next to a somewhat battered block of squash
courts.

But it was a very nice clubhouse even so, funded by
Lottery money and looking out onto a spotless new track
under sparkling floodlights. A handful of figures were

already warming up. They were bulked out by those odd garments with which runners shield themselves from the elements and their dyskinesiac expressions were those worn by all runners training on squally nights in January, a cross between eye-rolling despondency and grim make-the-best-of-it determination, as if they had been given only two options for spending the evening and the other one was having their kidneys removed without anaesthetic. Inside the clubhouse were showers and loos, somewhere to sit and a small kitchen on the wall of which a notice was pinned:

> Life membership £5
> Club nights (per session) £1.50
> Tea 15p
> If it's your birthday – you bring the cakes

After signing my life away to the East End Road Runners I went out with some of them on a training run. Over the ensuing weeks, on Tuesdays, Thursdays and, as the London Marathon approached, Sundays when we set out in a gloved and woolly-hatted pack for The Long Weekend Run, I discovered with a mean, competitive pleasure that among our number were runners even more deficient than me and that for other slow, dumpy women with creaking ligaments and a Rioja habit I might, if I worked on my form assiduously enough and perhaps renounced spitting *en passant* into hedgerows, aspire to be a role model. I also discovered that far better than to wipe your nose on your sleeve is to use your gloves.

In the eighteen months that I had been running, people sometimes asked me why I did it. No they didn't, they asked if I was mad. I didn't know why I ran, except that it made me feel great afterwards and even some of the time I was actually doing it. Around the time I started training with the East End Road Runners I had lunch at Christophers in Covent Garden with my friend Alice who, like me, had been cast adrift in the choppy waters of freelance life after the closure of 'Active'. She had recently landed the lucrative job on the women's pages of the *Mail on Sunday* that her talent, diligence and sweetness of nature deserved and after I had admired her new suit (shade anthracite) and modestly accepted her offer of an absurdly inflated sum of money for the journalistic equivalent of pissing in a pot, she asked me why I ran.

'Because', I said, 'it makes me feel completely in touch with my power.'

Clearly she wanted to follow that up with 'Are you mad?' but was far too well brought up to give voice to any such thing. But, well, why *did* I run? Because I loved it, actually. I loved running in races. I loved the East End Road Runners. I loved my purple vest (with which, incidentally, I wore a red hat that didn't go, though I like to think suited me in some jaunty, playful way). I loved running in a pack, to the rhythm of our silent song. The men's voices, strong and deep, would lead our music; the women's, lighter but more melodic, would respond. I loved running on my own through Blackheath in the early mornings, when the office workers were hurrying down the hill to the station. Just before closing their front doors the women had sprayed on their perfume and those were some of the sweetest-smelling roads I ever ran. I loved running with Fred, his long, loping style, the way he slowed down so I could keep up with him, the occasion on which a passing lady cyclist nearly tumbled off her bike when between splits he announced in his booming solicitor's voice, 'I shagged a Japanese girl last night, five times.' Running would not do away with all sadness and loss but it was a place to go. Took you out of yourself, as my late

Midlands mother-in-law used to say. A little away-day from life's harshnesses and deprivations.

I knew that these sentiments were deeply uncool and that running not only made me fit, hardy and thin (-ish) but also brought out a dreadfully earnest and proselytizing quality which for most of my adult life I had managed reasonably successfully to suppress but frankly, my dear, I no longer gave a toss.

That's self-esteem.

RUBBISH RUNS

Runner's World Training Log.
Day: Sunday. **Distance:** 15 m. **Time:** 2 h. 39.59 min.
Weather: Dry but nippy. **Course/notes:** The Benfleet
15. Went to Canvey mob-handed with the club and Fred.
Bleak cross-country course round the sea wall, through
spongey moor and a frightful stretch of mudslick. Didn't
finish last, by any means. East End Road Runners won
the ladies prize. Fred did 2 hours. He was a little
surprised, having visualized himself among the leaders.
But talent isn't enough, you need to train for endurance.

On the way back from races Mick liked us to eat together;
the meals had a Eucharistic quality. They were celebrations of the fact that in running there were no calamitous
defeats or engulfing sorrows; we might have run better
than last time, or worse; there would be other races and
some would be triumphs, some flops. Fred and I usually
sat opposite each other, so we could talk; it felt good
sometimes to recreate the days when he was growing up,
when we only had each other.

I've said those were the worst times in the world but
they weren't always. I've happy memories of the two of
us, some evenings, quietly reading among the unrolled
rugs. I don't know who protected who, really, but we got
by. He went to boarding school, got excellent O and A
Levels, shagged the housemaster's daughter, smoked,

drank and ran 5 miles in 25 minutes. Did it one sports day; it's still the school record. He was talent-spotted by a coach, who invited him to join one of the great harrier clubs, because Fred could have been a proper runner if he'd put his back into it. I'd already mentally awarded him his international vest and stuck him on the Olympic podium when he told me he'd turned the coach down.

Off he went instead to university where, like me, he was a stranger to the lecture hall. He was cleverer than me, though, and came out two marks short of a first. It was the summer my first novel was accepted. I guess I was so busy being An Authoress I didn't see how unhappy he was. Dumped by the girl he'd been with for two years, unable to get work, he went into a deep, foul pit of despair. Down and down he went till I thought he'd never come out again. He'd look in the mirror and say his face was ugly, and to hear my son talking of himself that way just ripped me up. For months and months I knelt at the edge of the pit calling out to him that he wasn't ugly, he was handsome; he couldn't hear me. My second novel went down and down too. I couldn't write, I couldn't sleep, I couldn't think of anything except where Fred was and whether he'd come back safely.

He got himself out in the end, turned the depression down the way he'd turned down the coach. Just got up one morning, went off to a graduate fair and came back as a trainee solicitor. Over the next couple of years it was sometimes tough, but he fought through. I might have handed on my depression to him, but he'd also inherited my rage, the rage of the survivor.

Running is too narrow, too planned, to work wholly as a metaphor for life; that isn't to say there are no instructive comparisons. Some nights I'd go out training and feel great. I'd come back buzzing and Mick would say, 'Yeah, and you'll have some rubbish runs.' And I did; I'd go out two nights later, gasp and stumble and get left behind by the pack. I decided after a while it was like writing books; my second novel was a rubbish run. Like all rubbish runs, it wasn't worth fretting about; you just tried to work out what went wrong, learnt from the experience and carried on running. It wasn't the most profound of insights, but it seemed as good a way of addressing life as any.

RUNNING FASTER
IS A SKILL

Runner's World Training Log.
Day: Tuesday. **Time:** 1 h. 30 min. **Distance:** around
4 m. **Course/notes:** Track night. Coaching by Albert, a
deceptively mild-mannered yoga fanatic wearing his
daughter's hand-me-down pastel sweatshirt. We did
speedwork: 200 metre relays and something enervating
called Bananas. Made the mistake of saying Albert looked
like Harry Redknapp. 'I was at school with Harry
Redknapp,' he snarled. 'I hated him.'

In the last weeks of 1997 and shortly before I set out for
Cap Ferret I had the opportunity to interview Alan Storey,
a very nice man who is not only a national coach but the
race director of the London Marathon. He had kindly
agreed to give me a chunk of his time to help me whittle
a few minutes off my marathon PB.

A PB is abbreviated running parlance for your personal
best and to everyone who runs for what we will euphemize
as fun the time it takes you to complete, let's say, a
half-marathon is, far more than the post-finish cup of tea
and a tin medal engraved with the insignia of your host
club, the Throgmorton Trotters, the emotionally loaded
focus of the race. It may be hard for those who do not
run to appreciate this; what I'm saying, though, is that

you've got to have something to strive for. At the level at which most of us compete, where you do not have to worry about bettering last year's World Championship silver or fretting as to where you will garage the third Mercedes you have won this season, a Personal Best is it.

Don't be misled by that joyous, festive damburst of humanity you see flooding through Charlton at the start of the London Marathon. Clap eyes on us around the 20-mile mark in Westferry Road and you will understand the nature of true wretchedness. A marathon is huge, cruel and long and, like life, even if you do it in company, you enter and leave it alone. The first time you cross the finish your overriding feeling is not of triumph but of deliverance. At last there is no pain, effort or boredom, no wizened fool in Throgmorton Trotters vest at your shoulder gibbering, 'If you think you feel bad now, wait till you've reached St. Katharine's Dock.' Only after a few minutes or so of savouring this sweet *absence* do you turn your thoughts towards the free cheese and tomato sandwich and somewhere to have a pee.

In due course, having passed through the stage of needing to walk around in carpet slippers and having to descend the stairs backwards, on all fours, you lose your grip on reason. Instead of saying to yourself, 'For six months I neglected my family and short-changed my workmates in order to train for one Sunday morning of utter hell; enough is enough and I'm going to take up Morris dancing,' you find yourself thinking, 'Well now, if I knock off the eleven minutes it took me to pass through the start line, and the six minutes queuing for the toilets at Poplar High Street, and all the times I had to stop and retie my laces, I finished in 4 hours 45, and next year if I train 80 miles a week instead of 40, wear slip-on trainers and have my bladder removed, I'll get round in 4.30, a personal best.'

For the last two thirds of 1997 I had secretly entertained the notion that within me was a sub-four marathon, rather in the way that girls of thirteen believed that David Beckham would marry them. I knew that, biomechanically, I had ridiculously unpromising material to work with; nevertheless, I fantasized about the miracle that would happen on my very next training run, when as I closed the front door behind me and set off up the gentle slope towards the heath my legs would not feel as though they were pulling a pair of suitcases. I would be light and supple and easy of breathing. I would be fast.

It never happened, of course. I'd come back six miles later, sweaty, tender-kneed, cheeks the colour of cough candy, and with something wrong with my watch. However much I put into my run the small hand had moved on one digit further but the big hand was stuck in exactly the same place as when I started out. It didn't matter whether I felt terrific out there or ran like a wheelbarrow. A mile for me always took ten minutes.

By the time I met Alan Storey I was resigned to that. All I wanted to know was how to keep running at tenminute mile pace for the duration of a marathon, rather than have my legs go from underneath me halfway along Narrow Street and be overtaken by the Pot Noodles and four men playing bagpipes, by which time I was too drained, footsore and hypothermic to care.

So I was quite surprised when Storey told me that running slowly was not necessarily an irreversible fate and that all I had to do, apart from perhaps losing half a stone in weight and not getting legless the night before a race, was just practise running fast.

There would be a point at which I *could* run no faster

because when it came to being an athlete I had not chosen my parents carefully enough, and while my genetic inheritance included a very useful dollop of linguistic skill and flair for interior decoration from my mum and from Dad, as well as an instinctive knowledge of the best way to cook turkey, a kind of dogged optimism that helped with life's vicissitudes, what neither had been able to pass on to me were legs like Sebastian Coe's. I would, if I practised, indeed run faster but it might – almost certainly *would* – be that 26.2 miles in under four hours was, for someone of my age and physique, a simple impossibility. But at least I would have done the best of which I was capable at something which gave me pleasure and healing and meaning and a place to go.

It is an ability of the best coaches – and in this category I include not only Alan Storey but Mick down at the East End Road Runners – to encourage you to embrace reality without ridding you of hope and self-regard. Having timed me on a bleak January night at a series of 1200 metre splits round the Terence McMillan Stadium track, Mick quietly pointed out that the pace at which I had been running – the pace at which I could not speak and in due course could not breathe and after several minutes of which I needed to sit down and have a nice cup of tea – was the very one which I needed to keep up for the duration if I wanted to attain my goal of a sub-four marathon. We agreed – when I could talk again, that was – that my ambition was therefore a bit on the extreme side of grandiose.

In the course of helping me to take all this on board Mick had highlighted two qualities which, he thought, I did possess. These were mental toughness and a long stride. I won't say it was quite like being told I had literary genius or was drop-dead gorgeous but, my goodness, how hearing that made my spirit grow. Presently I was devoting one night a week to running up and down hills twelve times in succession, and doing Bananas (don't even ask) and 200 metre relays and more 1200 metre splits. It was a desperately boring business executed in shrilly inclement weather but after two months I could run faster for longer and my revised ambition, to knock a few minutes off my last marathon time and perhaps in a year or so rustle up a little sub-4.30, was generally agreed to be entirely within my grasp.

But, I thought, I'd still look around for a pair of slip-on trainers and avoid the queue for the toilets at Poplar High Street, just to be on the safe side.

THE RIGHT SHOES

Runner's World Training Log.
Day: Sunday. **Distance:** 13.1 m. **Time:** 2 h. 11 min.
Weather: Sunny. **Course/notes:** The Brentwood Half-
marathon. Went with Flo and Kenny from the club and
raced in my new shoes. Flo and I enjoyed a pre-race
massage from a man with a speech impediment. Very
nice race, Brentwood: first two miles are downhill. Lost it
a bit in the middle stages, distracted by overwhelming
urge to take machine gun to young bloke in flapping
shoes who kept slowing to a walk. I'd keep passing him at
which, flap-flap-flap, he'd wheeze past me. Did him in
just beyond Blackmore. Stormed up final hill and
managed a sprint finish. Beat Flo by five minutes, and
personal best by two.

Thirty-odd years ago, if I'd been more trusting of adults
in general, if I'd accepted that not all of them were
hypocrites and that some genuinely wanted me to succeed
because, well, it would be nice for me, in short if I hadn't
been such a stroppy little arsehole, I would in all probabil-
ity never have become a sportswriter.

In my final term at Bristol, I went to see the careers
officer. We had an informative and exciting discussion
about my staying on at the university to do a B.Ed.,
during which, for a quarter of an hour or so, I forgot that
although I had just won a writing award I was almost

certainly pregnant, and that my internal world was black when outside it looked shining white. I sauntered away fantasizing I was a normal young adult with all of life in front of me, there for the taking. I could do whatever I wanted to do, and believe it or not what I wanted to do was become a teacher.

Now I don't want to give the impression for one second that I regard a career at an inner-city comprehensive as in any way less rewarding than one on Fleet Street, or that spending evenings and entire weekends drowning in government-inspired paperwork, having thirty years' worth of chalkdust lodged in my eyebrows or being roughed up by fourteen-year-old girls built like James 'Bonecrusher' Smith is not a satisfying and soul-nurturing way to earn a crust but, on the other hand, had I been in a position to make a rational career choice at the age of twenty I would not in all likelihood have been at Wembley the day Trevor Brooking won the F.A. Cup for West Ham with a thirteenth-minute header. I would never have got to meet Danny Blanchflower, Muhammad Ali or Alex Ferguson. I would not have reported three World Cups, been at Centre Court in 1981 to watch Borg beat McEnroe in the greatest final ever played at Wimbledon, or indeed, as a babe in the press box (well anyway, a good deal prettier than Ronan Goldblatt), have been invited by the manager of Stoke City to come upstairs and see his European pennants.

And I would not, in the sleep-deprived exhaustion of the days following the birth of my third and last son, have hallucinated myself into a dimension beyond conventional time and space where I found myself standing atop some mountain in the ether (look, you don't have to tell me it sounds barmy) regarding the thirty-nine years of my life thus far with distant awe and gratitude while the following soundbite floated through my head: 'I was a football reporter. Why, how wonderful that I was allowed to do that.'

Whenever I attempted to impart this revelation, together with its sundry accompanying intimations of heaven and eternity, to close friends and family, they would nod and say, 'Fancy that. Did you remember to put brillo pads on the shopping list?' and I only mention it now to show that had it been left to me to plan my future in a sensible and self-aware manner on a late spring day in 1969 instead of falling chaotically two years later into a rubbish secretarial job on the sports desk of a Sunday newspaper because that was the only place that would have me, a whole load of wondrous things would never have happened to me. Though I would, of course, have my own carriage clock presented by the PTA on the occasion of my early retirement after nervous collapse.

In short, there was no historical reason whatsoever to trust my judgement when it came to deciding how I wanted to earn a living for the second half of my life, and enormous sections of my being were saying that it was a very bad idea indeed to turn my back on what had always been, by and large, an enviably fulfilling line of work. But what else could I do when it made me feel so phoney? The nub of it was that as a woman in her twenties I'd enjoyed a great time being Fleet Street's first female football reporter but I felt too old now to sit in a press box banging out febrile intros about Cup Magic and pretending that Jurgen Klinsmann scoring four for Spurs against Wimbledon was the apogee of my week.

Some years back, on the first of my many renunciations of football writing, I took it into my head that what I would really like to do was return to university – one, perhaps, not a million miles from Cambridge, where I would make amends for not getting in the first time around by being offered a place to study psychology. After I had gained a degree of, I hoped, somewhat greater distinction than my shabby little BA in philosophy, I would carry on learning with a view to becoming a psychotherapist. This was something I had wanted to do ever since the kindly Hampstead shrink had restored me to the land of the reasonably sane and well-balanced in the early eighties.

My ambition to retrain had foundered primarily on two fronts. The first was practical: with numerous dependent children and stepchildren of various ages, I lacked the resources to fund myself through any course longer than Introduction to Aromatherapy at our local college of education. At the same time, I would not qualify for a grant because I'd already had my wedge of taxpayers' money, and goodness me, how ashamed I felt of the wilful silliness with which I'd frittered it away. The second obstacle to enlightenment led on from the first: it was that the degree I had obtained from Bristol in the closing years of the sixties was a shit one which owed nothing to my effort or application and everything to Stephen Korner's kindness, and as soon as anybody looked at my educational record they'd realize that I was an intellectual damp squib, a bad bet, a wrong 'un who was incapable of learning or training or seeing anything through, so there was no point trying. And meanwhile I'd gone and run up a bill on my Monsoon credit card and in short it seemed a pretty good idea to forget all about changing direction and to go back to football reporting.

Like I've said, I know that you can only go so far using running as an exemplar for life but in the short time I had been training with the East End Road Runners the most pressing of my feelings of inadequacy had gone. The only way I can explain it was that by paying attention to what the coaches were telling me and no matter how cold or silly or untalented I felt, I had become faster and stronger and more determined. And as my shrivelled self-esteem grew I was able to put aside the dafter of my dreams; though I still wanted to learn something new, I didn't have to be accepted by Cambridge so I could heal the wound of an old rejection. I could go to a university near where I lived, on a part-time course that would allow me to keep working and earning while I studied.

Around the end of January 1998, in the *Guardian*, I saw advertised a Postgraduate Diploma and M.Sc. in Psychotherapy at the South Bank University. A phone call elicited the news that not only were there places still available on the course but that, subject to interview, one of them might be made available to a forty-nine-year-old sports journalist with a shit first degree in an unrelated subject and whose only experience of the healing art of therapy was on the wrong side of the couch.

My interview clothes:
  Black fur coat (Monsoon)
  Brick red cotton jersey (Racing Green)
  Black Levi's
  Black suede loafers (Hobbs)
  Lots of Chloe

The South Bank University's School of Counselling and Psychotherapy was based at the Whittington Hospital in Archway, North London, and rather endearingly shared a floor with the maternity department. I travelled up to the appropriate level in a lift shared with a mother and her recently delivered infant and I don't know whether some of that new life rubbed off on to me but the whole interview was brilliant from beginning to end:

amongst other subjects we talked of transference, love, lust, nuns, Melanie Klein and above all knees, because the course director was, like me, a runner, though his preferred distance was the 10k. Later that week, a letter arrived with the offer of a place and details of the course. I read these and was suddenly scared almost witless by the cost, the commitment, the immediacy (the term was to start in four weeks) and the sheer emotional and academic enormity of what would be demanded of me. So I turned the offer down, though not for ever.

And now, before I go any further, I'd like to deviate briefly on the subject of shoes. In the months leading up to my interview at the School of Counselling and Psychotherapy, I had been running in a pair of Nikes which, apart from a slightly clunky feel and some tightness around the toe box, had served me comfortably and well. Alas, after more than 400 miles of wear they were no longer providing the cushioned ride on which my ageing skeleton depended. I therefore replaced them, with a pair of what I shall refer to as Brand Xes.

At first I was highly pleased with my Brand Xes, which – apart from being £20 cheaper and having gay yellow stripes – were so light they might have been soled in rice paper. However, after six weeks of Bananas and Long Weekend Runs and a couple of half-marathons, I had developed a distressing and utterly terrifying collection of symptoms in my legs, back and side which, when I checked them out with our *Family Doctor Home Adviser*, implied that far from taking part in the 1998 London Marathon I might, with a very strong effort of will, just survive long enough to watch it on television from my bed in the neighbourhood hospice.

I won't dwell on the anguished hours I endured worrying about how the twelve-year-old would manage without me to make sure he'd remembered to pack his box on cricket squad practice days, or mourning that I would never see Fred take a bride, or hoping that the ten-year-old would get over my death in time to pass his eleven-plus, but to say that I was in pretty much of a state hardly hints at my condition. In fact, I was so distraught by my imminent departure from this life that, having decided to visit the Terence Mcmillan Stadium to bid a tearful adieu to the East End Road Runners and run around their track one last time, I forgot to take my Brand Xes. But as luck would have it, my old Nikes were hanging around my kitbag because I'd been too lazy to chuck them out, so that night I did Bananas in them instead.

Well, you'll never guess what happened. As soon as I began running in my old shoes again, all my symptoms disappeared rapidly and in their entirety apart from one slight twinge at the front of my left foot. This, when I disrobed later that night, turned out to be due to a carelessly cut nail which had dug into my big toe. But I reckoned I could cope with one bloodied Thousand Mile Sock when the alternative was a premature grave, so I junked my Brand Xes and slipped gratefully back into my old shoes. They weren't perfect but they were there when I needed them and once they had carried me through the London Marathon I would buy a new pair which suited me just as well.

This is not quite the end of the story. Just after my successful interview at the South Bank University, I took a phone call from a former colleague. Like me, he had moved on but we had kept in touch and when 'Active' had closed I had contacted him to see if there was any chance of some freelance work at the paper for which he now worked. At the time he had been unable to offer very much but now, out of the blue, he was ringing to ask whether I would be interested in contributing a weekly sports column.

When I found out that it would not entail any driving up and down motorways, eating at Little Chefs or ringing up managers, and after I had stipulated that a clause would have to be written into my contract to confirm that under no circumstances should I be required to use the expression Cup Magic or set eyes on Ronan Goldblatt, I told him that I would indeed be interested in contributing a weekly sports column. So, just as I had gratefully slipped back into my old shoes for the time being, I returned to sports journalism, and very good it was too.

What I'd realized, I suppose, was that I didn't have to make a drastic and irrevocable switch of direction. I had enough affection for my old life to want to continue living it in circumstances that suited me. At the same time, I still wished to pursue my goal of becoming a psychotherapist, at my own pace and level of experience, not to mention ability to pay. So I reapplied to the South Bank University and in due course found myself welcomed on to its diploma course in Humanistic-Integrative Counselling and beginning the long and strange journey through the next half of my life.

ANOTHER BLOODY SUNDAY

Runner's World Training Log.
Day: Thursday. **Distance:** 5.5 m. **Time:** 55 min.
Weather: Warm. **Course/notes:** Ran with Flo and
Julie O. Last Woolwich-and-back before London.

Non-running friends and family have always failed to spot
the charm of the London Marathon, which as I have
already indicated in these pages is a way of spending a
Sunday morning in spring which might, with hindsight,
have been more entertainingly devoted to assessing vinyl
wall coverings in Texas Homecare or trying out bondage.
It seems inadequate to explain that I like running it
precisely because it offers periods of utter awfulness which
are not always redeemed by lacunae of gaiety and joy.
There is a limit to non-runners' comprehension and that
limit is reached long before your post-race recital arrives
at the bit where you threatened your good friend and
running partner with grievous bodily harm.

Let me put you in the picture. In the weeks leading up
to London, I had done much of my training with my
fellow East End Road Runner Flo who, while younger
than me, was not so adrift in years as to make it embarrassing. We shared a good deal in common, having both
been single parents who had eventually won the struggle

to make something of our professional and personal lives. At weekends we slogged companionably around the pavements of Blackheath and Beckton and sometimes we took in a half-marathon or 20-miler. When we first raced together, I finished well ahead of her and though, as the weeks went on, I began to notice that I was barely started on my post-race cup of tea before she came steaming in it was a matter of quiet satisfaction to me that here, at least, was someone I could beat.

Then came the day, two weeks before London, when we ran in the Docklands Half-marathon and far from my gradually leaving Flo behind in the heaving throng she floated upfield of me before the first mile-marker and I never did catch her. We both achieved personal bests that morning; indeed, she beat hers by five minutes and I thought it was very sporting of me to embrace her afterwards while issuing warm words of congratulation, being as I was as sick as it was possible for a pig to be.

Because, of course, our rivalry had only been enjoyable as long as I came out tops and I am not proud of the turn events took a fortnight later on the streets of London. What happened was, a quarter of an hour before the start in Greenwich Park, Flo was moved to make a last-minute comfort stop. I agreed to wait for her but the queue for the Nurds was of great length and ponderousness and with thirty seconds left till the off Flo had still not returned to our meeting place. Nevertheless, with what I later realized on mature reflection was not only unasked-for but quite half-witted loyalty, I continued to wait. It was only when the race started that I realized I had better join it and, hurling myself through spectators and over a crash barrier, I joined the pack, not in my allotted starting position for Slow But Not Entirely Disastrous Runners but in the section for Really Crap Runners and People Wearing Exceptionally Cumbrous Fancy Dress.

And now we move on, more than two hours and thirteen miles later, to Cable Street where, in conditions of lashing rain and average despondency, I heard my name called by someone in the crowd and found myself gazing on the soaked but smiling face of Ricky, one of the East End Road Runners coaches. By way of encouragement, Ricky informed me that Flo had passed this way not a minute before and if I got a move on I might catch up with her.

Goodness me, I'm embarrassed just thinking now of the slanders I heaped on my poor innocent friend and running partner. I called her a cow. The expression 'I'll deck her' was heard throughout E1. I screamed and ranted as the pack swept me forward. I may even have turned to the person running next to me and embarked on a long, vicious monologue about the perfidy of so-called friends who ask you to wait outside toilets for them then steal a march on you by skipping into the start section reserved for Not Bad At All, Considering Runners while leaving you to take your chance with Big Ben and the Wombles.

In short, I ran the rest of the 1998 London Marathon in a mood of paranoia and infantile rage that only abated as I heaved my weary legs up the Blackfriars underpass. It was here that I enjoyed the sublime and never-to-be-repeated experience of overtaking one of the Fast Blokes from the East End Road Runners. The poor guy had badly sprained his ankle at Tower Bridge but out of sheer, mad, brave grit was dragging himself to the finish line. 'Ha ha!' I thought as I lumbered by. I tell you, there's no one so pitiless as a slow runner given a whiff of superiority.

Well, that was about it, really. On the clock when I finished was 4 hours 51 minutes 59 seconds. I collected my medal and free cheese and tomato sandwich and was soon indulging in those calculations made by all London Marathon finishers, the ones which begin, 'There were twelve minutes on the clock when I crossed the start line, and if I take off another two minutes for . . .' and by the time I had hobbled and pushed my way through the crowded park to meet my husband and children I was in the state of reasonable complacency that comes from having covered 26.2 miles in just under 4 hours 40 minutes. Not a sub-four, not even sub four-thirty, but by no means to be sneered at, I like to think.

In the days following the marathon, there was the pleasure of discovering how everyone else had fared, of hearing how on the morning of the race Fred had boarded a train at London Bridge which took him not to the start on Blackheath as he had been informed but several miles further on to the dozing suburb of Chislehurst from where, at ten minutes to nine, he boarded a train to take him back. This deposited him at Lewisham just after a quarter past the hour and by dint of running up Lewisham Hill (a pretty considerable mound) and remaining thereafter in motion he was able to cross Blue Start at 9.39, in the company of Mr Punch. He did 3 hours 51, before deploying the calculations exemplified above. Not sub three, not even sub three-thirty, but by no means to be sneered at.

My son in whom I am well pleased.

Thoroughly decent sort that she is, Flo phoned me the day after the race (word about my shame-making outburst having Got Back) to apologize and explain that as the queue for the Nurds had been so long she had eventually, in desperation, availed herself of the back of a shed. Unable to locate me and with the race about to begin, she had then joined her allotted place in the start. Her finishing time was two minutes ahead of mine, a personal best for her by a good half hour and one, moreover, achieved despite having to stop at the St. Johns' Ambulance station halfway through to have plasters placed on her bloodied feet. I told her how determinedly she had trained and how much she deserved her medal and I meant it. And even as I spoke, even as I was mentally admiring her physical courage and unquenchable spirit, I heard myself thinking, 'It's the Southend Half-Marathon in six weeks and I'm going to leave you for toast.'

THE ANCESTOR RIDE

Runner's World Training Log.
Day: Thursday. **Distance:** 4 m. **Time:** 42 min.
Weather: Bountiful. **Course/notes:** Blackheath Hill
down to Lewisham, back through Blackheath Park.
Stopped at polling station en route to vote Yes to mayor
for London. Wistaria, pigeons, schoolkids bunking off.
On the heath, bluebottles on a dog turd. Amazed at how
darkly jewel-like their colour is. The paparazzi of the
insect world. **Life quality:** Beckoning.

I went back to the site of my old house. I travelled there
on my Raleigh bike. I'd left it to grow dusty in the garden
shed while I was training for the London Marathon; it
was good to be reunited with its gel-filled seat, 12-speed
grip-shift gears and British Legion poppy which I had
never got around to disentangling from the spokes after
Pedal to Paris in 1996. (Note to Raleigh: if you want any
further mentions, we will have to come to some arrangement, possibly involving one of your new racing models.)

It was on a Saturday, just after 10.30, that I set off.
Two years before, almost to the day, my dad had died; I
had a bunch of bluebells from my back garden to lay on
his grave. The chestnuts and hawthorns of London were
in full bloom and I thought how much he would have
enjoyed being alive on this sunny May morning. He
enjoyed being alive most of the time, actually, singing in

the bathroom even when old and frail. His favourite was 'The Mountains of Mourne': 'Oh Mary, this London's a wonderful sight/The folk are all working by day and by night.' These sentiments, heard from childhood, left me with a romantic enthusiasm for our capital city and for gainful activity which has never dissipated. If, after the Mountains of Mourne, his bathroom tasks were not yet complete he would launch into one of John Wesley's more feelgood numbers.

I steered a course through New Cross and the Old Kent Road, where modest travel shops advertised flights to Nigeria and Jamaica on boards that competed for pavement space with crates of furrowed green melons belonging to adjacent general stores. At the Elephant and Castle, roads fragmented outwards in every direction like cracks around holed glass, the hole being a roundabout that had the feel of a small abandoned town. I stood on it and took a drink. Unexplained walls grew out of waste ground and dandelion clocks flourished beside subways where no one walked. Over the road was an empty office block with postered-up windows. They promised EXCITING OPPORTUNITY, LAST CHANCE and PANORAMIC VIEWS. My panoramic view was of the underground, whose reddish-brown tiled walls and old-fashioned canopy saying Elephant & Castle Station had not yet been ravaged by modernization.

I rode over Blackfriars Bridge, remembering that once, oh, a lifetime ago, I had contemplated casting myself upon the waters of the Thames that rushed beneath. This sad thought was fleeting because almost immediately I was wheeling the bike across the underpass where, a mere fortnight back, I had briefly experienced what it was like to outrun a Fast Bloke. Before me, next to Temple, was the grid of narrow streets lined with fusty buildings. Past these, as a twelve-year-old, I had hurried from Blackfriars Station to the school where I turned into a dolt.

I went slowly up Temple Avenue. Still there was the basement restaurant from which, as The Girl Who Reported Football, I'd staggered away late on many a seventies afternoon after interviews over lunch and brandies with permed midfield dynamos. At the corner of Tallis Street stood an old block of offices like a dark theatre; its window panes were grimy, dust everywhere. On its roof was a pretty clock with a weathervane on its tower and pale green face, hands stuck for ever at six minutes past eleven.

Soon I came upon Carmelite Street. Where the school had been was a new commercial building, between old ones that had been buffed up and knocked through. It being Saturday, everywhere was silent and echoing; only a low hum of traffic from Victoria Embankment told me that life on this planet had not ceased. I tried to work out where the school's entrance door had stood, the huge one under a stone arch, dungeon-like, painted black, but it was gone without trace, along with the Porter's Lodge that had been on the left-hand side as you went in. In this cranny with nicotine-coloured walls resided Stringer, a school employee of such antiquity that he was fabled to have lost close relations in the Fire of London. He seemed a good-natured old geezer, allowing me the use of his phone to place a successful bet on Rockavon in the 2000 Guineas of 1960, although for all I know he might also have watched us changing for gym from a cunningly placed spyhole.

For a moment I was with the friends I made in that place, the lively Jewish girls from North London who taught me about life, death and Tottenham Hotspur. Here we huddled, the four of us in maroon tunics and laddered nylons, listening again on a transistor radio to the '60–'61 F.A. Cup fourth round draw behind the bolted door of one of the pungent downstairs lavatories. What had they become? Psychotherapists, housewives, performance artists? I would never know; I didn't need to. I waved them goodbye and pushed the bike a bit further up the road. Here a line of shutters barred what had once been a familiar, welcoming doorway.

This had been the home of Scribes, a Fleet Street drinking den in which many a sottish and debauched afternoon was passed on expenses and where, as increasingly flushed husband and wife of a few hours, Ron and I had enjoyed our wedding reception (and to this day I still cannot fathom how all those muddy footprints of different sizes came to be on my train). Beyond me was Tudor Street. The former *Evening Standard* and *Daily Mail* building – Bourgeois Triumphalism House, had it been called? – remained, but was boarded up and abandoned. A London Electricity repair vehicle stood parked where once the news vans waited in revving line. It was a depressing sight, so I headed across New Bridge Street to gaze upon what had once been the *Observer*.

This was still siamesed to Printing House Square, which up till the end of the seventies had housed *The Times*. The walls were an unchanged grey-green, though mottled now with accumulated dirt and rain. The plate glass windows that had afforded a spacious if majestically uninteresting view of the ground floor reception desk were obscured by large sheets of plywood. Once I had walked in there, aged twenty-two, in a mini-dress and the kind of shoes you fell off, to be interviewed for the post of secretary to the sports editor. The first person I met on that far-off June day was Ron. I remember that he wore a brown suit with lapels the size of car doors. But didn't everybody? It was a long time before he was free to be what I wanted him to be to me, but I like the notion very much that he was the first person I ever met there. Even if, as he later confessed, he had strongly advised the sports editor to give the job to the only other applicant, to whom I was inferior in both shorthand speed and breast measurement.

Now, above the entrance of the newspaper where once I was a girl just starting out on her working life hung a board with the name of a demolition company and the legend 'It all comes down to experience'. How true, how very true, I muttered, my thoughts turning to a swift and, I hoped, soul-restoring visit to the Cockpit up the road. It was there in 1983 that, fresh and blushing from Hatton Garden, Ron and I had announced our engagement to Liam the landlord. And as I thought with increasing dolefulness that the Cockpit would now be a themed pub, that Liam would be long returned to his native Donegal soil, might very possibly be *in* his native Donegal soil, and that Ron and I were now a pair of penurious and unwanted old hacks whose good times were all behind us, the bells of St Andrew by the Wardrobe rang out.

I can't begin to tell you how wonderful it was to hear those bells and trot with my bike just twenty yards up the road to the porch of the church where the wedding guests were hurrying inside, the women in big hats and bright narrow dresses, the men in black tie, the unmarried friend in the lime green bomber jacket. I propped the bike against the railings and scrabbled inside my rucksack for a drink; the day had turned very hot. Just then, the bridal car drew up alongside and the bride looked out. She was holding her bouquet against her neck and she gave me a little smile, though it must have come as some surprise to her to be greeted not by her bridesmaids but a simpering beetroot-faced woman in a sun hat with Lucozade dribbling down her chin. A breeze swept along the street as she stepped on to the pavement. The petals of her bouquet flapped, her veil streamed back like car exhaust, her tiara wobbled. She had little pearl studs in her ears; her dress was made of cream silk. She went up the steps and into the old dark church. Silently I wished on her all the blessings I had had, and went pedalling away up Farringdon Road.

Just after Islington I found my way onto Kingsland High Street, which under the alias of the A10 funnels traffic out from the City and Shoreditch towards Hertfordshire. It was a long, clogged artery of a road, passing through shopping parades of little distinction, dull and vaguely municipal buildings set back from the pavement, establishments of an arcanely religious nature, occasional lines of stunted trees, purveyors of dubious motor cars. It wasn't that I only had eyes for the hideous and dreary that morning; this had never been an easy thoroughfare to love, and the one part of it that had once filled me with pride and fondness, White Hart Lane with its mighty wooden-floored stands, each roof ornamented with the badge of the cockerel, had undergone a Balfour Beatty makeover somewhere around 1980. Bit by bit, the lovely place had crumbled, to be replaced by grey and brutal monsters. I hated it.

Sadly I sat on a low wall opposite and gazed on the last remnants of the old Spurs, my Spurs and the Spurs of Brown, Baker, Henry, Blanchflower, Norman, Mackay, Jones, White, Smith, Allen, Dyson and Medwin who played sometimes. The gates were still there, tall, black, iron ones which used to send shivers of awe down my spine. They just weren't in scale any more. Dwarfed by the monsters, they seemed like out-takes from someone's front garden. Beside them, the redbrick lodge had so far evaded extinction. Round the side I could still see the painted sign saying 'Complimentary tickets and passes collection point', beside the familiar blue door. On the other side, bridging the gap between the lodge and the Tottenham & Edmonton Dispensary (its name was engraved on the elegant stonework above the long closed and unwanted concern) stood a barred gateway under a wallflower sign that said TOTTENHAM HOTSPUR V. Now you could look up, to the very top of the chief monster, and read, courtesy of an electronic noticeboard, that 'This is White Hart Lane. The famous home of the *Spurs*. And The Spurs Go Marching On.'

Well, I suppose they do, after a fashion, and presently I did too, pedalling away past an incredibly depressing block of abandoned shops and businesses to the Edmonton branch of Sainsbury's where I filled my rucksack with sandwiches, crisps, water, more crisps and Cadbury's fruit and nut and quickly emptied it again by consuming them in a car park with panoramic views of abandoned trolleys.

Actually, I'd always liked this little part of the world, the land of my ancestors, where Tottenham became Edmonton and the road stopped being the A10 and turned almost leafy and villagey. Vestigial hints of North-East London's rural past remained in street names: Greens, Groves, Leas, Lanes. How lovely the place must have been a century and a half ago, when this highway was no more than a track, rucked and holed in winter but on a sunny May afternoon sweet-smelling and full of peace. It was the dawn of the age of cycling; how the people must have relished the new freedom to ride far away from home on something that didn't neigh or shit. Somewhere here the youthful Great-Uncle King had his workshop, inventing and constructing not just bikes but cameras, lamps, sundry widgets, toys for his friends and vast collection of younger siblings, Daisy sitting quietly in a corner watching him, fourteen years old and already smitten. Here, too, was the shop of Tonkin the butcher where, as a girl, Grandma Belle helped her father serve customers; he wore one of those blue-and-white-striped aprons and a tall stiff hat. The family was Cornish by descent, apple-cheeked and reddish-haired. It was very pleasant to think of them, grouped behind the counter under a pergola of Norfolk hams and barons of beef.

From Edmonton I turned east onto the North Circular and wished I hadn't. Lorries thundered, exhausts spewed foully, gears crashed. I strayed onto a flyover and devoted the next ten minutes merely to trying to stay alive before the vile edifice expelled me onto a residential road and thence a cycle path that wound between allotments planted with flighty lettuces and slouching beans and in due course deposited me in Chingford.

I moved on, as in time my ancestors had done, to Woodford. Some of them had settled there; it was where Dad was born, a village then, of course. Beyond the green, screened by a row of fat chestnuts, was where the House of Gloom had been. Here were places where, as a little girl, I'd done things with Mum: taken afternoon tea in cafés with linen cloths on each table and terrifyingly genteel waitresses, shied stale bread at ducks on one of three algae-cloaked ponds; we were spoiled for choice. The main road through Woodford was where a girl in my dancing class was knocked down by a Morris Cowley in 1955. She became the heroine of a cautionary tale told by all mothers in the district: crossed the road without looking and was snuffed out at eight years old. I have one memory of her – a tall child with bouncing Shirley Temple curls, pirouetting around the scuffed floor of the church hall, arms outstretched like wings. I *always* look very hard before I cross the road.

I left Woodford behind and was soon passing the churchyard where Dad was buried. I gave a nod of ackowledgement to my first school before freewheeling down the hill into the place where I grew up. In those days, it too still qualified for the term 'village' though the big houses were already beginning to be pulled down to be replaced by the Higher Suburbia. Now it's half town, half London and the main street where Jo and I mooched in school holidays is full of expensive frock shops for footballers' wives. Residentially, it's convenient for Arsenal, Spurs and West Ham. I was going to say Leyton Orient as well, but I fancy their players' wages wouldn't run to it. Once Mum saw Paul Gascoigne, then a wearer of the Tottenham jersey, in the off licence. They made eye contact. 'That's Gazza,' she gasped to Dad. Gazza winked at her, put his finger to his lips and sauntered out, leaving Mum as pink and thrilled as a girl.

Goodness, was it me or had the hill leading to our old house got steeper? Jo and I used to pedal up here in no time at all but halfway up, I found I had to dismount and start pushing. It was extraordinary to me how little the road had changed, though. There was the house where all the fat children had lived; one of the girls was in my class at school, even her plaits were obese. Next door was the house which had had the foghorn-voiced Mummy; Mum hadn't thought much of her, found her guilty of having a swimming pool in the back garden. There, over the road, was the pile built by the common family who had more money than they knew what to do with so they spent it on fancy architectural crap like a lych gate the size of Brighton Pier. A little further along, as the hill levelled out, was the house with the Mummy who'd had the affair.

And then I came upon it – the place where our dear house had been, the place to which I had never returned, and I tell you, I was just *choked*. For years and years, in some little art gallery in my mind had hung a picture of a huge Victorian house, a barn of a place, no one seemingly very happy in it, but *ours*, *mine*. Now, even as I looked, the huge triangle of roof with its little attic window and space for the dovecote, the oriole window of my bedroom, the conservatory stuffed with cacti and fluttery ferns, the tall pine where my trapeze had hung, the apple trees and vegetable plot, the weeping willow and lily-padded pond and coal shed and rabbit hutch, the gardener's privy and the plump hollies and laurels and rhododendron bushes were slowly, slowly dissolving. For a moment there was nothing left but sky and then, still slowly, a new picture formed, the real picture which belonged to here and now.

And actually, as Mum said, it was quite nice, considering.

I left my bike lying on the pavement and strolled nearer. The houses were big, though wedged somewhat uneasily into the space, like travellers on a crowded tube. They were built of dark reddish brick in no particular style and – what is it estate agents say? oh yes – benefited from double garages. The first house had retained our old number and occupied most of what had been the main lawn. The front door of the middle house opened on to where our magnolia tree used to be. The third house was at a right angle to the others, facing onto the forest. They'd kept one of our trees, I was happy to note, the one which stood half in the garden, half on the pavement, the one on which Dad had espied the 'For Sale' board that day forty-two years back when we drove past.

No one was around and the gate hung open. Faintly I seemed to hear my mum say, 'You can't do that,' but

I wandered in. There were three lawns where our drive had been. For a moment I was back at our kitchen table with Mum and Jane, listening to Dad draw up in his car after a council meeting. It was late; the fine details of plans to reduce high street congestion had obviously taken some time and several gin and tonics to thrash out. We heard him fumble with the handle of the back door; he entered via the scullery where he bumped into the hoover. 'I beg your pardon, madam,' he said to it, raising his hat.

What used to be our living room was now almost the entire ground floor of a house. There were no ghosts, no happy trio of pensioners: Mum, Dad and Jane bending over the Scrabble board, a tray of ham sandwiches beside. It was just somebody's well-kept suburban castle, with inoffensive carpets and a table laid for supper. The new residents had retained some of our hedge so on my way out I plucked a bit and stuck it in my hat.

I walked past the high fence which had once divided my house from Jo's. Hers was gone, too: the ballroom, rose garden, bespoke Wendy House, the oak trees which in spring had always grown a gold skirt of crocuses. In its place was a cul-de-sac and more new houses. There were a greater number of them but not, I decided, as attractive as ours.

As I walked back to where the house had stood a bit of a breeze began to get up. For some reason a recent conversation I'd had with Mum jumped into my mind; she'd been recalling the time when she, Dad and Jane, returning from an outing to town, had searched for somewhere to eat. The only place which seemed open was the Wimpy Bar in Walthamstow. 'I'm not going in there,' Dad had harrumphed. So he and Mum sat in the car while Jane went in to order a take-away.

'We sat for ages,' said Mum, 'wondering what could

have become of her. And suddenly we saw her waiting at the tables. Apparently there was only one waitress and she had to cook as well, so Jane had said, "Right, you cook and I'll serve."' Mum sighed then. 'She was a real comic,' she said, 'and I miss her very much.'

The breeze was quite powerful now. Across the road, in the forest, trees rustled and whispered, the burbling of the birds suddenly stopped and for a moment I thought I saw a flash of sharp colour, a woman in a green dress slipping out through the fence where once our five-barred gate had been. But I can't swear to it and anyway she was soon gone.

It was getting late and after twenty miles my rucksack felt hot and heavy on my back. I'd debated dumping it at the site of the house in a gesture to symbolize the getting rid of old baggage but at the last minute I couldn't bring myself to renounce £150-worth of Berghaus so I fumbled in it and presently my hand closed on a very old and misshapen Power Bar, which I lobbed into the forest. That would have to do. Then I took the bluebells which had been meant for Dad's grave and laid them at the foot of the tree, half in and half out of the road.

Well, I thought, here goes.

Mum and Dad, I'm sorry I messed up my education.

I'm sorry I struck at everything that was dear to your hearts.

I'm not sorry I had Fred because that was meant to be and, anyway, look how he's turned out.

After that, there seemed no reason to hang about any longer so I picked up my bike and pedalled off to re-engage in battle with the North Circular, a middle-aged woman with a plume of privet in her hat.